EMOTION,
DISCLOSURE,
& HEALTH

EMOTION, DISCLOSURE, & HEALTH

JAMES W. PENNEBAKER, EDITOR

AMERICAN PSYCHOLOGICAL ASSOCIATION

WASHINGTON, DC

Fourth printing April 2006

Published by
American Psychological Association
750 First Street, NE
Washington, DC 20002

Copies may be ordered from
APA Order Department
P.O. Box 92984
Washington, DC 20090-2984

In the UK and Europe, copies may be ordered from
American Psychological Association
3 Henrietta Street
Covent Garden, London
WC2E 8LU England

Typeset in Minion by University Graphics, York, PA

Printer: Sheridan Books Inc., Ann Arbor, MI
Cover Designer: Anne Masters Design, Washington, DC
Cover Illustrator: James Yang
Technical/Production Editor: Edward B. Meidenbauer

Library of Congress Cataloging-in-Publication Data
Emotion, disclosure, and health / edited by James W. Pennebaker.
        p.   cm.
    Includes bibliographical references and index.
    ISBN 1-55798-308-9 (acid-free paper).—ISBN 1-55798-943-5 (pbk.)
    1. Emotions—Health aspects.   2. Mental health.   3. Self
-disclosure.   I. Pennebaker, James W.
    RC455.4.E46E46   1995
    616.89—dc20   95-16989
                                                                                    CIP

British Library Cataloguing-in-Publication Data
A CIP record is available from the British Library.

Printed in the United States of America

APA Science Volumes

Best Methods for the Analysis of Change: Recent Advances, Unanswered Questions, Future Directions

Cardiovascular Reactivity to Psychological Stress and Disease

The Challenge in Mathematics and Science Education: Psychology's Response

Cognition: Conceptual and Methodological Issues

Cognitive Bases of Musical Communication

Conceptualization and Measurement of Organism—Environment Interaction

Developmental Psychoacoustics

Emotion and Culture: Empirical Studies of Mutual Influence

Emotion, Disclosure, and Health

Examining Lives in Context: Perspectives on the Ecology of Human Development

Hostility, Coping, and Health

Organ Donation and Transplantation: Psychological and Behavioral Factors

The Perception of Structure

Perspectives on Socially Shared Cognition

Psychological Testing of Hispanics

Psychology of Women's Health: Progress and Challenges in Research and Application

Researching Community Psychology: Issues of Theory and Methods

Sleep and Cognition

Sleep Onset: Normal and Abnormal Processes

Studying Lives Through Time: Personality and Development

The Suggestibility of Children's Recollections: Implications for Eyewitness Testimony

Taste, Experience, and Feeding: Development and Learning

Temperament: Individual Differences at the Interface of Biology and Behavior

Through the Looking Glass: Issues of Psychological Well-Being in Captive Nonhuman Primates

APA expects to publish volumes on the following conference topics:

Attribution Processes, Person Perception, and Social Interaction: The Legacy of Ned Jones

Changing Ecological Approaches to Development: Organism— Environment Mutualities

Conceptual Structure and Processes: Emergence, Discovery, and Change

Converging Operations in the Study of Visual Selective Attention

Genetic, Ethological, and Evolutionary Perspectives on Human Development

Global Prospects for Education: Development, Culture, and Schooling

Maintaining and Promoting Integrity in Behavioral Science Research

Marital and Family Therapy Outcome and Process Research

Measuring Changes in Patients Following Psychological and Pharmacological Interventions

Psychology of Industrial Relations

Psychophysiological Study of Attention

Stereotype Accuracy

Stereotypes: Brain–Behavior Relationships

Work Team Dynamics and Productivity in the Context of Diversity

As part of its continuing and expanding commitment to enhance the dissemination of scientific psychological knowledge, the Science Directorate of the APA established a Scientific Conferences Program. A series of volumes resulting from these conferences is produced jointly by the Science Directorate and the Office of Communications. A call for proposals is issued several times annually by the Science Directorate, which, collaboratively with the APA Board of Scientific Affairs, evaluates the proposals and selects several conferences for funding. This important effort has resulted in an exceptional series of meetings and scholarly volumes, each of which has contributed to the dissemination of research and dialogue in these topical areas.

The APA Science Directorate's conferences funding program has supported 35 conferences since its inception in 1988. To date, 24 volumes resulting from conferences have been published.

WILLIAM C. HOWELL, PhD
Executive Director

VIRGINIA E. HOLT
Assistant Executive Director

Contents

Contributors

Nekane Basabe, Basque Country University, Spain

Roger J. Booth, University of Auckland, New Zealand

Thomas D. Borkovec, Pennsylvania State University

Wilma Bucci, Adelphi University

Kathryn P. Davison, Southern Methodist University

Benjamín Domínguez, National Autonomous University of Mexico

Eugenia Georges, Rice University

Susan Lee Goldman, Yale University

Ioseba Iraurgi, Basque Country University, Spain

John Kinyon, Pennsylvania State University

John P. Kline, University of Arizona

Julie D. Lane, University of Virginia

Michael J. Mahoney, University of North Texas

Gloria Martínez, National Autonomous University of Mexico

John D. Mayer, University of New Hampshire

Victor Manuel Méndez, National Autonomous University of Mexico

María de los Angeles Meza, National Autonomous University of Mexico

Yolanda Olvera, National Polytechnic Institute, Mexico City

Dario Paez, Basque Country University, Spain

Tibor P. Palfai, Yale University

James W. Pennebaker, Southern Methodist University

Sara Lidia Pérez, National Autonomous University of Mexico

Keith J. Petrie, University of Auckland, New Zealand

Bernard Rimé, University of Louvain, Belgium

Lizabeth Roemer, Pennsylvania State University

Peter Salovey, Yale University

Gary E. Schwartz, University of Arizona

Amparo Silva, National Autonomous University of Mexico
William B. Stiles, Miami University, Ohio
Harald C. Traue, University of Ulm, Germany
Carolyn Turvey, Yale University
Pablo Valderrama, National Autonomous University of Mexico
Maite Valdoseda, Basque Country University, Spain
Carmen Velasco, Basque Country University, Spain
Daniel M. Wegner, University of Virginia
Jane Wellenkamp, University of California, Los Angeles

Preface

Emotional upheavals can disrupt virtually all aspects of our lives. Illness rates, levels of rumination, and social conflict typically increase following traumatic experiences. A central psychological question concerns how people overcome these events. On the basis of research over the past decade, psychologists now have a strong sense that talking or even writing about emotions or personal upheavals can boost autonomic nervous system activity, immune function, and physical health. Although the links between disclosure and health have now been firmly established, why such links exist is still unknown. The purpose of this book, then, is to address some of the most basic issues of psychology: How do people respond to emotional upheavals in their lives and why? Why does translating an event into language affect physical and psychological health? How can our understanding of disclosure and health be applied in clinically useful and cost-effective ways?

The guiding idea of this book was to bring together a diverse group of thinkers and researchers to address why translating upsetting experiences into words can promote physical and mental health. This is a broad problem that is not the exclusive domain of any subdiscipline within psychology. Rather, if researchers are to understand the links among disclosure, emotion, and health, work in cognitive, physiological, clinical, social, personality, and health psychology as well as allied areas in medicine and anthropology must be considered.

In order to establish a common focus, an international group of researchers met at Fort Burgwin, the Southern Methodist University campus in Taos, New Mexico, in the summer of 1994. The three-day meeting included approximately 40 faculty and graduate students who had been selected on the basis of their research and clinical work related to the broad topic of emotion, disclosure, and health. Following this meeting, participants wrote chapters drawing on their own and others' research. The final product is a series of intriguing perspectives that should be of interest to students, researchers, clinicians, and a general lay audience.

This book and the Taos conference could not have been accomplished without the generous help of Southern Methodist University (SMU) and the Science Directorate of the American Psychological Association (APA). From the beginning, SMU Deans James Jones and Michael Best have offered financial and moral support. Within APA, I am indebted to Virginia Holt and Mary Lynn Skutley for their help. The conference itself would not have been possible without the generous efforts of Nadine Pearce in the SMU-in-Taos office, and the help of the following graduate students at SMU: Michael Crow, Kathy Davison, Sun-Mee Kang, Roberta Mancuso, and Anne Vano. Finally, the conference coordinator, Jane Richards, deserves more praise than anyone. Since this is not an academy award thank-you speech, suffice it to say that dozens of others have been invaluable and have not gone unnoticed.

JAMES W. PENNEBAKER
DALLAS, TEXAS

PART ONE

Introduction

Emotion, Disclosure, and Health: An Overview

James W. Pennebaker

I n the psychological and medical literatures, there is overwhelming evidence that traumatic experiences provoke mental and physical health
problems. A central tenet of most psychotherapies is that talking about
these experiences is beneficial. Indeed, meta-analyses of therapy outcomes
indicate that virtually all therapies—irrespective of their theoretical
orientation—bring about improvements in both psychological and physical health. An important nonspecific feature of therapy is that it allows
individuals to translate their experiences into words. The disclosure
process itself, then, may be as important as any feedback the client receives
from the therapist.

Until the mid-1980s, the scant psychological research on disclosure
focused on interpersonal relationships (Jourard, 1971), the role of confession in healing (Frank, 1961), the broad value of social support (Cobb,
1976), and disclosure within the therapeutic relationship, especially as it
related to transference (Freud, 1920/1966; Rogers, 1951). Occasional stud-

The preparation of this chapter was made possible, in part, by a grant from the National Science Foundation, SBR9411674.

ies in anthropology reported that medical healing ceremonies in Native American, African, and ancient Asian societies typically involved some form of confession or disclosure of secrets by the person who was to be healed (see Georges, chapter 2).

For the past 5 to 8 years, a growing number of researchers from several disciplines have begun investigating why talking or writing about emotional upheavals can influence mental and physical health. For example, investigators have now found that writing about traumatic experiences produces improvements in immune function, drops in physician visits for illness, and better performance at school and work (e.g., Esterling, Antoni, Fletcher, Margulies, & Schneiderman, 1994; Pennebaker, 1993a; Spera, Buhrfeind, & Pennebaker, 1994). Similarly, other studies indicate that the failure to talk or acknowledge significant experiences is associated with increased health problems, autonomic activity, and ruminations (e.g., Rimé, Mesquita, Philippot, & Boca, 1991; Wegner, 1994). Yet other investigations from the cognitive and clinical realms are now finding that traumatic experiences affect basic cognitive and memory processes (Freyd, 1993) and the abilities to construct coherent narratives (Mahoney, 1991).

The increasingly clear links among traumatic experiences, emotional expression, cognitive processes, and language have been difficult to study because they cross several areas of expertise within psychology. The purpose of this book is to bring together a diverse group of thinkers to address some of the central features of the disclosure–health relationship. As suggested by the organization of the book, three of these features include the cognitive, emotional, and social dimensions of disclosure.

COGNITIVE PROCESSING IN INHIBITING AND DISCLOSING

When upheavals occur in our lives, we think differently. Common symptoms of thought disruptions include ruminating and worrying. Why do these cognitive changes occur? One argument that has roots in Freud's dream analyses as well as in the Gestalt views of perception is that individuals are psychologically attempting to reach closure or, in some way, resolve the upheaval (cf. Horowitz, 1976; Martin, Tesser, & McIntosh, 1993). Recent work on thought suppression provides another perspective: The reason that we ruminate about events is because we are trying not to ruminate about them (Wegner & Lane, chapter 3, this volume). The mere act of thought suppression— whether about distressing traumas or titillating secrets—makes the thoughts more accessible and difficult to dislodge from our minds. Several ongoing clinical investigations are examining techniques that may reduce people's levels of worrying and ruminating. Borkovec and colleagues (chapter 4, this volume) provide exciting evidence to suggest that disclosure and worry may be opposite sides of the same coin. Whereas future-oriented worry may disrupt health, disclosure about the past may reduce worrying and improve health.

If talking about the past reduces ruminations and worries, how does it work? One idea is that translating experiences into words forces some kind of structure to the experiences themselves. Through language individuals are able to organize, structure, and ultimately assimilate both their emotional experiences and the events that may have provoked the emotions. In his analyses of client disclosure within a therapeutic setting, Stiles (chapter 5, this volume) proposes that talking about an event accomplishes two important goals. First, talking both reflects and reduces anxiety. Second, repeated disclosure over time gradually promotes the assimilation of the upsetting event. Interestingly, Bucci (chapter 6, this volume) offers a complementary explanation. Coming from a psychoanalytic perspective, she suggests that an effective psychotherapeutic discourse progresses from a concrete description of an event to the creation of a more abstract narrative of it.

EMOTIONS, EXPRESSIVENESS, AND PSYCHOSOMATICS

When individuals write or talk about emotional events, important biological changes occur. During confession in the laboratory, for example, talking about traumas brings about striking reductions in blood pressure, muscle tension, and skin conductance during or immediately after the disclosure. These biological effects are most apparent among participants who express emotion. Indeed, other laboratory studies indicate that long-term health benefits of disclosure are only apparent if individuals are encouraged to write about or express their emotions as opposed to providing factual accounts of their upheavals (Pennebaker, 1989). The disclosure–health link, then, is closely tied into our understanding of emotions and their biological concomitants.

A traditional debate within psychology and psychosomatics has surrounded the definition of emotion. Is it more important, for example, to consider emotion as a subjective experience or as its expressive or biological manifestations? As the contributors to this volume indicate, this overlooks the fact that all components of an emotional experience may have important health correlates. Salovey and his colleagues (in chapter 7 of this volume) make a compelling case that the subjective ways by which we perceive and cope with our emotions can influence health and social behaviors. Traue (chapter 8, this volume), drawing on the rich and sometimes controversial assumptions of Harold G. Wolff (e.g., Wolf & Goodell, 1968) and Wilhelm Reich (1949), provides impressive data that link inhibited emotional expressiveness in various parts of the body to headache and back pain. In short, both subjective experienced emotion and the bases of emotional expressiveness are tied to health and illness.

One reason that researchers in psychology have shied away from studying emotion and its links to illness is that they have not known how to deal with the concept of *repression*. Clinical signs of emotional repression and denial are observed quite frequently. When a friend assures one that he is happy and relaxed in the midst of an emotional upheaval and, at the same time, his facial muscles are rigid and his speech is clipped and hostile, one knows something is amiss. A discipline that relies too heavily on straightforward self-reports cannot, by definition, see or measure repression (cf. Shedler, Mayman, & Manis, 1993).

The repression or inhibition of emotion is central to an understanding of disclosure. In theory, individuals who attempt to confront traumatic experiences without acknowledging emotions should not benefit and could, perhaps, suffer from disclosure. The work by Schwartz and Kline (chapter 9, this volume) indicates that individuals who are classified as repressive copers are, indeed, hyperresponsive to emotional stimuli as measured by brain wave and even immune system activity. Paez and his colleagues (chapter 10, this volume) extend this thinking by focusing on the often-maligned but intuitively appealing concept of *alexithymia*—a conceptual cousin of repression. In their work with cancer patients, the authors are discovering that alexithymics may be at greater risk for both psychological and biological problems. Finally, Petrie, Booth, and Davison (chapter 11, this volume) offer an important overview of repression, disclosure, and immune function. Their chapter describes how and why the immune system taps psychologically relevant dimensions associated with emotions.

CLINICAL AND SOCIAL DIMENSIONS OF DISCLOSURE

Disclosure of one's deepest thoughts and feelings is a powerful social phenomenon, whether in a therapeutic setting or in daily life. Talking about intimate topics with another person typically assumes a particular level of trust between the participants. Furthermore, the degree to which one discloses personal experiences may have profound positive or negative effects on the relationship. Whereas talking about a trauma may make the discloser feel better, it can make the listener feel worse (Pennebaker, 1990, 1993b).

Within a clinical setting, the client's disclosure of powerful negative emotions can provoke meaningful thoughts and images within the therapist. Drawing on a constructivist perspective, Mahoney (chapter 12, this volume) suggests that the most effective therapy occurs when both the therapist and client are able to build on their shared emotions together. To accomplish this, the therapist must be attuned to both his or her own emotions as well as to those of the client. Whereas Mahoney examines the joint emotional world of the therapist and client, Domínguez and colleagues (chapter 13, this volume) take a very different strategy in dealing with clients' emotions. They believe that the ultimate goal of therapy is to help people learn to reverse their emotions quickly, going from negative to positive states.

Moving beyond the laboratory and clinic, Rimé and Wellenkamp (chapters 14 & 15 of this volume, respectively) address the nature of the social sharing and disclosure of emotions among people in the real world on a daily basis. In an intriguing series of studies, Rimé demonstrates that an overwhelming majority of people share most of their emotional experiences with others. This natural tendency, however, is most likely to be blocked for the emotions of shame. In addition, he finds that social sharing is powerful in reducing anxiety and psychological distress with a variety of populations. Wellenkamp, an anthropologist, supports many of these observations on the basis of her field work with the Toraja culture from the remote regions of Indonesia. Wellenkamp, like Georges (chapter 2), helps to put disclosure into the broader cultural perspective. That is, many but not all cultures look favorably on the sharing of emotions. In addition, the types of emotions and the modes of expression vary considerably.

SUMMARY

The links among emotion, disclosure, and health exist at multiple levels of analysis. Within Western culture, the disclosure of traumatic and emotional experiences can promote physical and psychological health. The underlying mechanisms for this phenomenon are cognitive, emotional, biological, and social. Each of these systems of understanding are intimately interrelated. Shakespeare's King Lear, Rostand's Cyrano de Bergerac, the Truly Guilty person in any of Erle Stanley Gardner's Perry Mason books, or even the wolf in Little Red Riding Hood all change once they reveal their true identities. Their thoughts, behaviors, probable physiology, and relationships to others are immediately transformed—usually, but not always, for the best. Once the disclosure is made, however, the person (or wolf) becomes an internally consistent creature, wherein all features of mind and body become synchronous.

REFERENCES

Cobb, S. (1976). Social support as a moderator of life stress. *Psychosomatic Medicine, 38,* 300–313.

Esterling, B. A., Antoni, M., Fletcher, M., Margulies, S., & Schneiderman, N. (1994). Emotional disclosure through writing or speaking modulates latent Epstein-Barr virus reactivation. *Journal of Consulting and Clinical Psychology, 62,* 130–140.

Frank, J. D. (1961). *Persuasion and healing.* Baltimore: Johns Hopkins Press.

Freud, S. (1966). *Introductory lectures in psychoanalysis* (J. Strachey, Trans.). New York: W. W. Norton & Co. (Original work published 1920)

Freyd, J. J. (1993). *Theoretical and personal perspectives on the delayed memory debate.* Center for Mental Health at Foote Hospital's Continuing Education Conference: Ann Arbor, MI.

Horowitz, M. (1976). *Stress response syndromes.* Northvale, NJ: Jason Aronson.

Jourard, S. M. (1971). *Self-disclosure: An experimental analysis of the transparent self.* New York: Wiley-Interscience.

Mahoney, M. J. (1991). *Human change processes: The scientific foundations of psychotherapy.* New York: Basic Books.

Martin, L. L., Tesser, A., & McIntosh, W. D. (1993). Wanting but not having: The effects of unattained goals on thoughts and feelings. In D. M. Wegner and J. W. Pennebaker (Eds.), *Handbook of mental control* (pp. 552–572). Englewood Cliffs, NJ: Prentice Hall.

Pennebaker, J. W. (1989). Confession, inhibition, and disease. In L. Berkowitz (Ed.), *Advances in experimental social psychology: Vol. 22* (pp. 211–244). New York: Academic Press.

Pennebaker, J. W. (1990). *Opening up: The healing power of confiding in others.* New York: William Morrow.

Pennebaker, J. W. (1993a). Putting stress into words: Health, linguistic, and therapeutic implications. *Behaviour Research and Therapy, 31,* 539–548.

Pennebaker, J. W. (1993b). Mechanisms of social constraint. In D. M. Wegner & J. W. Pennebaker (Eds.), *Handbook of mental control* (pp. 200–219). Englewood Cliffs, NJ: Prentice Hall.

Reich, W. (1949). *Character analysis* (3rd ed.). New York: Orgone Institute Press.

Rimé, B., Mesquita, B., Philippot, P., & Boca, S. (1991). Beyond the emotional event: Six studies on the social sharing of emotion. *Cognition & Emotion, 5,* 435–465.

Rogers, C. R. (1951). *Client-centered therapy: Its current practice, implications, and theory.* Boston: Houghton Mifflin.

Shedler, J., Mayman, M., & Manis, M. (1993). The illusion of mental health. *American Psychologist, 48,* 1117–1131.

Spera, S. P., Buhrfeind, E. D., & Pennebaker, J. W. (1994). Expressive writing and coping with job loss. *Academy of Management Journal, 37,* 722–733.

Wegner, D. M. (1994). Ironic processes of mental control. *Psychological Review, 101,* 34–52.

Wolf, S. & Goodell, H. (1968). *Harold G. Wolff's stress and disease* (2nd ed.). Springfield, IL: Charles C Thomas.

2

A Cultural and Historical Perspective on Confession

Eugenia Georges

The disclosure of deeply personal topics as a therapeutic technique is an entrenched and long-standing feature of Western culture. Cross-culturally, as well, confession-as-therapy is found in a widely diverse array of societies. However, in other cultures, confession is absent—and even actively discouraged—on the premise that the disclosure of intimate thoughts and feelings would compromise health and well-being.

In a number of essays, Pennebaker and his colleagues have demonstrated the health benefits of confession for middle class Americans (see, e.g., Pennebaker, 1993). Beyond the objective manifestation of these benefits, such as reduced number of doctors visits and enhanced immune function, Pennebaker's subjects themselves consistently described the practice of disclosure, even when it occurs under experimental conditions, as highly meaningful and valuable to them. In this chapter, I examine the meanings attached to confession in cultures that rely on the practice to effect healing, as well as in those that explicitly proscribe it in order to maintain health. In addition, I briefly sketch the long pedigree of confession-as-therapy in the Western tradition. My objectives are, first, to add (albeit in a brief and programmatic way) an ethnographic dimension to the study of the therapeutic implications of confession and, second, to apply to the research on the relationships among disclosure, emotions, and health some of the central insights to have emerged from the cross-cultural study of health-related beliefs and practices within anthropology. I hope that, through such a comparative perspective, the question of what is culturally-specific about the relationship between disclosure and health, and what is universal, can be more fruitfully explored in future work.

CONFESSION AS SYMBOLIC HEALING

From the perspective of medical anthropology, disclosure is usefully categorized as a form of symbolic healing: a therapy that is based on the ritual use of words and symbols (cf. Kleinman, 1988). It is important to note that ritual can be secular as well as religious, and that here it refers simply to a repetitive, patterned and symbolic enactment of a cultural belief or value (Davis-Floyd 1992). The efficacy of symbolic therapies is contingent on a shared symbolic universe that ensures that a given therapy carries culturally specific meaning. In other words, a symbolic therapy is meaningful and can be said to "work" insofar as it is related to the theories of illness-causation of a particular culture and, more broadly, to other aspects of that culture (this is anthropology's hallmark *holism*).

Healing is facilitated when symbolic therapies are used to effect changes in emotional and physiological states, although the links between the symbolic and the physiological are as yet not well understood. The central anthropological insight here is that historically determined cultural values and social processes give meaning to a symbolic therapy and, in doing so, facilitate its ability to heal within a given context. Early socialization into this symbolic system, through the acquisition of language and culture, provides the framework that enables people to make sense of their interior experiences (Kleinman, 1980). Symbols carry unique force in this regard because they are simultaneously internalized and are, thus, an integral part of internal experience. Yet they also exist externally, as part of the individual's "objective" and "commonsense" experience at the level of action (Munn, 1974; Comaroff, 1983). Thus, from the perspective of the anthropology of healing, forms of symbolic therapy, such as confession, must be analyzed and explicated as intimately embedded within the context of specific sociocultural processes.

In the following three sections, I first trace the long historical presence of confession-as-healing modality in the West and point to some of its associations with widely held lay and professional beliefs. Second, I turn to examples of non-Western cultures in which confession plays a prominent role in healing and health promotion and discuss the distinctive interpretations of confession-as-healing characteristic of each of these cultures. Third, I present examples of cultures in which disclosure is regarded as detrimental to health and subject to negative sanctions, as well as cultures in which nondisclosure is believed to promote health.

WESTERNERS: THE "CONFESSING ANIMALS"

Self-disclosure has been an important technique of both specialist and folk understandings of the self through some two millennia of Western history, prompting one observer of this history to call Westerners "confessing animals" (Foucault, 1978). Although the practice of self-disclosure has been remarkably persistent in the West, the meanings and ends have varied considerably at different times.

Disclosure as a method of self-knowledge can be traced at least as far back as the Stoic philosophers of the first two centuries A.D. For the Stoics, daily inscription of one's thoughts and actions in diaries, journals, and letters was a means of knowing one's self in order to overcome flaws and refashion the self according to a specific ethos or model. The objective of this reflective process was both moral and medical well-being, and ongoing attention to health maintenance was one of the significant features of contemplative self-disclosure (Foucault, 1988).

In early Christianity, confession also played an important role as a technique for understanding the self. However, confession for Christians was put to quite different ends from those of the Stoics. Whereas the Stoics recorded daily conduct in order to measure it against the rules of proper comportment and make corrections in the future, for Christians confession was directed at exposing the hidden thoughts and sins they harbored and at engaging in continual struggle with the enemy lurking within. Despite these differences, the association of confession with medical ends made by the Stoics can also be found in early Christianity. The identification of the pastor–confessor as a "physician of souls" is probably traceable to the notion of Christ as a healer and to the medical ministrations of early Church Fathers. The use of medical metaphors in connection with confession goes back as far as the influential writings of John Cassian (360–435 A.D.), founder of Christian monasticism. An association between confession and healing is also found in the early Christian penitential literature (Jackson, 1985).

When confession was declared obligatory by the Fourth Lateran Council early in the thirteenth century, a large body of literature appeared to codify and catalogue the cardinal sins and to detail the guidelines for their ritual confession. These penitential manuals and handbooks often associated sins with afflictions that could be healed through the technique of confession. The Fourth Lateran Council also made it obligatory for pastors to preach regularly to their parishioners. With this obligation, the idea that sins were afflictions that could be treated and cured, at least in part, through confession, became widely diffused as well as more standardized as preachers drew on the penitential manuals and handbooks for their guidelines (Jackson, 1985, p. 49).

Although obligatory confession to a priest was rejected by the Protestant revolution, the practice of confessional self-inspection nonetheless persisted. For the Puritans in the seventeenth century, for example, daily writing in confessional diaries was a technique for monitoring one's state of sin. However, in contrast to earlier Christian traditions in which confessions were made to a spiritual guide, in the Protestant tradition, the individual now served as both sinner and judge of his or her own self (Rose, 1990).

Foucault (1980) has called attention to Freud's appropriation of the technique of spoken confession from the Catholic Church. However, in psychoanalysis a break occurs in the long tradition of self-disclosure in the West, as confession loses its overtly ethical or religious purposes and becomes thoroughly directed to medical ends (Hutton, 1988). In the twentieth century, as professional medicine (including psychotherapy) has extended its influence into and control over a wide variety of human activities previously outside its purview (through the process of medicalization), the practice of confession has spread more widely and become even more entrenched.

Thus, confession in the West has a long history as a culturally authorized "idiom of distress" that is associated with some benefits to body and soul. The authority of confession as a form of healing is strengthened by its long history of therapeutic associations in the West and the more recent imprimatur of health psychology and psychosomatic medicine. In short, confession in the West takes place in a cultural context "defined as one that will make us better and taking place within the powerful ambit of a tradition, an authority, a history of cases and cures" (Rose, 1990, p. 246).

Beyond this long lineage in the specialized discourses of philosophy, religion, and medicine, and adding further to its cultural authority, is the fact that in American culture, disclosure also fits well with a prevalent folk model of the emotions—particularly of negative emotions—and of the benefits to be had by their verbalization. The linguists Lakoff and Kovecses (1987), in their analysis of metaphors of anger, for example, have demonstrated the pervasiveness of the metaphorical folk conception of the body as a "container for the emotions." Furthermore, like many other commonly used metaphors of the body and its functioning, this is a mechanical metaphor that is based on a hydraulic analogy. Thus, in American English, anger is metaphorized as heat or fluid that can dangerously accumulate in the bodily container, causing physiological damage if not allowed to exit. Although the specific implications for healing and health maintenance are not pursued by Lakoff and Kovecses, folk understandings clearly mark "letting off steam," "getting something off your chest," and the like as salutary processes.

In short, in the West, and perhaps most intensely in the contemporary middle class in the United States, in which psychology and psychotherapy has more pervasively influenced popular culture, self-disclosure is a technique that has long-standing implications for health and its maintenance. In the following section, I turn to ethnographic examples of disclosure from two very different cultural contexts.

DISCLOSURE IN NON-WESTERN SOCIETIES

One problem in examining disclosure in non-Western cultures is that, with some exceptions, the practice is rarely the central focus of ethnographers' descriptions of healing and health beliefs. Among the exceptions are the detailed descriptions provided by A. Irving Hallowell, a psychoanalytically trained anthropologist who has provided a very detailed description of confession as part of Ojibwa healing, and Victor Turner, who has thoroughly described health beliefs and healing practices of the Ndembu of West Africa.

From Hallowell's (1963) descriptions of relatively unacculturated Ojibwa living in the 1930s and 1940s in Canada, it is clear that confession was an important technique used to effect healing in cases of serious illness. The Ojibwa, like many other peoples cross-culturally, regard serious illness as a penalty for violating social norms and moral precepts. Serious illnesses understandably generated fear and anxiety and, given the Ojibwa's view of their etiology, became a matter of reflection on the connections between the individual and the social body. Serious illness signaled the violation of cultural norms highly significant to this egalitarian, hunting–fishing society: failure to share food and other material possessions, failure to reciprocate with others who had previously shared with you, manifestations of competitiveness, and acts of cruelty and of proscribed sexual activity.

Healing was believed to occur after a healer elicited a confession from the sick person. However, in contrast to much of the Western tradition, confessions were not private, dyadic transactions, and patients were not isolated. On the contrary, confessions were public statements of transgression, made to the group. They were also in a real sense compulsory, for even if the patient wanted to withhold the disclosure of her or his transgressions, the healer would find out anyway through the assistance of his "other-than-human" helpers ("grandfather" spirits who routinely interacted with humans). In essence, then, serious illnesses forced the sick

16

person to accept responsibility for culturally disapproved conduct in full public view. Ritual confession thus provided a recurrent public forum for stating and restating the core values of Ojibwan culture to members of the group as well as a venue for the socialization of children. In Hallowell's (1963) opinion,

> . . . insofar as primary moral values could be linked with the un-predictable and periodic occurrence of the illness of individuals, a workable psychological means was provided for reinforcing confor-mity with approved values, through the generation of fear, anxiety and guilt. While such an interpretation of sickness could not lead to any kind of treatment that promoted the survival of individuals . . . a disease sanction would become adaptive in relation to the maintenance and persistence of socio-cultural systems. (Hallowell, 1963, p. 264)

For the Ndembu of West Africa, confession is also an important tech-nique for effecting the healing of serious illness. As in the Ojibwa case, confession is publically performed. Furthermore, for the Ndembu, seri-ous illness occasions *multiple* confessions of wrong-doing and wrong-thinking. The Ndembu healer orchestrates the confessions of not only the patient, but also those of relatives, neighbors, and other members of the community who must all confess in order that the sick person get well. As Turner has shown in a series of studies (see especially 1967), the Ndembu, like the Ojibwa, believe that individual illness is an indication that some-thing has gone awry in the social body. According to Turner, the Ndembu doctor heals by tapping into the various streams of affect associated with conflicts and inter-personal disputes that have built up in the community over time. Confessions are thus used as a mechanism (along with other cultural practices) for transforming ill-feeling into well-wishing, for re-structuring relationships to restore social harmony, and for reintegrating the sick person into the social group.

For the Ndembu and the Ojibwa, as for many Westerners, there is a clear and positive association between the disclosure of personal events and the restoration of health. Yet, in comparing Western practices of dis-closure with those other cultures, some striking differences are also evident (moreover, these differences are seen in the organization of healing more generally).

Whereas the Western practice of disclosure is dyadic and private, occurring between an individual and a confessor, who may be only symbolically present, confession for the Ojibwa and the Ndembu is public and embedded within, and oriented toward, the social group (the family and the larger community). While for Westerners the goal of disclosure is enlightenment through the process of self-reflection or alleviation from the "work" or "burden" of containing negative emotion, for the Ojibwa and the Ndembu the goal of therapy is collective: to restore social relations to a harmonious keel. Indeed, in such "sociotherapy," the patient and his or her affliction would appear to serve as the pretext for effecting the broader social goals of confirming social norms and restoring both cosmological and social balance (Mullings, 1984). Yet given a sociocentric, relational view of the self, that is, one in which the self is defined and presented in social interaction (Gaines, 1992), it follows that therapies will also be concerned with social relations. Such a sociocentric focus contrasts sharply with the emphasis on the needs and rights of the individual in the Western practice of confession.

SWALLOWING THE SEEDS OF THE BITTER MELON: NONDISCLOSURE AS A TECHNIQUE FOR MAINTAINING HEALTH

In stark contrast to the examples above, in other cultures disclosing negative emotions and one's "deepest thoughts and feelings" is believed to be directly responsible for poor health, illness, and general misfortune. Here I also select two ethnographic examples, Bali and Taiwan, once again primarily on the basis of the richness of the available literature on the cultural meanings assigned to nondisclosure.

Probably the most detailed description of a culture that negatively values disclosure is provided for north Bali in Unni Wikan's recent ethnography, *Managing Turbulent Hearts* (1990). According to Wikan (1990), Balinese are socialized from infancy not to disclose negative emotions such as sadness and anger. Children are taught that such emotions can be conquered by the strategies of "not caring" and "forgetting" as well as by laughing and joking, even in the most somber of circumstances. These strategies are regarded as techniques essential to "managing the heart" and presenting a "a clear and happy face" to others, a culturally appropriate and highly valued style of dealing with negative events and emotions. Thus, by this logic, Balinese do not cry at funerals and may laugh at hearing the news of someone's death.

For the Balinese, "not caring" and "forgetting" are explicitly linked with the preservation of sanity and health. Balinese do not disclose emotional difficulties often, even to family and close friends, for two reasons. The first is compassion for others, since it is believed that sadness spreads when it is verbally and nonverbally expressed. The second is to maintain their own mental calmness, since by not disclosing emotion and "forgetting," it is thought to be possible to shape inner feeling itself. According to the Balinese, not to think about something is not to feel it. This is not to say that Balinese do not feel anger, sadness, and envy. These emotions are felt, often intensely, and the Balinese can provide detailed physiological descriptions of their effects. Thus, anger, for example, gives a characteristically "hot" feeling because it causes the blood to push through body too quickly. It weighs on the heart and causes an inner pressure. However, these undesirable feelings cannot be eliminated by going more deeply into them. The only appropriate technique for their elimination is to try not to think about and not to care about the experience that aggravates the feeling. In this effort, laughter is regarded as especially effective.

It is important to stress that Balinese acknowledge that these strategies involve much emotional work, effort, and struggle. Not caring may be difficult to accomplish, but there is a moral obligation to engage in that struggle, on the one hand, and an imperative for health maintenance and the prevention of illness, on the other. When a person succeeds in not caring, he or she is believed to emerge fresh and strong and with an enhanced sense of self-worth. Disclosing negative emotions and experiences is thought to increase susceptibility to illness by weakening one's life force. Not caring, in contrast, strengthens this force and helps maintain good health. In addition, and of equal importance, is the association of nondisclosure with Balinese understandings of black magic. Black magic is believed to be an omnipresent potential threat to well-being. Because strong emotions such as sadness or anger can blur judgment, they can result in a person offending, disappointing, or hurting others and provoking their magical attacks. Under these circumstances, disclosure could threaten an individual's very survival.

The second example of positive valuation of nondisclosure draws on the nearly two decades of research in Taiwan and the People's Republic of China by the psychiatrist and anthropologist Arthur Kleinman (1980, 1988). According to Kleinman, emotions for the Chinese are private and embarrassing, or shameful, events, with polluting qualities. Thus, they are best left unscrutinized and are almost never disclosed to others. What would be called psychological insight in the United States, the Chinese regard as self-absorption. Thus, children learn from an early age not to attend to their emotional states. When feelings are expressed, it is generally in somatic terms, using idioms of bodily organs and their functioning. Kleinman (1980) writes that when practicing psychiatry in Taiwan he continually experienced exasperation and helplessness in his attempts to get his Chinese patients to talk about their negative emotions. This was not a matter of denial or suppression; rather, the Chinese did not think in terms of the intrapsychic qualities of these emotions and lacked a language for their expression. Finally, like the Balinese, the Chinese believe that the excessive expression of feelings will disturb the harmony of the body and lead to illness (1980).

From studies of Chinese psychiatrists and their clinical encounters with patients also conducted by Kleinman, it is evident that this understanding of emotions underlies professional ideology as well. For instance, in a transcript of a psychiatric interview from the People's Republic, a psychiatrist advises a female patient suffering from depression and anxiety that "You must contain your anger. You know the old adage: 'Be deaf and dumb! Swallow the seeds of the bitter melon! Don't speak out!' " (1988, p. 97). American psychiatrists find such prescriptions superficial, Kleinman (1988) observes, because American psychiatry is heavily influenced by "implicit Western cultural values about the nature of the self and its pathologies which emphasize a deep, hidden, private self" (p. 98). In China, common implicit cultural values also underlie professional and lay knowledges. In the Chinese case, however, these values affirm an understanding of the self that is more sociocentric, more attuned to and resonant with relational and situational contexts than to inner, private states. In China, as in the United States and elsewhere, it is the existence of these commonalities between lay and professional understandings and, more specifically, of congruent expectations regarding the clinical encounter, that is the requisite for the credibility and efficacy of specific therapies (Gaines, 1992; Kleinman, 1988).

In this chapter, I have argued for the examination of confessional practices within the framework of culturally and historically specific contexts. From this perspective, it becomes evident that no single, universal meaning or function can be attributed to the institutionalized disclosure of intimate thoughts and feelings. Rather, I have attempted to show that both disclosure and nondisclosure are related to particular cultural expectations of health and of cure. Furthermore, the fact that both disclosure and nondisclosure are deployed to therapeutic ends in a wide variety of cultures suggests the possibility that a range of habitual strategies exists for dealing with negative emotions, and that the specific strategy chosen may vary according to a culture's understanding of emotions, the self, and the maintenance of health.

REFERENCES

Comaroff, J. (1983). The defectiveness of symbols or the symbols of defectiveness? On the cultural analysis of medical systems. *Culture, Medicine and Psychiatry, 7,* 3–20.

Davis-Floyd, R. (1992). *Birth as an American rite of passage.* Berkeley: University of California Press.

Foucault, M. (1978). *The history of sexuality: An introduction.* (Robert Hurley, Trans.). New York: Pantheon.

Foucault, M. (1980). The confessions of the flesh. In C. Gordon (Ed.), *Power/knowledge: Selected interviews and other writings* (pp. 211–213). New York: Pantheon.

Foucault, M. (1988). Technologies of the self. In L. Martin, H. Gutman, and P. Hutton (Eds.), *Technologies of the self: A seminar with Michel Foucault* (pp. 16–49). Amherst: University of Massachusetts Press.

Gaines, A. (1992). Ethnopsychiatry: The cultural construction of psychiatries. In A. Gaines (Ed.), *Ethnopsychiatry: The cultural construction of professional and folk psychiatries* (pp. 3–49). Albany: State University of New York Press.

Hallowell, A. I. (1963). Ojibwa world view and disease. In I. Goldston (Ed.), *Man's image in medicine and anthropology* (pp. 258–315). New York: International Universities Press.

Hutton, P. (1988). Foucault, Freud and the technologies of the self. In L. Martin, H. Gutman, and P. Hutton (Eds.), *Technologies of the self: A seminar with Michel Foucault* (pp. 121–144). Amherst: University of Massachusetts Press.

Jackson, S. (1985). Acedia the sin and its relationship to sorrow and melancholia. In A. Kleinman and B. Good (Eds.), *Culture and depression: Studies in the anthropology and cross-cultural psychiatry of affect and disorder* (pp. 43–62). Berkeley: University of California Press.

Kleinman, A. (1980). *Patients and healers in the context of culture.* Berkeley: University of California Press.

Kleinman, A. (1988). *Rethinking psychiatry: From cultural category to personal experience.* New York: The Free Press.

Lakoff, G. and Kovecses, Z. (1987). The cognitive model of anger inherent in American English. In N. Quinn and D. Holland (Eds.), *Cultural models in language and thought* (pp. 195–221). Cambridge: Cambridge University Press.

Mullings, L. (1984). *Therapy, ideology and social change: Mental healing in urban Ghana.* Berkeley: University of California Press.

Munn, N. (1974). Symbolism in a ritual context: Aspects of symbolic action. In J. Honigmann (Ed.), *Handbook of social and cultural anthropology.* Chicago: Rand McNally.

Pennebaker, J. W. (1993). Putting stress into words: Health, linguistic, and therapeutic implications. *Behavior, Research and Therapy* 6: 539–548.

Rose, N. (1990). *Governing the soul: The shaping of the private self.* London: Routledge & Kegan Paul.

Turner, V. (1967). *The forest of symbols: Aspects of Ndembu ritual.* New York: Cornell University Press.

Wikan, U. (1990). *Managing turbulent hearts: A Balinese formula for living.* Chicago: The University of Chicago Press.

PART TWO

Cognitive Processes in Inhibiting and Disclosing

3

From Secrecy to Psychopathology

Daniel M. Wegner and Julie D. Lane

E veryone has certain thoughts that are not shared with others. Whether these thoughts are sexy, pathetic, grotesque, malevolent, or merely ordinary, psychologists since Freud (e.g., 1913/1953) have placed considerable emphasis on such thoughts in the analysis of mind and behavior. It seems sensible, after all, that any thought a person would keep secret might somehow be important to the person's psychological makeup. Usually, the logical progression here is understood as going from thought importance to secrecy: It may be that important or diagnostic or central thoughts are kept secret because they are fundamental. What we wish to suggest in this chapter is the reverse of the usual progression: Secret, innermost thoughts may start out unimportant, but then grow through the processes involved in maintaining secrecy to become fundamental preoccupations in the individual's life. Eventually, innermost thoughts may become the seeds of psychopathology. One of the reasons that opening up and sharing one's hidden thoughts is beneficial may be that disclosure staves off the nega-

We wish to thank Cheryl Witt for her help in preparing this chapter. Preparation of this chapter was supported by National Institute of Mental Health grant MH-49127.

tive psychological, and oftentimes pathogenic, effects produced by keeping secrets (Ellenberger, 1966).

This chapter begins with an analysis of the kinds of thoughts that people keep secret. We then consider a *preoccupation model of secrecy* that suggests how it is that any thought might, when kept secret, become a target of obsessive thinking and attention. Evidence for this model is reviewed briefly, and finally, we examine some implications of the model for the study of the role of secrecy in psychopathology more generally.

CATEGORIES OF SECRET THOUGHTS

What makes anyone keep a secret? As a first step in understanding secret thoughts, it is useful to have a picture of the kinds of pressures that might make individuals want to keep their thoughts from others. A first general idea represented in many literatures, of course, is the notion that secret thoughts are kept inside as a result of a person's concern about the social consequences of disclosure (e.g., Bok, 1982; Burnam, 1991; Hillix, Harari, & Mohr, 1979; Larson & Chastain, 1990; Simmel, 1950; Stiles, 1987; Wegner & Erber, 1993). People keep secrets because they anticipate ostracism, retaliation, derision, maniacal laughter, armed intervention, or worse—all the results of social disapproval. We hoped to refine our understanding of this general motive for secrecy, and so we conducted an analysis of data on secret thoughts collected by Lane and Wegner (in press).

For this study, a group of 237 college students at the University of Virginia (126 women, 97 men, and 14 lost souls who did not provide gender information) spent a few minutes rating the degree to which they kept their thoughts about each of a series of topics secret from others. Each participant received a list of 50 thought topics and was asked to rate each one on a 5-point scale according to the degree to which he or she tried to keep thoughts on that topic secret. The set of topics included both those that might be highly secret for most people and those that might be secret for only a few, and were derived from an examination of the literatures on secrecy, disclosure, worry, obsessive thinking, and thought suppression (see Lane & Wegner, in press). Each participant in the group administration was asked to be as forthcoming as possible in making these ratings, and confidentiality was guaranteed by arranging for the return of anonymous response sheets through a slot atop a sealed box that participants understood would only be opened when the sheets from all participants were inside and were not distinguishable.

The ratings were submitted to a principal axis factor analysis that accounted for 44% of the rating variance, and a varimax rotation was performed on the four factors with eigenvalues over 1.75. The solution for items loading above .40 on any factor is shown in Table 1. We find that the 4 factors can be understood to represent distinct categories of secret thoughts: *offenses, worries, sorrows,* and *sins.* Before we comment on the categories individually, it is worth noting that they each formed fairly reliable scales in this sample (Cronbach's α for the 4 factors, respectively, was .86, .84, .79, and .77). Also, in the population we studied, the degree of secrecy for these different topics varied. Averaging over topics within each category, secrecy was greatest for sorrows ($M = 2.81$), less for offenses ($M = 2.31$), even less for sins ($M = 1.80$), and least for worries ($M = 1.67$), with all differences significant at $p < .05$. It should be remembered, though, that ratings of keeping thoughts secret are likely to be predicated on a participant's *having* such thoughts; if a person seldom thinks of offenses at all, for example, ratings of the secrecy of thoughts of offenses might well be reduced accordingly. This could influence both the category means and reliabilities. Suffice it to say that at this exploratory stage in our research, these categories form a reasonable first sorting of the kinds of thoughts that people keep secret.

The category of *offenses* includes primarily acts of violence and taboo sexual practices. Many of these are actually crimes, although there are some topics that are merely offensive in some way. They appear to represent overt acts that tend to harm others and that are thus not only socially disapproved but are also often punished by society or by their victims. Most of the acts have a victim other than self, and it is tempting to suggest that the emotional state underlying many if not all of these activities might be anger

Table 1

Factor Analysis of Secret Thought Topics

Topic	Offenses	Worries	Sorrows	Sins
Killing someone	.70	—	—	—
Stealing things	.69	—	—	—
Touching a stranger sexually	.66	—	—	—
Incest	.62	—	—	—
Cheating in school	.61	—	—	—
Fantasies about a teacher	.60	—	—	—
Being a homosexual	.59	—	—	—
Watching X-rated videos	.52	—	—	—
Hitting someone	.50	—	—	—
Masturbation	.49	—	—	—
Rape	.48	—	—	—
Cheating on a lover or friend by seeing someone else	.41	—	—	—
Getting mugged	—	.65	—	—
Getting bitten by a dog	—	.62	—	—
Sleeping in through an important class	—	.61	—	—
Having someone hit me	—	.58	—	—
Being hit by a car	—	.57	—	—
Losing my keys	—	.53	—	—
Leaving my door unlocked	—	.53	—	—
Wearing clothes that aren't clean	—	.53	—	—
Forgetting to put on deodorant	—	.48	—	—
Failing a test	—	.46	—	—
Germs	—	.43	—	—
Being lonely	—	—	.71	—
Someone I am jealous of	—	—	.61	—
Someone I have a crush on	—	—	.56	—
A lie I told	—	—	.54	—

(*continues*)

Table 1 (cont.)				

(Continued)

Topic	Offenses	Worries	Sorrows	Sins
Doing poorly at school	—	—	.52	—
My body	—	—	.52	
Dying	—	—	.49	—
Being in love	—	—	.47	—
Getting AIDS	—	—	.44	—
Sexual intercourse	—	—	.42	—
Using marijuana	—	—	—	.64
Drinking alcohol	—	—	—	.59
Smoking cigarettes	—	—	—	.53
Crack or cocaine	—	—	—	.52
God	—	—	—	.51
Devil	—	—	—	.48
Going crazy	—	—	—	.42
Making myself throw up	—	—	—	.41

or hostility. For the most part, these are the kinds of thoughts that are kept secret in Dostoevsky's *Crime and Punishment* and Poe's *Telltale Heart*.

Worries represent a different category of secrets, thoughts about things that could happen that would victimize oneself. Many of these worries are no doubt very real, and they seem likely to be accompanied by fear or anxiety. They involve potential violence against the self in several cases, but more often consist of the more minor concerns or doubts (e.g., losing one's keys) that come to mind from time to time and prompt checking or a desire for reassurance. By and large, however, these topics represent fairly unlikely occurrences that probably come to mind too often and so prompt thinking—but not disclosure. A person who keeps these things secret would seem to be trying to look brave in the face of worry about the multiple risks of everyday life.

Sorrows are a third category of secrets. The first impression of this category is that it is more of a hodgepodge than the others, dominated by secrets pertaining to close relationships and then containing several other lacks or embarrassments. On reflecting on the conglomeration of topics, however, we came to realize that every item involves a potential for failure or sadness, and that, more so than the other topics, these could be the kinds of things one would want to keep from others as a means of protecting one's self-esteem or avoiding depressive emotion. The relationship orientation of this category may represent the precariousness of relationships and their potential for frequent heartache in the lives of the college students sampled in this study.

We couldn't help but call the final category of secret thoughts *sins.* In part, this was because the category includes several victimless crimes, activities that are socially disapproved but that do not hurt others in any immediate way. Unlike the offenses, then, these thoughts center more on personal moral weaknesses. Curiously, though, the religious thoughts of God and the Devil appeared on this factor as well, and this is what prompted us to view the whole package as sin-relevant. The self-control of disapproved appetites might not be a religious matter in every culture, but it could still be a subset of thought topics whose secrecy covaries reliably.

We are not yet willing to claim that these four factors of secret thoughts are necessarily a precise or exhaustive analysis of the domain. Indeed, we began with an idiosyncratic selection of secret thoughts, and these were rated in only one way by one college sample. And too, we want to reemphasize the preliminary nature of the factor analytic work that led us to this set of categories. We retain a certain enthusiasm for this category system despite these shortcomings, however, because of its interesting mapping on the major negative emotions (anger, fear, sadness, and guilt), and because it thus provides a straightforward way to understand why any thought might be kept secret. In essence, this analysis suggests that people keep thoughts secret to avoid the social consequences that may arise from the creation or expression of the negative emotions underlying those thoughts. Given such a range of motives to keep thoughts secret, it makes sense that people would avoid talking about many things. This is the point of departure for our preoccupation model of secrecy.

THE PREOCCUPATION MODEL OF SECRECY

We have formulated a model that may help to explain part of the connection between secrecy and the development of or maintenance of certain psychological disorders (Lane & Wegner, in press). According to this preoccupation model, secrecy sets into motion certain cognitive processes that can create an obsessive preoccupation with the secret thought. This model comprises these steps: (a) *secrecy causes thought suppression,* (b) *thought suppression causes intrusive thought,* (c) *intrusive thought causes renewed efforts at thought suppression,* and (d) *steps b and c continue in cyclic repetition, as each occurs in response to the other.* We will describe each of these steps in further detail, and then present several studies that provide support for this model.

Secrecy Causes Thought Suppression

The development of a cycle of obsessive preoccupation with a secret has its beginnings in the selection of the mental control strategy of thought suppression to help keep the secret. Secret-keepers are often placed in the unnerving position of having simultaneously to think about their cover-up and not to think about it. Thinking is required because it is important for a secret-bearer to at least be aware of the secret information so that it can be stopped from coming to light. In a sense, then, thinking about the secret is a good thing and it may even be done intentionally in hopes of reminding oneself what should not be revealed. Whenever the secret-keeper is in the presence of someone who must not know the hidden information, however, any thoughts of the secret that come to mind may well threaten to reveal themselves through nonverbal leaks or slips of the tongue. In order to defend against this mental assault it seems that a secret-keeper would be best served by choosing the proactive strategy of attempting to banish all unwanted, secret thoughts from consciousness. This predicts the use of thought suppression as a likely mental control strategy when keeping a secret. Thought suppression may also be used as a preemptive strategy, even before any actual social interaction takes place, to curb the occurrence of secret thoughts during upcoming social encounters.

31

Thought Suppression Causes Intrusive Thought

Unfortunately for secret-keepers, attempts to push thoughts of the secret out of mind often do not work. Past research has found that suppressing thoughts results in those thoughts returning to mind intrusively. Wegner, Schneider, Carter, and White (1987) found that trying not to think of a white bear was extremely difficult for participants, and that when suppression attempts had ended, participants actually experienced a rebound of thoughts of the white bear. A wide array of research now indicates that thought suppression (at least in the short run) is inclined paradoxically to increase the accessibility and return of the unwanted thought, even as compared with intentional concentration on the thought (Wegner, 1989, 1992).

When people attempt thought suppression, two cognitive processes are shifted into gear at the same time (Wegner, 1994). The process of which we are aware, the *operator*, actively tries to direct our thoughts toward anything other than the unwanted thought. At the same time, below the surface of our consciousness the *monitor* is at work automatically searching for occurrences of the unwanted thought. Once the monitor discovers the unwanted thought it hurls it into consciousness where the operator again attempts to suppress it. The operator is usually the dominant process but under conditions of cognitive load its resources are taxed thereby giving the monitor free reign. When the automatic processing becomes the default response, as is the case under high load, the unwanted thought is highlighted and projects into consciousness without a stopguard. In this sense the unwanted thought becomes hyperaccessible to consciousness (Wegner & Erber, 1992). Secret-keepers who rely on thought suppression to rid themselves of thoughts of the secret will quickly find that this strategy backfires and makes the secret likely to spring to mind.

Intrusive Thought Causes Renewed Efforts at Thought Suppression

For a secret-keeper, the recurrence of thoughts of the secret in consciousness represents a potential difficulty in maintenance of the secret. If thoughts of the secret intrude while the person is engaged in an interaction with someone from whom the secret must be kept, immediate efforts are made to push the unwanted thought from mind so as not to reveal the secret. The secret thought can also intrude even when the bearer of the secret is not actively engaged in the endeavor to conceal. The thought can be particularly worrisome in this instance because of its frequent appearance at such irrelevant moments. Again, attempts are made to relegate the secret thought to the unconscious realm whence it came. Thought suppression is likely when intrusions of the secret thought come to mind.

Thought Suppression and Intrusive Thoughts Occur Cyclically, Each in Response to the Other

Secrecy sets into motion a self-sustaining cycle of obsessive preoccupation with the secret. Attempts made to suppress the secret thought are responded to with intrusive thinking of the secret, which in turn engenders further efforts to eliminate the secret thought. Once this loop has been started, removing the secret nature of the information does not guarantee that obsessive preoccupation with the secret will cease. The cognitive consequences of secrecy may haunt the mind for quite a while after the secrecy itself is gone.

EVIDENCE FOR THE PREOCCUPATION MODEL

A set of studies by Wegner, Lane, and Dimitri (1994) shows evidence for the workings of the preoccupation model in secret relationships. In a first survey study, participants reported the former loves and crushes that they still ruminated about were more likely to have been secret at the time of the relationship. Along the same vein, a second survey study revealed that participants who reported their past relationship was secret also reported that relationship continues as the target of their obsessive preoccupation. It seems that the imposition of secrecy on a relationship can have the unintended long-term consequence of promoting an obsessive preoccupation with that relationship. As this model would predict, secrecy seemed to foster obsessive preoccupation with partner-related and relationship-related thoughts that lasted for years after the relationship had ended.

In a third study, Wegner, Lane, and Dimitri formed impromptu couples in the laboratory and gave half of them instructions to play "footsie" with their partners during a card game. Of the couples making foot contact, half were asked to keep this contact a secret. As compared with couples who did not touch feet or couples who touched openly, couples who kept secret contact reported greater attraction to each other after the game. The specific combination of suppression and intrusive thinking—obsessive preoccupation—was found only in the secret contact condition. This pattern suggests that there is something unique about the social situation of secret-keeping that helps cultivate the ground upon which obsessive preoccupation grows.

A series of studies conducted by Lane and Wegner (in press) focused on cognitive consequences of secrecy beyond just the context of romantic relationships. We will discuss here the results of each of these studies in terms of what evidence they provide for the preoccupation model of secrecy. The first of these studies was intended to examine whether keeping a secret created increased accessibility to thoughts of that secret. As mentioned previously, Wegner and Erber (1992) found that participants suppressing thoughts of a word while they were under cognitive load showed hyperaccessibility of those suppressed target words to consciousness. If keeping secrets involves suppressing thoughts of the secret, as proposed in step one of the preoccupation model, then participants keeping secrets under high load should experience increased sensitivity to occurrences of the secret thoughts. The prediction for this study, then, was that participants who kept secrets under high load would show greater accessibility of thoughts of the secret target word than when not under load and than participants who did not keep secrets.

Participants in the study read instructions that the experimenter either knew or did not know their target word (e.g., *mountain*). Participants who thought the experimenter did not know the target word were instructed to keep it secret from her during the entire experiment. Participants were then given either a two-digit (low cognitive load condition) or a nine-digit number (high cognitive load condition) to rehearse during a subsequent computer task. After receiving the number, participants performed a two-color Stroop reaction time (RT) task on the computer. For each of a series of words appearing on a computer monitor the participants pressed either a red key or blue key corresponding to the color in which the word was printed. The task consisted of naming the colors of target words, (e.g., *mountain*), nontarget words (e.g., *car*), and target-related words (e.g., *climb*). The experimenter stood looking over participants' shoulders while they performed the computer task. Participants who were trying to keep a secret from the experimenter were told that she would be watching their reactions on the computer to try to guess their target word, whereas participants not keeping a secret were told the experimenter would just be watching their reactions. After the computer task, participants completed a short questionnaire.

As predicted, keeping a secret under cognitive load resulted in enhanced accessibility of the secret thought (as shown by higher color-naming RTs), compared with keeping a secret under low load or not keeping a secret. RTs to secret targets followed a similar pattern to those of suppressed target words in the Wegner and Erber (1992) study, suggesting that keeping a secret does indeed entail suppression of thoughts of the secret. The finding that keeping a secret under high load created an interference of thoughts of the secret with color naming is consistent with the idea that suppression leads to intrusions of the secret and, one step further, that secrecy leads to intrusions of the secret through the mechanism of thought suppression. The self-report measure participants completed after the computer task also showed evidence for secrecy causing thought suppression. Participants instructed to keep the target secret reported greater attempts to suppress the target than participants given no instructions.

According to the preoccupation model, the cognitive consequences of secrecy should endure beyond the specific attempts at secrecy. To assess this possibility, Lane and Wegner performed a second study, now looking at the effect of secrecy on memory. It was predicted that participants instructed to respond to an experimenter's questions about a target topic with a secret, rather than with the truth or a lie, would show earlier recall of the secret words 10 minutes after the questioning. While being videotaped, participants answered questions about 24 topic words (e.g., *date*) by responding according to instructions with either a truthful statement on the topic, a lying statement on the topic, or an irrelevant statement on the topic during which the participant kept his or her true sentiments secret. Also, after answering each question aloud, participants wrote down a statement. If they had just told a truth or a lie they were supposed to write down exactly what they had stated. On the other hand, if they had just told a secret they were supposed to write down their true feelings on the target topic rather than record the irrelevant statement they had made verbally. After participants had answered all of the experimenter's questions, they completed a 10 min filler task. Participants were then asked to write down as many of the 24 target topics as they could recall.

There was no overall difference in the number of secret, truth, or lie topics recalled. However, analyses revealed that more secret items were remembered in the first half of the list than truth or lie items. Secret topics were remembered less than truth or lie topics in the second half. So, although secrets were no more frequently recalled, they were recalled earlier. This finding of earlier recall for secret items points to the idea that secrecy might prompt intrusive thinking or rumination over an extended period of time. Secret-keepers may try to push thoughts of the secret from mind, but these thoughts continue to intrude into consciousness even after the attempts at secrecy are ended. The unwanted, secret thoughts are poised on the brink of consciousness, ready to spring to mind from memory before other thoughts.

The third study in this series was intended to obtain a broader perspective on the relationship between secrecy and the elements of obsessive preoccupation—thought suppression and intrusive thinking. It was predicted that participants who read instructions to keep a word secret during a stream of consciousness task would report increased attempts to suppress thoughts of the secret, and that the suppression effort would be correlated with self-reports of unintentional thinking of the word. Four target words were presented, one at a time, to participants along with one of four possible instructions regarding what to do with that target word when writing stream of consciousness for 5 min. The instructions indicated participants should (a) try to think about the target word, (b) try not to think about the word (suppress), (c) try to keep the word a secret, or (d) write their stream of consciousness with no special instructions regarding the word. After each writing task, participants completed a short questionnaire assessing aspects of their cognitive functioning during the writing task.

This study provided an overarching view of the relationship between elements in the preoccupation model. First of all, the link between secrecy and suppression was again found by observing participants' self-report measures. When receiving instructions to keep a target word secret, participants showed higher levels of thought suppression than when they received instructions to think about the target word or when they were given no instructions at all. Along these same lines, self-reports of secrecy and suppression were significantly positively correlated in every condition, a finding in accord with the idea that thought suppression may be the strategy of choice for secret-keepers.

A positive correlation between self-reports of unintentional thinking and thought suppression in the suppression and secret conditions was found and is consistent with the preoccupation model's steps of suppression leading to intrusions and in turn, intrusions creating more thought suppression. This positive relationship between suppression and intrusions was not found when participants were given no instructions and, in fact, the two variables were negatively related for participants attempting to think about the target word. Expanding on other research that has shown that obsessive thinking of given thoughts may be a product of thought suppression (Wegner & Zanakos, 1994), this study suggests that secrecy may also be a mental task that touches off a cycle of obsessive preoccupation with thoughts of the secret.

Using yet another paradigm, Lane and Wegner completed a fourth study to examine the relationships among secrecy, thought suppression, and intrusion within individual participants across a wide range of possible thought topics. Participants completed a "Secret Thoughts" questionnaire divided into three parts. In the first section, participants indicated how secret their thoughts were on 50 diverse, preselected topics (these were the ratings on which we based the factor analysis shown in Table 1). The second section asked participants to rate how much they tried to suppress thoughts of each of these same 50 topics whenever they came to mind. Lastly, participants rated how much they found each of these 50 thought topics coming intrusively to mind. It was hypothesized that topics about which a participant suppressed thoughts and topics that were likely to be intrusive were also more likely to be secret topics for that participant, and that suppressed topics and intrusive topics would also tend to be positively correlated within each participant.

A significant positive mean within-subject correlation across 50 topics was found between participants' self-ratings of secrecy and suppression. Although this finding may represent the preoccupation model's assertion that secrecy creates thought suppression, the direction of causation, of course, cannot be determined from correlational analyses. It may be the case that attempts to try not to think particular thoughts spur on people to try actively to keep them secret from others so they don't remind them of the unwanted thoughts.

A significant mean within-subject correlation was also found between thought suppression and intrusive thinking, thus providing additional support for the preoccupation model's steps of suppression creating intrusive thinking, which then leads to further suppression. Although the causal direction of this relationship also cannot be determined from these data, the preoccupation model would predict a causal link between suppression and intrusions in both directions. A path from secrecy to intrusions via thought suppression can also be inferred from the significant positive within-subject correlation between secrecy and intrusive thinking. Although it is possible that this finding may be interpreted as meaning that people tend to keep secret those items that intrude into consciousness, it seems that these thoughts would serve as likely topics of conversation. Considered together with findings from the other three studies, it seems more probable that secrecy creates intrusive thinking by initiating the process of thought suppression. Together, these studies trace the road leading from secrecy to obsessive preoccupation. This journey may begin with the simple initial decision to keep information hidden, but as it progresses, the cognitive repercussions of the secret oftentime make for a long, winding, and wearying misadventure.

SECRECY AND PSYCHOPATHOLOGY

The preoccupation model suggests that when people have good reasons to keep their thoughts in some area a secret, they may eventually find that those thoughts return repetitively and intrusively, perhaps to the point that the thoughts become so bothersome that they lead to the self-perception of disordered thinking. We suspect that this may be a common pathway. A person might hide a particular thought from others because it represents an offense, for example, or a fear, sorrow, or sin, and for this reason engage the preoccupation cycle. As a result, the person would soon find thoughts of this topic returning to mind often—in fact, too often. The sources of this apparent obsession might not be clear, as we believe that most people do not appreciate the possibility that their secrets can turn into "fixed ideas" that absorb them and guide much of their conscious life. Unexpected and unexplained obsessions, then, form the bases for all sorts of inferences about the self. People begin to think they are crazy.

Let us consider how this might happen for each of the four categories of secret thoughts. As we review these sources of secrecy, we will consider what kinds of psychopathology might be engendered in each case.

Offenses

Thoughts about sexual and aggressive crimes are, of course, not very smart to reveal to others. Even talking about a bomb near airport security can get you into prison, as there are multiple penalties for mentioning thoughts or intentions of offenses to others. This cloak of secrecy should prompt the occurrence of the very thoughts that society abhors, and so should serve to initiate a variety of forms of psychopathology centering on intrusive thoughts of harm to others.

Research on this topic has typically indicated that secrecy is indeed an important part of disorders involving hostility and sexual harm to others, especially including the paraphilias (cf. Denko, 1976; Moser, 1988; Summit, 1983). As a rule, the observation of secrecy in these circumstances is taken to indicate that offenders are simply avoiding apprehension—not that they may be creating or aggravating their own disordered behavior in the process of keeping it undisclosed. But this may be a real possibility that deserves investigation in studies of the etiology of such problems. The finding that sexual offenders often retrospectively report repressive approaches toward sexuality in their families is one sort of evidence in this direction (Goldstein & Kant, 1973; O'Connor, Leberg, & Donaldson, 1990). If a person becomes involved in thinking about a crime, the very pressure he or she perceives to avoid reporting those thoughts could eventually come around to motivate the criminal behavior.

Worries

It is common for people who have anxiety problems to keep secret the things that they worry about (Stekel, 1962). This is particularly evident in the case of obsessive–compulsive disorder. The point is highlighted in two books on this topic: "Obsessionals are more secretive than other sufferers from psychological problems" (Toates, 1990, p. 78) and "Secrecy is part of the disorder. . . . We see new patients every week who have suffered in silence for years" (Rapoport, 1989, p. 13). It makes sense that the forms of anxiety disorder that are particularly related to thinking would be most susceptible to the obsession-generating effects of secrecy (see also Wegner, 1988). Unfortunately for individuals keeping secret their worries, any attempts to control worry may pave the way for its uncontrollability (Roemer & Borkovec, 1993).

It may be that secrecy has a role in the production of anxiety disorders more generally, however, as it is quite possible that people might be embarrassed or keep secret the thoughts they have about minor fears. Even more plausible, in turn, is the idea that serious ongoing fears could be kept secret, so to evolve into preoccupations that emerge into psychopathology. Although the literature on the topic of multiple personality or related dissociative disorders is currently under flux, for example, there are some commentators in this area who attribute the development of such responses to anxiety to the early strategic use of secrecy (e.g., Buchele, 1993; Coons, 1986).

Sorrows

In a way, this source of secrecy and psychopathology is the flipside of the offenses category examined above. Just as the perpetrators of offenses keep secrets, so do the victims and potential victims, and this is one way in which secret sorrows develop. Offenders often coerce their victims into secrecy to avoid being caught, and it is widely reported that the shame and fear of retaliation surrounding victimization can complicate responses to trauma by the victim for this reason (e.g., Pennebaker, 1990; Summit, 1983; Swanson & Biaggio, 1985). But there is much more here to keep secret. The kinds of sorrows implied by incest, sexual or physical abuse in childhood, torture, betrayal, or other deep traumas remind us that the sorrowful secret thoughts in our college student questionnaire just begin to scratch the surface of the experiences in this category that people may live through and then feel compelled by shame or disgrace to conceal from others.

Considered most broadly, sorrows may be understood as the sorts of events that precipitate depression. People commonly keep their failures, losses, and lacks secret from others, as advertising these things is a quick route to social rejection (Gurtman, 1987). It makes sense that the decision not to disclose such items could prompt the now-familiar cycle of preoccupation, and that this tendency could enhance the development of automatic negative thought and affect surrounding the secret thought topics (Wenzlaff, 1993). With this in mind, it is not surprising to find that a reticence to disclose to others is often found to be associated with depression (Burnum, 1991; Raphael & Dohrenwend, 1987). Our interpretation of such findings, and of the more general tendency for the lack of disclosure of trauma to produce ill health (Pennebaker, 1990), is that the active nondisclosure of these sorrows promotes their expansion into pathologies.

Sins

The various lapses in self-control that people keep secret include issues of eating, alcohol, drugs, *and beyond*. These "sins" are not necessarily as socially undesirable as some of the offenses or sorrows, and more resemble the worries as signs of personal weakness. Some of the sins are criminalized in our society, of course, and their disclosure has certain costs as a result. The sins seem to involve private struggles, or struggles with one's demons, that people strive to keep to themselves. Rather than admitting to one's "weakness of will" in succumbing to some vice, a person may keep the whole thing secret.

There are several sources of evidence indicating that psychopathological involvement in the private sins is indeed linked with secrecy. So, for instance, it appears that difficulties in abstinence from drug use are associated with keeping the use secret (Murphy & Irwin, 1992). Secrecy plays a role in eating disorders as well: The cycle of binge eating and purging in bulimia is exacerbated by the desire to keep these acts secret (Vognsen, 1985); obesity is often associated with secrecy surrounding eating (Ganley, 1989); and anorexia tends to occur in the presence of secrecy and shame about eating as well (Lemberg, Phillips, & Fischer, 1992). Selfcontrol activities often take on all the characteristics of full-blown preoccupations, and in some proportion of cases it may be that secrecy precedes and induces the obsession.

There could be other cases of secrecy leading to psychopathology that do not fit our four-category scheme. A review of the American Psychiatric Association's *Diagnostic and Statistical Manual of Mental Disorders,* 4th Edition (1994), indicates that secrecy is mentioned often in the contexts of a wide variety of disorders. Indeed, it may be that secrecy is tempting whenever issues of mental health are raised at all. Almost any mental disorder may be the target of secrecy, simply because the label of a mental disorder itself is stigmatizing. The label of "mental patient" or "former mental patient" is not usually something people freely disclose to others, nor is a diagnostic category something people show much pride in proclaiming ("Guess what, Mom, I'm a borderline!"). The desire to avoid discrimination or derogation based on these things may lead to ardent attempts at secrecy (Herman, 1993; Link, Cullen, Struening, Shrout, & Dohrenwend, 1989).

This recognition suggests that our basic model of the role of secrecy in psychopathology might need to be expanded to include postdiagnosis and posttreatment secrets. Although we have suggested that symptoms may be magnified when secrecy is imposed at points well before any diagnosis is made or treatment is offered, it is also true that the stigmatization of the mentally ill contributes to still another layer of preoccupation and turmoil following any initial secrecy. The further concealment of a diagnosis or treatment would seem to create yet another focus for concern and intrusive doubts and worries.

CONCLUSION

We have presented here the idea that secrecy is not always imposed on odd, crazy, or improper thoughts or behaviors *after* they have happened. Rather, in some cases secrecy may precede and cause these things. Currently, we can only point to two general sources of evidence on this claim, neither of which "nails it," but both of which are supportive and suggest that further research is warranted. First, it appears that secrecy imposed on a thought is linked with the intrusive and obsessive return of that thought, probably through the mechanism of thought suppression. These lab findings suggest that the link is indeed causal, in that manipulations of secrecy lead to indications of cognitive intrusion. The second line of research findings that is consistent with our idea involves the cases in which secrecy is associated with disordered thought and behavior. One can always claim that secrecy is a response to such behavior, not a cause, of course, and it certainly is true that the social history of the treatment of madness includes a strong impulse to hide its victims in the basement. But if secrecy does have the role in the etiology of psychopathology that is suggested by this laboratory work, it would seem wise to open up the basement to the light of day whenever we can. Breaking secrecy may be a first step toward the successful treatment of several forms of psychological disorder.

REFERENCES

American Psychiatric Association. (1994). *Diagnostic and statistical manual of the mental disorders* (4th ed.). Washington, DC: Author.

Bok, S. (1982). *Secrets: On the ethics of concealment and revelation.* New York: Pantheon.

Buchele, B. J. (1993). Group psychotherapy for persons with multiple personality and dissociative disorders. *Bulletin of the Menninger Clinic, 57,* 362–370.

Burnum, J. F. (1991). Secrets about patients. *New England Journal of Medicine, 324,* 1130–1133.

Coons, P. M. (1986). Treatment progress in 20 patients with multiple personality disorder. *Journal of Nervous and Mental Disease, 174,* 715–721.

Denko, J. D. (1976). Klismaphilia: Amplification of the erotic enema deviance. *American Journal of Psychotherapy, 30,* 236–255.

Ellenberger, H. F. (1966). The pathogenic secret and its therapeutics. *Journal of the History of the Behavioral Sciences, 2,* 29–42.

Freud, S. (1953). Totem and taboo. In J. Strachey (Ed.), *The standard edition of the complete psychological works of Sigmund Freud* (Vol. 13). London: Hogarth. (Original work published 1913)

Ganley, R. M. (1989). Emotion and eating in obesity: A review of the literature. *International Journal of Eating Disorders, 8,* 343–361.

Goldstein, M. J., & Kant, H. S. (1973). *Pornography and sexual deviance.* Berkeley: University of California Press.

Gurtman, M. B. (1987). Depressive affect and disclosures as factors in interpersonal rejection. *Cognitive Therapy and Research, 11,* 87–99.

Herman, N. J. (1993). Return to sender: Reintegrative stigma-management strategies of ex-psychiatric patients. *Journal of Contemporary Ethnography, 22,* 295–330.

Hillix, W. A., Harari, H., & Mohr, D. A. (1979). Secrets. *Psychology Today, 13,* 71–76.

Lane, J. D., & Wegner, D. M. (in press). The cognitive consequences of secrecy. *Journal of Personality and Social Psychology.*

Larson, D. G., & Chastain, R. L. (1990). Self-concealment: Conceptualization, measurement, and health implications. *Journal of Social and Clinical Psychology, 9,* 439–455.

Lemberg, R., Phillips, J., & Fischer, J. E. (1992). The obstetric experience in primigravida anorexic and bulimic women: Some preliminary observations. *British Review of Bulimia and Anorexia Nervosa, 6,* 31–38.

Link, B. G., Cullen, F. T., Struening, E. L., Shrout, P. E., & Dohrenwend, B. P. (1989). A modified labeling theory approach to mental disorders: An empirical assessment. *American Sociological Review, 54,* 400–423.

SECRECY TO PSYCHOPATHOLOGY

Moser, C. (1988). Sadomasochism. *Journal of Social Work and Human Sexuality, 7,* 43–56.

Murphy, S., & Irwin, J. (1992). "Living with a dirty secret": Problems of disclosure for methadone maintenance clients. *Journal of Psychoactive Drugs, 24,* 257–264.

O'Connor, M. A., Leberg, E., & Donaldson, C. R. (1990). *Working with sex offenders.* Newbury Park, CA: Sage.

Pennebaker, J. W. (1990). *Opening up.* New York: Morrow.

Raphael, K. G., & Dohrenwend, B. P. (1987). Self-disclosure and mental health: A problem of confounded measurement. *Journal of Abnormal Psychology, 96,* 214–217.

Rapoport, J. L. (1989). *The Boy Who Couldn't Stop Washing.* New York: Dutton.

Roemer, L., & Borkovec, T. D. (1993). Worry: Unwanted cognitive activity that controls unwanted somatic experience. In D. M. Wegner & J. W. Pennebaker (Eds.), *Handbook of mental control* (pp. 220–238). Englewood Cliffs, NJ: Prentice Hall.

Simmel, G. (1950). *The sociology of Georg Simmel.* (Kurt H. Wolff, Trans.). Glencoe, IL: Free Press.

Stekel, W. (1962). *Compulsion and doubt.* (E. A. Gutheil, Trans.). New York: Grosset and Dunlap. (Original work published 1949)

Stiles, W. B. (1987). "I have to talk to somebody": A fever model of disclosure. In V. J. Derlega & J. H. Berg (Eds.), *Self-Disclosure: Theory, research, and therapy* (pp. 257–282). New York: Plenum Press.

Summit, R. C. (1983). The child sexual abuse accommodation syndrome. *Child Abuse and Neglect, 7,* 177–193.

Swanson, L., & Biaggio, M. K. (1985). Therapeutic perspectives on father-daughter incest. *American Journal of Psychiatry, 142,* 667–674.

Toates, F. (1990). *Obsessional thoughts and behaviour.* Wellingborough, England: Thorsons.

Vognsen, J. (1985). Brief, strategic treatment of bulimia. *Transactional Analysis Journal, 15,* 79–84.

Wegner, D. M. (1988). Stress and mental control. In S. Fisher & J. Reason (Eds.), *Handbook of life stress, cognition, and health* (pp. 685–699). Chichester, England: Wiley.

Wegner, D. M. (1989). *White bears and other unwanted thoughts.* New York: Viking/Penguin.

Wegner, D. M. (1992). You can't always think what you want: Problems in the suppression of unwanted thoughts. In M. Zanna (Ed.), *Advances in experimental social psychology* (Vol. 25, pp. 193–225). San Diego, CA: Academic Press.

Wegner, D. M. (1994). Ironic processes of mental control. *Psychological Review, 101,* 34–52.

Wegner, D. M., & Erber, R. (1992). The hyperaccessibility of suppressed thoughts. *Journal of Personality and Social Psychology, 63,* 903–912.

Wegner, D. M., & Erber, R. (1993). Social foundations of mental control. In D. M. Wegner & J. W. Pennebaker (Eds.), *Handbook of mental control* (pp. 36–56). Englewood Cliffs, NJ: Prentice Hall.

Wegner, D. M., Lane, J. D., & Dimitri, S. (1994). The allure of secret relationships. *Journal of Personality and Social Psychology, 66,* 287–300.

Wegner, D. M., Schneider, D. J., Carter, S., & White, T. (1987). Paradoxical effects of thought suppression. *Journal of Personality and Social Psychology, 53,* 5–13.

Wegner, D. M., & Zanakos, S. (1994). Chronic thought suppression. *Journal of Personality, 62*(4), 615–640.

Wenzlaff, R. M. (1993). The mental control of depression: Psychological obstacles to emotional well-being. In D. M. Wegner & J. W. Pennebaker (Eds.), *Handbook of mental control* (pp. 239–257). Englewood Cliffs, NJ: Prentice Hall.

4

Disclosure and Worry: Opposite Sides of the Emotional Processing Coin

Thomas D. Borkovec, Lizabeth Roemer, and John Kinyon

Research by James Pennebaker and colleagues has repeatedly documented the beneficial effects that follow from the disclosure of past traumatic events, irrespective of whether that disclosure is in oral or written form (see Pennebaker, 1989, for a review). Such disclosure has been found to promote better health in studies employing retrospective report (Pennebaker & Susman, 1988), immune function assessment immediately following disclosure (Pennebaker, Kiecolt-Glaser, & Glaser, 1988), and prospective report of health care utilization following disclosure (Pennebaker & Beall, 1986). To some degree, it is not surprising that verbal disclosure of traumatic events would lead to beneficial results. This is an assumption upon which the majority of verbal psychotherapy rests. Obviously, therapists, regardless of whether their orientation involves psychodynamic, experiential, or cognitive behavioral perspectives, are invested in one way or another in the belief that verbalizing emotional events is therapeutic. However, the mechanisms by which either psychological or

Preparation of this chapter was supported in part by National Institute of Mental Health Research Grant MH-39172 to the first author.

physical benefits occur through this verbal process remain as unclear as they are crucially important to identify.

Our own research has focused on exploring a form of verbal–linguistic activity—worry—which actually interferes with health. Given that worry and emotional disclosure both involve verbal–linguistic activity with a focus on negatively valenced affective material and yet have diametrically opposite effects on well-being, comparing and contrasting these two processes may be useful in determining what it is that humans do with emotional material in their minds that can either facilitate the resolution of negative emotional experience or perpetuate emotional disturbance. We begin with a review of what we know about worry that is potentially relevant to emotional disclosure and then discuss dimensions along which these two phenomena dramatically differ.

WORRY

Worry as Verbal–Linguistic Suppression of Imagery, Affect, and Emotional Processing

Worry involves primarily thinking, or talking to oneself, about possible future negative events in response to perceived threat. In its clinically severe form, worry is the central feature of generalized anxiety disorder (GAD), and it is pervasive throughout the other anxiety and mood disorders as well. In contrast to other emotional disorders, worriers do not typically report experiencing intense negative affect; rather, they chronically feel low to moderate degrees of emotional discomfort.

The predominance of thought in worry is a highly significant characteristic for understanding its mechanisms and functional effects: If a person merely thinks in words about emotional material, very little physiological reaction will occur; when the person visualizes an image that represents the same emotional material, significant physiological response will be elicited (Vrana, Cuthbert, & Lang, 1986). Evolution wisely insulated thinking from immediate affective and behavioral expression so that creative exploration of and experimentation with possible response choices could take place in the absence of any immediate internal or environmental consequences that may interfere with the freedom of that process. However, if one processes emotional topics only at the abstract, conceptual level, other processes that are crucially required for the resolution of the dysfunctional emotions associated with those topics may be circumvented, and little or no change in emotional distress will take place. For example, in the area of anxiety disorders, empirical research supports the theory that accessing all of the associative network which is stored in memory and defines the psychological meaning of an emotional topic, including those stored elements having to do with affect and behavior, appears to be fundamentally important if therapeutic change is going to occur (Foa & Kozak, 1986). Therein resides the immediate, negatively reinforcing mechanism of worry. Its conceptual predominance prevents the occurrence of imagery and the otherwise intense negative affective experience associated with the emotional material. But it purchases this short-term phenomenological benefit at the high cost of perpetuating the original emotional disturbance. Worrisome thinking, therefore, by its very avoidance of affective and behavioral meaning elements and its engagement of emotional material solely at an isolated conceptual level, guarantees the maintenance, and quite possibly causes the further strengthening, of anxious meanings.

The empirical foundation for these above conclusions about worry has become quite extensive just in the last few years. Chronically anxious GAD clients have been found to engage in much more thought (and more negatively valenced thought) than nonanxious individuals during relaxation periods, both groups have shown large reductions in imagery and increases in negatively valenced thinking when asked to engage in worrying, and the ratio of thoughts to images and their affective valence have normalized for the clients after successful psychological intervention (Borkovec & Inz, 1990). The occurrence of worrisome thinking has been found in two investigations to have a significant impact on the processing of emotional information. If a phobic individual worries just prior to presentations of phobia-relevant images, he or she will show no cardiovascular response whatsoever to any of those images, whereas a phobic subject who thinks neutral or relaxing thoughts prior to each presentation will display marked responses (Borkovec & Hu, 1990; Borkovec, Lyonfields, Wiser, & Deihl, 1993). Because the presence of a strong physiological reaction is taken as evidence of (a) a more complete accessing of the fear structure surrounding the threatening topic, (b) greater emotional processing of the material, and (c) therefore a greater likelihood of therapeutic changes in meaning (Foa & Kozak, 1986), the results of these phobic imagery studies suggest that worry *prior* to confronting an internal representation of an emotional stimulus can prevent therapeutic change. The prevention of emotional processing by means of worry is also not limited to worry that occurs before the emotional event. Even though worrying immediately after an external emotional event does successfully distract the person from the subjective distress caused by the event in the short term, long-term negative emotional consequences occur in the form of increased cognitive intrusions during subsequent days (Butler, Wells, & Dewick, 1992).

The Psychophysiology of Worry: Autonomic Inflexibility

Surprisingly, early studies had found no differences between chronic worriers and nonworriers or between periods of rest and periods of worrying on tonic measures of physiological activity. It turns out that the typical, sympathetically based, fight-or-flight reaction so well documented in the other anxiety disorders is not at all characteristic of GAD clients or other chronically worried subjects. Rather, the latter groups show a restriction in the range of variability of various autonomic indicators, a deficiency in parasympathetic tone, and an autonomic rigidity; moreover, these same effects can be seen among nonanxious subjects when they are asked to worry (Friedman, Thayer, Borkovec, & Lyonfields, 1993; Hoehn-Saric & McLeod, 1988; Lyonfields, Borkovec, & Thayer, in press). Worry thus mitigates physiological changes, thereby lessens the perception of somatic activation and the intensity of the affects associated with such activation, and creates within the individual a rigidity of autonomic functioning that is ill-suited for flexible responding to moment-to-moment environmental demands.

50

Uncontrollability, Topical Domains, Trauma, and Childhood: Reflections of Unresolved Emotional Experience

The feature of worry that most distinguishes GAD clients from nonanxious control subjects is its uncontrollability. Nonanxious people readily postpone or dismiss their worrying; GAD clients cannot. The results of empirical studies documenting this difference were sufficiently compelling to result in the addition of uncontrollability to the diagnostic criteria for GAD in the recently published *DSM-IV* (American Psychiatric Association, 1994). GAD subjects are also distinctive in that they worry about many diverse topics, whereas nonanxious people, when they do worry, do so only about a few major topical domains (e.g., work, family, finances, health) (Shadick, Roemer, Hopkins, & Borkovec, 1991). GAD subjects also report the more frequent occurrence of physically threatening past trauma, even though injury and illness rank among the topics of *least* current worrisome concern (Molina, Roemer, M. Borkovec, & Posa, 1992; Roemer, M. Borkovec, Posa, & Lyonfields, 1991). Furthermore, they have significantly less memory of their childhood, but what they do remember indicates role-reversed and enmeshed relationships with their primary caregiver, that is, they had to take care of the physical and emotional needs of their mothers rather than their mothers taking care of them (Cassidy, 1992). Finally, an important distinguishing characteristic of GAD was discovered that potentially ties together all of the above findings. Subjects were asked to rate themselves on several scales that gave possible reasons for engaging in worry (e.g., worry as a problem-solving method, as a motivator to achieve, as a way of preparing for the future). The largest and most consistent difference between GAD and non-GAD groups found in two separate studies was that GAD subjects believed that they worried about all the things they worried about in order to distract themselves from even more emotional topics, things that they did not want to think about (Roemer et al., 1991).

This latter result suggests that worry may be functioning as a cognitive avoidance response in more ways than one. As described earlier, worry hypothetically serves to avoid imagery, physiological activation, and affect and is thereby negatively reinforced. But the actual content of daily worrying may also serve as a distraction in an effort to avoid accessing information about more distressing emotional material from the past. Thus, the worries cover many topics (including minor matters, Abel & Borkovec, in press), and the worrier experiences uncontrollable thinking about those topics because of the strong motivation to avoid the more disturbing content.

What those more emotional topics might be, and therefore what past history of psychologically meaningful events laid the motivational foundation for chronic worrying, remains to be determined empirically. However, the trauma and childhood reports of GAD subjects described above provide hints of what its source may be. Any occurrence of trauma in a person's life could provide sufficient evidence that the world is a dangerous place and that he or she may not be able to cope with it. Such a generalized perspective is central to GAD. Remarkably, however, GAD subjects do not worry very much about those areas of life concern that are most directly related to the past traumas that they have experienced. Hypothetically, then, they worry because their past histories have shown them that danger exists, but worrying about the things about which they do worry allows for an avoidance of the traumatic memories of events that taught them this lesson. Secondly, GAD subjects in their role-reversed relationships with the primary caregiver had less psychological safety throughout childhood, and therefore a greater sense of danger, by virtue of the absence of a secure attachment figure who would protect them from threat. An anxiety-laden childhood because of this could certainly lead in adult life to generalized worries about the future, and the current worries that they do have allow for distraction from thoughts about that earlier time of life, leading to motivated avoidance of childhood memories in general. The future is perceived to be filled with threat because the past, too distressing to think about directly, has actually been that way.

Worry thus involves habitual, uncontrollable, abstract thought which has developed as a result of unresolved emotional experiences from the past. It has immediate beneficial effects in terms of reduction of physiological activation and negative affect but long-term deleterious effects in terms of inhibited emotional processing and maintained distress. It is our proposal that this process differs from emotional disclosure in that the latter is adaptive by virtue of the fact that it heightens the very process which worry prevents; disclosure facilitates emotional processing. For the remainder of this chapter, we will contrast the maladaptive process of worry with emotional disclosure on dimensions which we feel contribute to this facilitative–inhibitory difference between the two phenomena.

EMOTIONAL DISCLOSURE AND WORRY: OPPOSING PROCESSES ON THE SAME DIMENSIONS

Disinhibition Versus Inhibition

One important underlying dimension along which disclosure and worry dramatically differ involves disinhibition and inhibition. As discussed above, worry is primarily an inhibitory process, whereas emotional disclosure encourages disinhibition. Pennebaker (1989) has proposed that disclosure is beneficial precisely because it puts an end to the behavioral inhibition required not to disclose information about a past event. Such inhibition places a strain on the body immediately, as reflected by increases in skin conductance, and ultimately causes long term health difficulties. He therefore views disclosure as a release of this inhibition, leading to decreases in skin conductance levels (Pennebaker, Hughes, & O'Heeron, 1987) and long-term improvements in health. Emotional suppression or inhibition has also been associated with increases in skin conductance in studies instructing subjects to inhibit their emotional experience (Gross & Levenson, 1993). If inhibition causes a strain on the body as proposed, it may be that the disinhibition required for disclosure reduces this strain and facilitates complete processing of the emotional experience.

Research has similarly proposed deleterious effects from the suppression or inhibition of any types of thoughts (e.g., Wegner, Schneider, Carter, & White, 1987). Suppression of neutral thoughts has been associated with subsequent intrusiveness of the target thought (Wegner et al., 1987) and increases in electrodermal fluctuations immediately preceding the target thought (Merckelbach, Muris, van den Hout, & de Jong, 1991), possibly indicating increased salience of the suppressed thought. In addition, suppression of emotional material has been associated with subsequent increases in tonic arousal (Wegner, Shortt, Blake, & Page, 1990; Wegner & Gold, submitted). Finally, suppression of thoughts, irrespective of whether they were about neutral, anxious, or depressing situations, was found to lead to increases in the subjective anxiety associated with the target situation, indicating that inhibition or suppression may in fact incubate the negative affect associated with the target (Roemer & Borkovec, 1994). Although the intrusiveness following suppression has not always been replicated (cf. Merckelbach et al., 1991), the above studies as a whole indicate the potentially deleterious effects of thought suppression.

Elsewhere (Roemer & Borkovec, 1993), we have speculated about ways in which worry and thought suppression may involve similarities in process. Worry is first initiated as an attempt to suppress thoughts about more distressing emotional material and to avoid unwanted somatic activation that would otherwise be elicited by the perception of threat. But worrisome thinking then becomes an unwanted cognitive activity in and of itself, toward which further specific suppression attempts are frequently made. There is thus little in worry process that involves disinhibition of any type. Indeed, everything about worry suggests its multiply inhibitory nature. Worriers use their verbal–linguistic activity to inhibit somatic activation and affect and then subsequently to inhibit this bothersome verbal activity. Although GAD clients report historically using a variety of distraction and suppression devices to try to stop their worry, the fact that GAD has a relatively early age of onset and a chronic course (Barlow, 1988) indicates the extent to which such coping methods are unsuccessful. Even among relatively healthy students, the majority report that efforts to terminate worry only result in a later return of the worrisome thoughts, and this occurs significantly more often for worriers than nonworriers (Tallis, Davey, & Capuzzo, 1994).

Further support for the inhibitory nature of worry is found in studies of two manipulations shown to reduce worry and possibly involving its disinhibition. In one manipulation, worriers who are asked to worry deliberately in a laboratory setting show a lessening of negative thought intrusions, as long as they do this for 30 min (Borkovec, Robinson, Pruzinsky, & DePree, 1983). Because 15 minutes of deliberate worrying produces, in contrast, an increase in thought intrusions, worry incubates in a way that is similar to fear: Brief periods of exposure to feared stimuli can result in a worsening of the fear, whereas longer durations of exposure produces fear reduction. Thus, extended exposure to worry appears to be required to allow access to a sufficient amount of the emotional information. It may well be the case that emotional disclosure would also show a similar incubating tendency if enough time was not provided to allow for a complete processing of the emotions. Indeed, experiential therapists would agree with this point (e.g., Greenberg & Safran, 1987). On the other hand, we also know that lengthy disclosure of worry process to a therapist does not necessarily lead to reduced anxiety. A therapy condition that involved only reflective listening was found to have only modest therapeutic effects, most of which were lost by one-year follow-up, in the treatment of GAD (Borkovec & Costello, 1993). Other crucial differences must therefore exist between merely talking about one's worries and disclosing information about a past traumatic event. Our clinical experience as well as the combination of results from worry research reviewed above suggest that worriers will merely talk about superficial concerns in therapy unless interventions explicitly focus their attention on the deeper meanings and emotions underlying them.

In the second manipulation, a stimulus control treatment program that includes a daily half-hour worry period has been found to be effective in reducing worry. Subjects are asked to learn to catch their daily worries early, to postpone those worries until a 30 min worry period later in the day, and to worry about these concerns only during that worry period. Reductions of 35% have been found among college student worriers using this method for four weeks (Borkovec, Wilkinson, Folensbee, & Lerman, 1983).

In both of the above manipulations, the 30 min deliberate worry period may involve greater internal identification and expression of affect (more similar to what occurs in emotional disclosure) than is the case with naturalistic daily worry, which tends to be sporadic and occurring more in background (rather than focal) awareness as the worrier simultaneously deals with moment-to-moment environmental demands. Alternately, deliberate worry may reduce or eliminate attempts to suppress the worrying itself. Finally, deliberately generated worry differs from naturally occurring worry in the controlled processing involved in the former as opposed to greater automaticity of processing in the latter, and this difference may underlie the therapeutic value of disclosure. This possibility is discussed in greater detail later.

If Pennebaker (1989) is correct in asserting that inhibition places a strain on physical process, and if the worrying constantly present for GAD subjects is predominantly inhibitory in its effects and is associated with chronic autonomic inflexibility, then one would expect this disorder to be related to significant physical health problems. Although we have found no extant research specifically addressing this prediction, there is indirect evidence that it is likely to be true. Increased autonomic rigidity is associated with the aging of the autonomic nervous system (Kaplan et al., 1991), and rather consistent findings have revealed a significant relationship between measures of stress and anxiety and indices of coronary heart disease (Byrne & Byrne, 1990). Thus, we can speculate that worry and emotional disclosure represent opposites along a dimension of mechanism ranging from general cognitive and somatic inhibition predictive of ill health to a release of such inhibition that leads to greater physical and psychological well-being.

Emotional Experiencing

Another important dimension that differentiates worry and emotional disclosure is degree of emotional experiencing that occurs during each process. According to the experiential tradition, one of the essential components of emotional processing is the full subjective experience of emotion in present-moment awareness (Greenberg & Safran, 1987). Similarly, the cognitive–behavioral tradition emphasizes the importance of functional exposure to the entire fear structure stored in associative memory (Foa & Kozak, 1986). As discussed above, worry is not associated with somatic activation (considered indicative of functional exposure by Foa & Kozak) and is thought to interfere with full access to the fear network (Mathews, 1990). In contrast, disclosure is often associated with characteristics prototypic of functional exposure and fully experienced emotion. First of all, instructions to subjects in the emotional disclosure paradigm emphasize the experiencing of "deepest" thoughts and feelings, and subjects are repeatedly advised that they may become upset during the procedure, providing a context in which intense experiencing of emotions is expected (Pennebaker, 1989). In contrast to the restricted physiological activity and low to moderate affect inherent to the worry process, subjects who participate in the emotional disclosure paradigms display increased heart rate while disclosing, report increases in anxiety and depression immediately following the session, and frequently cry during exposure (Pennebaker, 1989). The association between emotional experiencing and beneficial effects of disclosure is supported by content analysis comparing the disclosures of those who demonstrate subsequent health improvement to those who do not: Improved health is related to the use of more negative than positive affect words (Pennebaker, 1993).

Deep Versus Superficial Processing

Another dimension that may be relevant to differential effects on emotional processing is that of level of meaning. Pennebaker (1985) proposes that one way to react to a traumatic event involves shifting to a "lower level of analysis" (e.g., focusing on a need to clean one's desk or wash the car). He proposes that a superficial focus on the stressful topic or unrelated issues serves to distract one from the underlying meaning and emotion associated with the trauma. This low-level thinking is one of the forms of inhibition that place significant strains on the body.

It may be that worry is also an example of the low-level thinking Pennebaker describes. As discussed above, GAD is characterized by worry about minor things and miscellaneous or idiosyncratic topics, the frequent occurrence of past trauma, and reports of worrying in order to avoid more distressing topics. Also, it has been proposed that worry's superficial nature serves to avoid the accessing of core, underlying meanings, the accessing of which would otherwise facilitate emotional processing (Vasey & Borkovec, 1992).

Pennebaker (1989) suggests that disclosure involves the construction of a more coherent and efficient processing of information by adding a verbal–linguistic component to a more emotional construct. Theories of emotional processing stress the importance of integrating the conceptual meaning component with the affective component (e.g., Greenberg & Safran, 1987) or accessing the full network of affect and cognition (Foa & Kozak, 1986). Disclosure may facilitate such complete processing by providing verbal–linguistic analysis of an emotional event in conjunction with deep emotional experiencing. In fact, subjects who display health benefits following disclosure demonstrate an increase in insight and cognitive restructuring terms over time in comparison with subjects who do not display improved health (Pennebaker, 1993). It seems then that disclosure is beneficial when it facilitates cognitive elaboration and restructuring, an outcome that rarely if ever occurs in the course of daily worrying.

Past Versus Future

A dimension on which worry and disclosure differ which may have implications for emotional processing is their temporal focus. Worry is predominantly oriented to future, possible events (Borkovec et al., 1983). Emotional disclosure, as defined by the studies designed to evaluate its influence, has involved a focus on past events encoded in memory with significant emotional meaning. The functional significance of this difference is two-fold: Recall of a past event will result in vivid images and their associated affective and physiological reactions (cf. York, Borkovec, Vasey, & Stern, 1987). Therefore, although the actual disclosure itself involves verbal process as one of its products, a subject engaging in instructed disclosure is likely to be experiencing greater amounts of imagery as he or she describes the event. Such imagery guarantees greater access to emotional meaning and thus greater emotional processing. This would explain why subjects experience increased heart rate during disclosure (Pennebaker et al., 1987), even though verbalization by itself is not highly related to physiological activation (Vrana et al., 1986). In contrast, worrisome thinking about the future is not closely associated with imagery and would thus have limited value for full processing of the related affective material. Nor is mere talking about future possible events (involved in the reflective listening therapy with GAD mentioned earlier) significantly facilitative of emotional processing.

Another possible significance of the temporal distinction is that disclosure may, by virtue of its focus on the past, involve greater elaboration than worry does. Worry is characterized by the first step of problem-solving ("What if . . . ?") and subsequent avoidance of crucial aspects of anxiety-related meaning stored in memory (Mathews, 1990). It is this avoidance that perpetuates the fear structure and therefore the occurrence of worry. By focusing on past events, on the other hand, disclosure allows for greater elaboration of the associative network of meaning and therefore greater processing of the traumatic event. It is of significance in this regard that subjects who experience health benefits following disclosure have tended to rely less on future statements than those who do not benefit (Pennebaker, 1993).

The differences of these two processes in temporal focus is intriguing. It appears to be possible that worry, with its future orientation, is looking for solutions in all of the wrong places. To the extent that worry finds its origins in either past traumatic events or difficult childhood histories, therapeutic change may be more likely to occur if the therapist aids the client in identifying these contributory events, in assessing their possible relationship to current perceptions that the world is a dangerous place and that coping with it may not be successful, and in fully processing the emotional content of those historical events. If these speculations contain some truth, then GAD and chronic worry bear a closer relationship to posttraumatic stress disorder than was previously believed, and new therapeutic avenues to the modification of chronic worry may find useful suggestions from the emotional disclosure literature to a degree not previously anticipated.

Controlled Versus Automatic Processing

Research in basic cognitive psychology has revealed at least two qualitatively different types of information processing systems: controlled and automatic (cf. Schneider & Shiffrin, 1977). Controlled processing is characterized as a relatively slow, effortful, capacity-limited, and subject-controlled process that is associated with the conscious focusing of attention. Automatic processing, on the other hand, is associated with non-conscious information processing and is characterized as preattentional, effortless, rapid, capable of parallel processing of multiple channels (e.g., visual, auditory), and making little or no demand on capacity-limited attentional resources. Typical attentional processing is thought to be composed of an interactional shifting between multiple levels of conscious and nonconscious processing represented by these information systems (Posner, 1982).

The distinction between controlled and automatic processing may represent a crucial difference in what occurs during disclosure and what takes place during worry, and may partly explain their differential impact on the storage and retrieval of emotional information. It is reasonable to speculate that disclosure primarily utilizes controlled processing, whereas chronic worry manifests aspects of both systems. Based on Pennebaker's (1989) descriptions, disclosure is a volitional, introspective exploration of stored information from the past that includes cognitions, expressive–motor reactions, subjective emotional experience, and other related emotional episodes that are meaningfully associated in representational memory with the past traumatic event. This process appears to occur through an effortful directing, or focusing, of capacity-limited attentional resources toward the experiencing and expression of immediate subjective feelings as they relate to this introspective process. Thus, disclosure utilizes attentional resources allocated to both the active encoding of immediate, subjective emotional experience and to both the processing and production of verbal–linguistic information.

Worry, on the other hand, is a mixture of automatic and controlled processing. Evidence for the automaticity of worry process stems from the research that has characterized its chronic form as relatively uncontrollable, intrusive, problematic since childhood (Borkovec, Shadick, & Hopkins, 1991), and most frequently originating from "out of nowhere" rather than being elicited by some environmental stimulus (Craske, Rapee, Jackel,

& Barlow, 1989). Thus, it shows signs of automaticity similar to that found in other types of automatic task performance, that is, execution is partly occurring outside of awareness. On the other hand, worry also shows some characteristics of controlled processing. Worry involves streams of negative thinking whose content is accessible to conscious awareness (Borkovec, et al., 1983) and can be voluntarily directed to some degree. Unlike automatic task performances in cognitive psychology wherein a freeing of limited-capacity attentional resources occurs (Schneider & Shiffrin, 1977), worry has been shown to draw upon attentional resources (Wells, 1994) as these resources are diverted toward abstract thoughts about a threatening future and away from the immediate experiencing of associations to an aversive past (Borkovec, 1994).

This hypothesized mixture of automatic and controlled processing likely occurs because of the constant repetition of worrisome thinking. Researchers have found that consciously controlled behavior, with consistency and repetition, can become automatized and executed outside of awareness as self-contained or "chunked" motor programs (Brown & Carr, 1989). Posner's (1982) review of empirical evidence indicates that complex semantic processing can also become automated. Thus, even though aspects of worry can involve controlled processing, repetition of worrisome verbal content so characteristic of GAD clients can create an automaticity of those linguistic segments. Instead of behavioral task performance, worry involves over-rehearsed, "chunked," conceptual programs which, once initiated either attentively or preattentively, can run to completion without input from the controlled processing system.

Worry, therefore, appears to be an at least partially automatic process, possibly taking the form of self-contained, conceptual "worry programs" and also involves aspects of controlled processing associated with the depletion of attentional resources available for the processing of immediate emotional information. All of this would mitigate the full experiencing and processing of emotional material associated with one's central threats and the past events from which perception of those threats derives. In contrast, disclosure appears to be composed primarily, or perhaps solely, of controlled processing that actively directs attentional resources toward emotional information. So the reason that disclosure facilitates emotional processing, whereas worry does not, may be that attentional resources must necessarily be focused upon both the active encoding of present-moment emotional experience as well as the verbal–linguistic processing of both the internal and external sources of the emotional response.

As implied earlier, the short-term advantage of "using-up" attentional resources in the process of worry is that aversive emotional experience and somatic activation are avoided. The disadvantage, however, of the automated aspects of worry is the reduced flexibility of response inherent in any automated, habitual behavior. Worry represents a rigid asymmetry in favor of a predominance of automatic, verbal–linguistic mental activity and a dearth of controlled processing available for the processing of both immediate emotional experience and new information available in the immediate environment that could otherwise modify one's beliefs and perceptions about threat and abilities to cope. Given such an analysis, perhaps interventions to reduce the phenomenon could be derived from cognitive psychology.

In the presence of a maladaptive, automated activity, the remedy for learning new behaviors from the cognitive psychology perspective involves (a) the effortful focusing of attentional awareness on habitual stimulus–response relationships, (b) the effortful application of controlled processing in order to generate different, more adaptive responses, and (c) the use of consistency and repetition of the new behavior to strengthen the likelihood of its occurrence and weaken the likelihood of the old, maladaptive habit. The first two processes at the very least are clearly involved in emotional disclosure. All three are fundamental to our cognitive behavioral therapy program for GAD (cf. Borkovec & Costello, 1993). Clients first learn in the therapy office, and then in daily living, to monitor anxiety-related reactions (especially worry) and to catch the beginnings of their occurrence earlier and earlier. As they subsequently learn relaxation and cognitive coping skills, the clients are encouraged to apply these new, alternative, more adaptive responses upon first detection of incipient anxiety. Emphasis is placed on (a) the effort required in paying attention to their anxious experience and in successfully generating new responses and

(b) the importance of frequent application of alternative responses in daily living. To facilitate practice of all of these skills, self-control desensitization is used in therapy sessions to provide multiple opportunities for application and rehearsal. Specifically in the latter technique, imagery (so often avoided by GAD clients because it generates affect) is used deliberately to initiate anxious experience, and the client practices shifting to the deployment of the alternative coping responses as soon as anxiety is generated. Although much remains to be learned about the successful psychological treatment of GAD, extant outcome research currently indicates that cognitive–behavioral therapies involving these types of methods produce the most long-lasting therapeutic change (Borkovec & Whisman, in press; Chambless & Gillis, 1993). So it seems that some of the processes that facilitate emotional processing in disclosure (i.e., controlled processes) may be similar to those that are therapeutic with chronic worriers.

CONCLUSION

This preliminary exploration of disclosure and worry suggests several dimensions along which these two processes dramatically differ, and each dimension appears to be crucially related to whether or not therapeutic emotional processing occurs. Due to the predominance of abstract thought in its process, worrying about emotional material is characterized by inhibition of affect and arousal, reduction of emotional experiencing, superficial level of processing, and future focus and reduction of the attentional resources available for complete processing. These features guarantee interference with the emotional processing of anxious material, maintenance of fear structures, and a prolongation of distress. In contrast, emotional disclosure is disinhibitory, encourages emotional experience, explores deeper meanings associated with emotional experience, elicits via imagery present-moment experiencing of past events, and focuses attentional resources on stimulus–response habits, all of which facilitate emotional processing and adaptive emotional change.

Perhaps the most significant outcome that emerges from this review of worry research and the relationship between worry and emotional disclosure is the hypothesis that worry may find its origins and continuing motivation in unresolved emotional events from the past. If this is indeed the case, then the disclosure literature suggests that accessing, experiencing, and verbally expressing the stored meanings surrounding those past events may provide an efficient and effective method of reducing worry and the chronically anxious condition that it generates. We know that merely talking about one's worries in a supportive, reflective–listening therapy produces some beneficial change, but the degree of change is not large, and whatever gains are made in reduced anxious experience are generally lost a year later (Borkovec & Costello, 1993). Disclosure of superficial worry content thus appears to be insufficient, even when this occurs over as many as 12 therapy sessions. Indeed, the reflective–listening environment may simply provide opportunities for the client to rehearse outloud and thereby strengthen the same worrisome streams that are taking place internally throughout the typical day. Accessing and disclosing past emotional information, rather than perserverative thinking and talking about an unknown future that is seen as dangerous because of that past, may thus be an important feature of any therapy developments that make use of what is known about emotional processing from disclosure research.

What we have learned thus far about the nature of worry also has one potential implication for further development of emotional disclosure interventions. Greater explicit emphasis on the generation of imagery during disclosure should maximize the degree of present-moment experiencing of affects associated with traumatic events and thus further facilitate a complete processing of their meaning.

Because the two processes appear to represent opposite sides of the same coin, future research on both phenomena is likely to reveal important mechanisms that lie at the heart of therapeutic change for emotional disorders. The more we learn about the nature and functions of one, the more we will be able to understand about the other. But the chapters of this volume present an opportunity to go even deeper. One of the striking features of the conference upon which this book was based was the degree of interrelationship that seemed to exist among the theoretical and empirically based ideas presented by each of the participants. This occurred despite the fact that the researchers came from a variety of disciplines and conceptual orientations. We mention here only a few of many such connections. A remarkable basis of agreement emerged between our view of the mechanisms of worry and disclosure and the importance of thought and imagery in these mechanisms from our neo-behavioristic point of view, on the one hand, and the fundamental processes of emotional disturbance, emotional change, and the importance of "concreteness" outlined by Bucci from a psychodynamic perspective (chapter 6, this volume). Both of the chronic pain researchers (Dominguez, chapter 13, and Traue, chapter 8) pointed to the role of psychophysiological processes in understanding the psychological aspects of pain, and in informal dialogue we discovered a shared recognition of the importance of human perception of time that may provide a foundation to the physical and psychological characteristics of our respective phenomenon: GAD clients are lost in the illusion of the negative future with its consequential anxiety, and our therapeutic goal is partly to encourage them in methods of living more in the present; chronic pain patients are psychologically stuck in the illusion of the negative past with its consequential depression, and therapy usefully moves them to the present. Both Schwartz and Wegner (chapters 9 and 3 respectively) emphasized for emotional distress the self-maintaining role played by efforts to remove cognitive–affective products from conscious recall, a notion that overlaps very nicely with our view of worry as cognitive avoidance of deeper, more emotionally disturbing material. Pennebaker has drawn the field's attention to the importance of language in emotion, and differing forms of complex verbal–linguistic activity clearly reside at the heart of both disclosure and worry effects. Wellenkamp's work in Thailand revealed some startling similarities in psychological strategies designed for coping with emotion and emotional expression, even though culture obviously gave rise to distinctive environmental conditions under which public expression of emotion could occur and provided ritualistic means for fully experiencing and expressing affect (chapter 15, this volume).

Taking only this one subset of interrelationships, one can easily infer directions for future research that are likely to yield significant fruit. We need to learn more about complex language activity, in and of itself, and apply that knowledge to increase our understanding of emotional processing, its prevention, and its facilitation. Cross-cultural influences will obviously play a significant role here, even at the level of syntax, grammar, and the etymology of the words of the language. Cultural similarities and differences will also inform us about the targets of thought and emotion suppression and the consequences of using such a device. Psychophysiology will continue to reveal at a very fundamental level both the physical consequences of facilitated or inhibited emotional experience and the restrictions physiological systems place on the range of possible cognitive, imaginal, affective, and behavioral states and processes. Suppression, repression, and disclosure research would usefully expand to detailing the effects of these processes when they are differentially applied to thoughts alone, images alone, affect alone, and their pairings.

The future looks bright. Thrill of discovery, joy in its sharing, and openness to the insights of others paid large dividends to all of the participants at the conference. Such collaborative spirit offers the prospect that we will soon be learning a great deal more about human nature as we continue to explore the connection between emotion, health, and the proclivities of human beings that lead them to heaven or hell.

REFERENCES

Abel, J. L., & Borkovec, T. D. (in press). Generalizability of *DSM-III-R* generalized anxiety disorders to proposed *DSM-IV* criteria and cross-validation of proposed changes. *Journal of Anxiety Disorders.*

American Psychiatric Association. (1994). *Diagnostic and Statistical Manual* (4th ed.). Washington, DC: Author.

Barlow, D. H. (1988). *Anxiety and its disorders: The nature and treatment of anxiety and panic.* New York: Guilford Press.

Borkovec, T. D. (1994). The nature, functions, and origins of worry. In G. C. L. Davey & F. Tallis (Eds.), *Worrying: Perspectives in theory, assessment, and treatment* (pp. 5–34). New York: Wiley.

Borkovec, T. D., & Costello, E. (1993). Efficacy of applied relaxation and cognitive behavioral therapy in the treatment of generalized anxiety disorder. *Journal of Consulting and Clinical Psychology, 61,* 611–619.

Borkovec, T. D., & Hu, S. (1990). The effect of worry on cardiovascular response to phobic imagery. *Behaviour Research and Therapy, 28,* 69–73.

Borkovec, T. D., & Inz, J. (1990). The nature of worry in generalized anxiety disorder: A predominance of thought activity. *Behaviour Research and Therapy, 28,* 153–158.

Borkovec, T. D., Lyonfields, J. D., Wiser, S. L., & Diehl, L. (1993). The role of worrisome thinking in the suppression of cardiovascular response to phobic imagery. *Behaviour Research and Therapy, 31,* 321–324.

Borkovec, T. D., Robinson, E., Pruzinsky, T., & DePree, J. A. (1983). Preliminary exploration of worry: Some characteristics and processes. *Behaviour Research and Therapy, 21,* 9–16.

Borkovec, T. D., Shadick, R. N., & Hopkins, M. (1991). The nature of normal versus pathological worry. In R. Rapee & D. H. Barlow (Eds.), *Chronic anxiety and generalized anxiety disorder.* New York: Guilford Press.

Borkovec, T. D., & Whisman, M. A. (in press). Psychological treatment for generalized anxiety disorder. In M. Mavissakalian & R. Prien (Eds.), *Anxiety disorders: Psychological and pharmacological treatments.* Washington, DC: American Psychiatric Association.

Borkovec, T. D., Wilkinson, L., Folensbee, R., & Lerman, C. (1983). Stimulus control applications to the treatment of worry. *Behaviour Research and Therapy, 21,* 247–251.

Brown, T. L., & Carr, T. H. (1989). Automaticity in skill acquisition. *Journal of Experimental Psychology: Human Perception and Performance, 15,* 686–700.

Butler, G., Wells, A., & Dewick, H. (1992, June). *Differential effects of worry and imagery after exposure to a stressful stimulus.* Paper presented at the meeting of the World Congress of Cognitive Therapy, Toronto.

Byrne, D. G., & Byrne, A. E. (1990). Anxiety and coronary heart disease. In D. G. Byrne & R. H. Rosenman (Eds.), *Anxiety and the heart.* New York: Hemisphere Publishing.

Cassidy, J. A. (October, 1992). *Generalized anxiety disorder and attachment: Emotion and cognition.* Rochester Developmental Psychopathology Symposium, University of Rochester.

Chambless, D. L., & Gillis, M. M. (1993). Cognitive therapy of anxiety disorders. *Journal of Consulting and Clinical Psychology, 61,* 248–260.

Craske, M. G., Rapee, R. M., Jackel, L., & Barlow, D. H. (1989). Qualitative dimensions of worry in DSM-III-R generalized anxiety disorder subjects and nonanxious controls. *Behaviour Research and Therapy, 27,* 397–402.

Foa, E. B., & Kozak, M. J. (1986). Emotional processing of fear: Exposure to corrective information. *Psychological Bulletin, 99,* 20–35.

Friedman, B. H., Thayer, J. F., Borkovec, T. D., & Lyonfields, J. D. (May, 1993). *Psychophysiological assessment of generalized anxiety disorder.* Paper presented at the meeting of the Midwestern Psychological Association, Chicago.

Greenberg, L. S., & Safran, J. D. (1987). *Emotions in psychotherapy.* New York: Guilford Press.

Gross, J. J., & Levenson, R. W. (1993). Emotional suppression: Physiology, self-report, and expressive behavior. *Journal of Personality and Social Psychology, 64,* 970–986.

Hoehn-Saric, R., & McLeod, D. R. (1988). The peripheral sympathetic nervous system: Its role in normal and pathological anxiety. *Psychiatric Clinics of North America, 11,* 375–386.

Kaplan, D., Furman, M. I., Pincus, S. M., Ryan, S. M., Lipsitz, L. A., & Goldberger, A. L. (1991). Aging and the complexity of cardiovascular dynamics. *Biophysical Journal, 59,* 945–949.

Lyonfields, J. D., Borkovec, T. D., & Thayer, J. F. (in press). Vagal tone in generalized anxiety disorder and the effects of aversive imagery and worrisome thinking. *Behaviour Therapy.*

Mathews, A. (1990). Why worry? The cognitive function of anxiety. *Behaviour Research and Therapy, 28,* 455–468.

Merckelbach, H., Muris, P., van den Hout, M., & de Jong, P. (1991). Rebound effects of thought suppression: Instruction dependent? *Behavioural Psychotherapy, 19,* 225–238.

Molina, S., Roemer, L., Borkovec, M., & Posa, S. (1992, November). *Generalized anxiety disorder in an analogue population: Types of past trauma.* Paper presented at the meeting of Association for the Advancement of Behavior Therapy, New York.

Pennebaker, J. W. (1985). Traumatic experience and psychosomatic disease: Exploring the roles of behavioural inhibition, obsession, and confiding. *Canadian Psychology, 26,* 82–95.

Pennebaker, J. W. (1989). Confession, inhibition and disease. *Advances in Experimental Social Psychology, 22,* 211–244.

Pennebaker, J. W. (1993). Putting stress into words: Health, linguistic, and therapeutic implications. *Behaviour Research and Therapy, 31,* 539–548.

Pennebaker, J. W., & Beall, S. K. (1986). Confronting a traumatic event: Toward an understanding of inhibition and disease. *Journal of Abnormal Psychology, 95,* 274–281.

Pennebaker, J. W., Hughes, C. F., & O'Heeron, R. C. (1987). The psychophysiology of confession: Linking inhibitory and psychosomatic processes. *Journal of Personality and Social Psychology, 52,* 781–793.

Pennebaker, J. W., Kiecolt-Glaser, J. K., & Glaser, R. (1988). Disclosure of traumas and immune function: Health implications for psychotherapy. *Journal of Consulting and Clinical Psychology, 56,* 238–245.

Pennebaker, J. W., & Susman, J. R. (1988). Disclosure of traumas and psychosomatic processes. *Social Science and Medicine, 26,* 327–332.

Posner, M. I. (1982). Cumulative development of attentional theory. *American Psychologist, 37,* 168–179.

Roemer, L., & Borkovec, T. D. (1993). Worry: Unwanted cognitive activity that controls unwanted somatic experience. In D. M. Wegner & J. Pennebaker (Eds.), *Handbook of mental control* (pp. 220–238). Englewood Crofts, NJ: Prentice Hall.

Roemer, L., & Borkovec, T. D. (1994). The effects of suppressing thoughts about emotional material. *Journal of Abnormal Psychology, 103,* 467–474.

Roemer, L., Borkovec, M., Posa, S., & Lyonfields, J. (1991, November). *Generalized anxiety disorder in an analogue population: The role of past trauma.* Paper presented at the meeting of the Association for the Advancement of Behavioral Therapy, New York.

Schneider, W., & Shiffrin, R. M. (1977). Controlled and automatic processing: I. Detection, search, and attention. *Psychological Review, 84,* 1–66.

Shadick, R. N., Roemer, L., Hopkins, M. B., & Borkovec, T. D. (1991, November). *The nature of worrisome thoughts.* Paper presented at the meeting of Association for the Advancement of Behavior Therapy, New York.

Tallis, F., Davey, G. C. L., & Capuzzo, N. (1994). The phenomenology of non-pathological worry: A preliminary investigation. In G. C. L. Davey & F. Tallis (Eds.), *Worrying: Perspectives on theory, assessment, and treatment* (pp. 61–90). New York: Wiley.

Vasey, M. W., & Borkovec, T. D. (1992). A catastrophizing assessment of worrisome thoughts. *Cognitive Therapy and Research, 16,* 1–16.

Vrana, S. R., Cuthbert, B. N., & Lang, P. J. (1986). Fear imagery and text processing. *Psychophysiology, 23,* 247–253.

Wegner, D. M., & Gold, D. B. (1994). Fanning old flames: Arousing romantic obsession through thought suppression. Manuscript submitted for publication.

Wegner, D. M., Schneider, D. J., Carter, S. R., & White, T. L. (1987). Paradoxical effects of thought suppression. *Journal of Personality and Social Psychology, 53,* 5–13.

Wegner, D. M., Shortt, J. W., Blake, A. W., & Page, M. S. (1990). The suppression of exciting thoughts. *Journal of Personality and Social Psychology, 58,* 409–418.

Wells, A. (1994). Attention and the control of worry. In G. C. L. Davey & F. Tallis (Eds.), *Worrying: Perspectives on theory, assessment, and treatment* (pp. 91–114). New York: John Wiley & Sons.

York, D., Borkovec, T. D., Vasey, M., & Stern, R. (1987). Effects of worry and somatic anxiety induction on thoughts, emotion, and physiological activity. *Behaviour Research and Therapy, 25,* 523–526.

5

Disclosure as a Speech Act: Is It Psychotherapeutic to Disclose?

William B. Stiles

D isclosure is at the heart of psychotherapy. Across the many alternative psychotherapeutic approaches and theories, expression of private thoughts and feelings is understood as beneficial, if not for its own
sake, then at least for providing material to work on. And many of the
psychotherapists' techniques appear aimed at facilitating clients' disclosure
(Sloan & Stiles, 1994).

Not all disclosure is expressive, of course. Speakers may use disclosure
strategically for self-presentation or management of relationships (cf.
Baumeister, 1982; Derlega & Grzelak, 1979; Goffman, 1959; Schlenker,
1980). For example, they may disclose to promote intimacy, or they may
suppress disclosures to avoid exposing inadequacies or vulnerabilities or
to avoid burdening or boring others. In psychotherapy, however, obser-
vance of confidentiality and injunctions against therapists treating friends
and relatives serve to minimize strategic motives for disclosure in favor of
expressive motives. Assurances of privacy and anonymity serve a similar
facilitating function in Pennebaker's writing paradigm (e.g., Dominguez,
chapter 13, this volume; Pennebaker, chapter 1, this volume; Petrie, chapter 11, this volume).

Investigating disclosure in psychotherapy requires a measure of disclosure, and I will begin this chapter with some conceptual distinctions among measures, as a way of introducing the measure used. After reviewing some of my research on disclosure in psychotherapy, I will conclude with some theoretical speculations.

MEASUREMENT OF DISCLOSURE

Disclosure has many meanings, and researchers have used varied measures, so that their findings about disclosure's relation to such things as emotion, health, and psychotherapy outcome (which have definitional problems of their own) can appear contradictory. Presumably, researchers invent new meanings and measures because they find the old ones unsatisfactory for their purposes. Explaining my meaning and my measure may not convert other researchers, but I hope it will facilitate clearer communication.[1]

Conceptual Distinctions

I have measured Disclosure (capitalized, to distinguish my use from other meanings) as defined within a general purpose taxonomy of speech acts (Stiles, 1992). This measure can be distinguished from alternatives as concerning:

Behavioral Observation Rather Than Self-report

Respondents to self-report questionnaires (e.g., Chelune, 1976; Jourard, 1958; Miller, Berg, & Archer, 1983) have a broader basis for assessing their own behavior and experience but less training and less objectivity.

Verbal Rather Than Nonverbal Expression

This is not to deny, however, that a gesture or a fleeting expression or a tone of voice or a pattern of emphasis can speak volumes.

---

[1] Readers who would rather not be bothered with measurement issues can skip to the section entitled "VRM Disclosure in Psychotherapy" on page 76.

Differentiated Rather Than Undifferentiated Discourse

I have distinguished disclosing from nondisclosing speech, but some researchers have considered any verbal output within a particular context to be disclosure (e.g., Post, Wittmaier, & Radin, 1978).

On-record Rather Than Off-record Communication

Different or even contradictory meanings can be conveyed at different levels (Stiles, 1986); for example, an on-record question, "Is it time to go home yet?" may hint at an off-record disclosure, "I want to go home now." As Brown and Levinson (1978) and others have pointed out, off-record communication is often used to be polite or to save face or avoid conflict when direct, on-record communication could result in a confrontation or some threat to the other's status or feelings. My coding of Disclosure has been limited to on-record meanings—not because off-record levels are unimportant or rare, but because it is inherently difficult to measure them reliably.

Coding Rather Than Rating

Coding involves classifying units of text into discrete categories, whereas rating involves placing some stretch of discourse on a continuum, such as how personal or intimate or potentially embarrassing the discourse might be (e.g., Pegalis, Shaffer, Bazzini, & Greenier, 1994).

Speech Acts Rather Than Content Categories

A speech act is what is done, as contrasted with what is said, when someone says something (Russell & Stiles, 1979; Stiles & Putnam, 1989, 1995). For example, in uttering "What's for breakfast?" the speaker has said something about food, but what the speaker has done is asked a question. Food is a content category; asking a question is a speech act. A disclosure content category might be defined as statements about personal topics such as family, sex, or emotional pain. Technically, *speech acts* here refers to what Austin (1975) and Searle (1969) called *illocutionary acts* (Stiles, 1981).

Taxonomy of Verbal Response Modes

My Disclosure category is embedded in a general-purpose classification of speech acts, which I call *verbal response modes* (VRMs; Stiles, 1978, 1992).

The coding unit is the *utterance,* defined grammatically as an independent clause, nonrestrictive dependent clause, multiple predicate, or term of address, evaluation, or acknowledgment.

According to this VRM taxonomy, each utterance from a speaker to an "other" can be classified according to three principles: first by whether it concerns the speaker's or the other's experience; second by whether it presumes knowledge of what the other's experience is, was, will be, or should be; and third by whether it uses the speaker's own frame of reference or one that is shared with the other. These three forced choices yield eight mutually exclusive VRM categories, as shown in Table 1.

For example, the Disclosure, "I am enjoying my breakfast," concerns the speaker's experience and makes no presumptions about the other's experience. By contrast, the Question, "Are you enjoying your breakfast?" concerns the other's experience. And the Advisement, "Please get me a cup of coffee," presumes to impose an experience on the other by directing his or her behavior. The Interpretation, "You're going to love this coffee," does both: It concerns the other's experience and presumes knowledge of it (Table 1).

Frame of reference refers to whose viewpoint the utterance takes. A Disclosure like "I am enjoying my breakfast" uses the speaker's internal frame of reference, whereas utterances that use an external frame of reference, like "Breakfast is in the dining hall" are called Edifications. A "litmus test" for distinguishing between Edification and Disclosure is whether an external observer in the right place at the right time with the right skills and equipment could tell whether the utterance is true or false. If the observer could tell, the utterance is Edification; if the observer would instead have to read the speaker's mind, the utterance is Disclosure. For example, an observer could check on whether breakfast was being served in the dining hall but would have to read my mind to know whether I was really enjoying it.

The VRM system codes each utterance's grammatical form as well as its pragmatic intent. Distinctive grammatical forms are associated with each of the eight taxonomic categories (see Stiles, 1992, for specifications). Disclosure form is first person, so that "I can't stop thinking about it" is coded as pure Disclosure (DD) and "I walked by his school today" is coded

Table 1

Verbal Response Mode Intents

Source of experience	Presumption	Frame of reference	
		Speaker	Other
Speaker	Speaker	DISCLOSURE (D) Reveals thoughts, feelings, perceptions or intentions	EDIFICATION (E) States objective information.
Speaker	Other	ADVISEMENT (A) Attempts to guide behavior; suggestions commands, permission prohibition.	CONFIRMATION (C) Compares speaker's experience with other's; agreement, disagreement, shared experience or belief.
Other	Speaker	QUESTION (Q) Requests information or guidance.	ACKNOWLEDGMENT (K) Conveys receipt of or receptiveness to other's communication; simple acceptance, salutations.
Other	Other	INTERPRETATION (I) Explains or labels the other; judgments or evaluations of other's experience or behavior	REFLECTION (R) Puts other's experience into words; repetitions, restatements, clarifications.

Note. UNCODABLE (U) is used only for incomprehensible utterances.

as Disclosure form with Edification intent (DE). It is possible to express
Disclosure intent in a variety of forms:

Q: Are you thinking about little Jimmy?   QQ
A: Yes, [contentless term of acknowledgment]   KD
   don't you know it! [inverted subject–verb order]   QD

You never really get over a child's death. [2nd person] RD
It's nearly always on my mind. [3rd person]   ED

Each of these utterances concerns the speaker's experience and uses the speaker's internal frame of reference, so all are Disclosure intent (Table 1).

Researchers whose disclosure classification is based on use of self-references (e.g., Jacobson & Anderson, 1982; Salovey, 1992; Wegner & Giuliano, 1980; Wood, Saltzberg, & Goldsamt, 1990) can be considered as using a speech act form category.

VRM DISCLOSURE IN PSYCHOTHERAPY
Clients Disclose a Lot

Early in our research, we found that therapists of different schools used systematically different modes (Stiles, 1979). Client-centered therapists used the client's frame of reference (cf. Table 1), including lots of Reflections. Gestalt and behavior therapists used the speaker's frame of reference including lots of Advisements. Psychoanalytic therapists used the patient's experience, including lots of Interpretations.

In contrast to these systematic therapist differences, however, psychotherapy clients used more-or-less the same profile of VRMs regardless of which type of therapy they were in (Stiles & Sultan, 1979). And in every therapy, the most common mode was Disclosure. Typically, clients used Disclosure intent for 40–60% of their utterances (McDaniel, Stiles, & McGaughey, 1981; Stiles & Shapiro, 1994; Stiles & Sultan, 1979).

The high levels of Disclosure distinguish the psychotherapy client role from other expository roles studied with the VRM system. For example, patients in medical interviews (Stiles, Putnam, & Jacob, 1982), participants in laboratory studies having social conversations (Premo & Stiles, 1983; Stiles, Chertkoff, Boyd, Williams, & Ickes, 1992), and courtroom trial witnesses during direct examination and cross-examination (McGaughey & Stiles, 1983) all used substantially less Disclosure than psychotherapy clients did. The people in the nonexpository roles in these studies—the psychotherapists, physicians, and attorneys—had far different VRM profiles and far lower levels of Disclosure.

Table 2

Correlations of Client Percentage of Pure Disclosure With Ratings of Good Process in Passages of Psychotherapy

Good process rating	Correlation with client DD percent
Experiencing Scale	.58*
Vanderbilt Psychotherapy Process Scale	
Patient Exploration	.66*
Therapist Exploration	.65*

Note. DD = pure Disclosure. Correlations of percent DD with the Experiencing Scale (Klein, Mathieu-Coughlan, & Kiesler, 1986) reported by Stiles, McDaniel, and McGaughey (1979), based on $N = 90$ segments of sessions. Correlations of percent DD with the Vanderbilt Psychotherapy Process Scale (Suh, O'Malley, & Strupp, 1986) reported by McDaniel, Stiles and McGaughey (1981), based on the mean DD percent in 3 coded sessions from each of $N = 31$ clients.
$*p < .001.$

Disclosure Correlated With Good Process

Disclosure's prominence in client VRM profiles suggested that it might be part of a common core of psychotherapy process. The search for a common core has been of particular interest because, despite the technical diversity of the many alternative psychotherapies, their demonstrated outcomes have been more-or-less equivalent (Elkin et al., 1989; Lambert & Bergin, 1994; Stiles, Shapiro, & Elliott, 1986).

In support, clients' percentage of Disclosure in passages of psychotherapy was found to be highly correlated with observers' impressions of the quality of the psychotherapeutic process in those passages. Table 2 shows correlations of clients' percentage of pure Disclosure (DD) with (a) the Experiencing Scale, which is drawn from client-centered research and is meant to measure the degree to which the client is aware of and working on his or her inner processes and feelings (Stiles, McDaniel, & McGaughey, 1979), and (b) the Therapist and Patient Exploration subscales from the Vanderbilt Psychotherapy Process Scale, which was constructed within a more psychodynamic perspective but also seeks to assess the degree to which the participants were exploring the patient's inner processes and feelings (McDaniel, Stiles, & McGaughey, 1981). That is, when clients use a lot of pure Disclosure, experts (i.e., the clinicians and trained raters who applied the rating scales) think they are doing what they are supposed to be doing in psychotherapy.

Disclosure Uncorrelated With Psychotherapy Outcome

If Disclosure is an important active ingredient in psychotherapy, then it might seem sensible to expect clients who Disclosed relatively more to improve more, whereas those who Disclosed relatively less should improve less. By this reasoning, rates of Disclosure should be positively correlated, across clients, with improvement in psychotherapy.

Table 3 shows some results from the first Sheffield Psychotherapy Project, based on VRM-coding half of all sessions in 16-session treatments for depression—over one third of a million utterances in all (Stiles & Shapiro, 1994). According to the design, each client received eight sessions each of a psychodynamic–interpersonal treatment and a cognitive–behavioral treatment, in counterbalanced order, with assessments at intake, midtreatment, and termination (Shapiro & Firth, 1987). Clients improved substantially and roughly equivalently in each treatment. The percentage of clients' utterances coded as Disclosure (in intent) was compared with the rate of change (i.e, the slope of the decay curve) across the whole 16-session therapies and across each of the separate 8-session segments on several standard symptom intensity measures, including the Present State Examination (Wing, Cooper, & Sartorius, 1974), the Beck Depression Inventory (Beck, Ward, Mendelson, Mock, & Erbaugh, 1961), and the Symptom Checklist-90 (Derogatis, Lipman, & Covi, 1973).

As Table 3 shows, none of the correlations was significant (Stiles & Shapiro, 1994). We redid these correlations using raw change scores as outcome indexes, and again using residual gain scores, with no better result. These results converge with the inconsistent and generally unimpressive results of other studies of the relation of Disclosure to psychotherapy outcome (Orlinsky, Grawe, & Parks, 1994; Sloan & Stiles, 1994).

These sorts of results have been confusing (Stiles, 1994b). They seemed

Table 3

Correlations of Client Disclosure Intent in Psychodynamic–Interpersonal (PI) and Cognitive–Behavioral (CB) Psychotherapy With Rate of Change on Assessment Measures

Statistic/Assessment measure	Client Disclosure intent
Correlation of mean Disclosure percentage in all coded sessions with rate of change from intake to termination	
Present State Examination	.02
Beck Depression Inventory	.23
Symptom Checklist—90	.07
Correlation of mean Disclosure percentage in PI sessions with rate of change across PI period	
Present State Examination	−.15
Beck Depression Inventory	.04
Symptom Checklist—90	−.03
Correlation of mean Disclosure percentage in CB sessions with rate of change across CB period	
Present State Examination	−.04
Beck Depression Inventory	−.08
Symptom Checklist—90	−.12

Note. N = 37 to 39 clients because of missing data on some measures. PI = psychodynamic-interpersonal treatment; CB = cognitive-behavioral treatment. Table entries for the separate treatments are correlations of residuals, corrected for order-of-treatment effects. Negative correlations indicate that higher Disclosure was associated with declining scores on assessment measures (i.e., with symptomatic improvement). (After Stiles & Shapiro, 1994.)

to imply that client Disclosure is irrelevant to psychotherapeutic success, whereas Disclosing is the main thing clients do in therapy, and a great deal of clinical effort goes into encouraging clients to Disclose. Of course, the possibility exists that one or another of the measures is insensitive. On reconsideration, however, I think that the problem is not the measurement or the clinical impression that Disclosure is important in therapy. Before saying why, though, I will note one further finding.

Table 4

Correlations of Client Disclosure Percentage in Three Sessions With Assessments of Symptom Intensity and Distress at Intake and Termination

Measure	Correlation With Client DD Percent	
	Intake	Termination
Client perspective		
MMPI Depression scale	.53**	.51**
MMPI Psychasthenia scale	.41*	.32
Therapist perspective		
Health–Sickness Rating Scale	.56**	.49**
Clinical Rating		
Overall intensity	.43*	.43*
Distress cluster	.49**	.48**
Independent clinician's perspective		
Health–Sickness Rating Scale	.32	.24
Clinical Rating		
Overall intensity	.19	.25
Distress cluster	.40*	.36*
Psychiatric Status Schedule rating		
Subjective distress	.51**	.51**
Behavioral disturbance	.30	.20

Note. N varied from 23 to 31 because of missing data on some measures. Clients were participants in the first Vanderbilt Psychotherapy Project (Strupp & Hadley, 1978). DD = pure Disclosure (Stiles, 1992). Coded sessions included the second, middle, and next-to-last session (out of a mean of 17.2 sessions, range 5–32 session) if available; if unavailable (e.g., tape missing or inaudible), an adjacent session was substituted. (After McDaniel, Stiles, & McGaughey, 1981.)
$*p < .05; **p < .01$.

Disclosure Correlated With Psychological Distress

Table 4 shows results of coding client Disclosure in the first Vanderbilt Psychotherapy project (McDaniel et al., 1981). The clients were male university students who presented with interpersonal difficulties, anxiety, and shyness (Strupp & Hadley, 1979). Although, again, Disclosure was uncorrelated with improvement (not shown), it was strongly associated with the absolute levels of distress and psychopathology at the beginning and end of treatment, including MMPI measures of depression and anxiety and ratings of global symptom severity and distress by the therapist and by a clinician who independently assessed the client. Other studies too have found associations of disclosure with distress among psychotherapy clients and psychologically disturbed groups (Burchill & Stiles, 1988; Mayo, 1968; McDaniel et al., 1981; Rippere, 1977; Stiles, 1984; Weintraub, 1981).

Experimental Link Between Anxiety and Disclosure

The observation that the level of Disclosure increases with distress has also been demonstrated experimentally in a nonclinical population (Stiles, Shuster, & Harrigan, 1992), some results of which are shown in Table 5.

High, moderate, and low-trait anxious university students were tape-recorded while they were speaking about events that they had identified as anxiety-arousing or happy in their personal past. This procedure can induce affect similar to that experienced originally (Laird, Wagener, Halal, & Szegda, 1982; Lang, 1985) while simultaneously providing a sample of verbal (and nonverbal) behavior (Harrigan, Lucic, & Rosenthal, 1991).

Table 5

Mean Disclosure Intent Percentages of High, Moderate, and Low Trait Anxious Students Speaking About Anxious and Happy Topics

Trait anxiety level	N	Topic		Contrast
		Anxious	Happy	F(1,20)
High	24	46.6	37.6	10.85**
Moderate	24	43.3	36.2	6.49*
Low	24	35.3	36.2	0.09

Note. Contrasts based on main within-subjects effect of topic in a separate $2 \times 2 \times 2$ (topic $\times$ order $\times$ gender) ANOVA for each trait group. (After Stiles, Shuster, & Harrigan, 1992.)
$*p < .05; **p < .01$.

The high- and moderate-trait anxious students Disclosed significantly more when describing their anxiety-arousing event than their happy event (Table 5). The lack of difference between topics among the low-trait anxious participants could reflect their relative lack of distress under this study's conditions, shown in a manipulation check (Stiles, Shuster, & Harrigan, 1992).

THEORETICAL ACCOUNTS: THE FEVER MODEL AND BEYOND

The Fever Model

To reconcile these findings and to rescue the clinical impression that Disclosure is therapeutic, I've proposed a fever model of self-disclosure (Stiles, 1987). The anxiety experiment was designed as a test of part of this model (Stiles, Shuster, & Harrigan, 1992). The fever model holds that people tend to Disclose more when they are psychologically distressed (anxious, depressed, frightened, angry, etc.) than when they are not and that this Disclosure helps relieve the distress—by catharsis and by promoting self-understanding. Thus, the relation of Disclosure to psychological distress is analogous to the relation of fever to physical infection: both an indicator of some underlying disturbance and part of a restorative process.

Theoretically, distress tends to promote attention to internal events over attention to external events (cf. Salovey, 1992; Tomkins, 1962, 1963). As distress increases, thoughts, feelings, wishes, sensations, intentions, and values become relatively more prominent in awareness, at the expense of ideas about external objects, events, or people. This tendency cannot be observed directly, of course, but its manifestation in speech can be assessed by VRM coding as a shift into the speaker's internal frame of reference (cf. Table 1).

The tendency to Disclose reflects a speaker's talking about what happens to be foremost in his or her awareness during a dysphoric affective state. People need not anticipate any benefits from disclosing, though they may come to recognize that there are benefits and seek opportunities to Disclose when they are distressed, by finding friends to talk to or seeking psychotherapy. Undisclosed distressing experiences may be felt as internal pressure (cf. Wegner, chapter 3, this volume); they may divert attention into superficial, automatic thoughts, and worries (cf. Borkovec, chapter 4, this volume); and they may have negative consequences for health (e.g., Pennebaker, chapter 1, this volume; Schwartz, chapter 9, this volume). Most theoretical accounts of disclosure's beneficial effects (including those by Bucci, chapter 6, this volume, and Pennebaker, chapter 1, this volume) emphasize the interplay of emotional expression and cognitive processing that is facilitated by extended disclosure.

In effect, the fever model suggests that Disclosure may be part of a psychological homeostatic system. Distress helps promote Disclosure and Disclosure helps relieve distress and hence reduce the need to Disclose. Under normal circumstances, people appear to talk about their emotionally significant experiences with their relatives, friends, and associates soon after the experience occurs (Rimé, chapter 14, this volume), suggesting that the personal system normally meshes with the social system to promote psychological homeostasis. On the other hand, such social support systems often have a limited tolerance for expressive disclosure (Coyne, Burchill, & Stiles, 1991). In the case of very problematic experiences (or individuals who for some reason are slow to assimilate their distressing experiences), extended and repeated disclosures may be required, and an individual's normal social support network may "burn out" and become unreceptive or even hostile. Perhaps psychotherapists, clergy, and other professional listeners can be regarded as social provision for such extenuating circumstances.

Importantly, although a high level of distress may promote Disclosure in psychotherapy, it is unlikely to predict positive outcome. Indeed, the opposite may be more likely; the most distressed clients may have poorer outcomes. Thus, Disclosure may have a null or even negative correlation with outcome, even though it is an essential ingredient in psychotherapeutic change (Stiles, 1987, 1988, 1989). Analogously, a high fever is not a particularly good predictor of full or rapid recovery from physical infection, and inducing a fever is rarely an effective treatment.

Responsiveness and the Process–Outcome Correlation Problem

The fever model is one version of a more general antidote to what David Shapiro and I (Stiles & Shapiro, 1989, 1994) have called the *drug metaphor:* the notion that the processes of verbal psychotherapy can be treated like the ingredients of pharmacological therapies (cf. Yeaton & Sechrest, 1981). If a process component is an active ingredient, according to the drug metaphor, administering a high level of it is supposed to yield a positive outcome. If it does not, the process component is presumed to be inert. In naturalistic studies, clients who get relatively higher levels of an active ingredient should improve relatively more, so the process component should be correlated with outcome across clients.

This process–outcome correlation logic overlooks people's responsiveness to their own and each other's varying requirements for process components. Human interaction is systematically appropriately responsive (e.g., Elliott, 1984; Elliott et al., 1994; Goodwin, 1981; Grice, 1975; Kent, Davis, & Shapiro, 1978; Labov & Fanshel, 1977). For example, if your question is not answered, you ask again; if it is answered, you do not. Thus, you respond to the effect of your own behavior.

Responsiveness implies that outcome feeds back to influence process. Clients and psychotherapists adjust what they say moment by moment in response to the effects of their previous behaviors on anticipated or ongoing outcomes (i.e., they attend to what seems to be working). Feedback can render relations between variables chaotic and unpredictable due to sensitive dependence on initial conditions (Barton, 1994; Gleick, 1987; Prigogene & Stengers, 1984). In conversations, minor fluctuations in phrasing can initiate cascades of reactions that may lead in unexpected directions and have large effects, for better or worse. Thus, the process–outcome system is inherently nonlinear, and it is unlikely that correlations or related linear statistics will adequately assess the relations between the process and outcome of any human encounter (Stiles, 1988, 1989; Stiles & Shapiro, 1994).

Paradoxically, finding flaws in the process–outcome correlation logic may restore confidence in the importance of Disclosure in psychotherapy.

Its negligible correlations with outcome do not demonstrate efficacy, but neither do they weigh against such evidence as the predominant use of Disclosure by psychotherapy clients, and expert judgments that client Disclosure represents good process (Table 2).

The Assimilation Model and Some Final Speculations

Recognizing the limitations of linear statistics for assessing process–outcome relations in psychotherapy has helped turn my attention to qualitative and narrative approaches (Stiles, 1993). One alternative has been to investigate an account of psychotherapeutic change called the *assimilation model* (Stiles, Elliott, et al., 1990). This model reconstrues psychotherapy outcome as something that takes place over time with respect to a particular problematic experience and seeks to describe common features of the process of change. Passages dealing with particular problematic experiences have been excerpted from sessions and examined qualitatively for the hypothesized sequence of changes (e.g., Stiles, Meshot, Anderson, & Sloan, 1992; Stiles, Morrison, et al., 1991; Stiles, Shapiro, & Harper, 1994).

The assimilation work has converged with work by Sloan (1990; Sloan & Stiles, 1990, 1994) to favor an alternative hypothesis about how disclosure is related to psychological problems. In this view, the most problematic experiences are initially warded off and emerge only as physical symptoms such as muscle tension and pain (cf. Traue, chapter 8, this volume), behavioral disturbances ("acting out"), projective identification, flashbacks, and other intrusions and nonverbal expressions (Stiles, 1994a). Talking about it directly would be too painful. As the experience emerges (if it does), it is seen as distant from the self, and expressed only indirectly, in the form of stories, perceptions of related problems in other people (projection), and other externalized verbalizations (e.g., expressed using Edifications). Only after the problem has been identified and owned— that is, as it is in the process of becoming intellectually and emotionally assimilated—is it recognized and expressed as being associated with the self, in the form of VRM Disclosures.

An implication of this view, consistent with the fever model, is that externalizing talk is an important link in the assimilation process. Only by keeping the material at some conceptual and grammatical distance can it be discussed at all. People may tell stories when they cannot label their feelings easily. They talk about the outside when they cannot talk about the inside. Conversely, Disclosing could amount to talking only about already-solved problems (Sloan & Stiles, 1994).

REFERENCES

Austin, J. L. (1975). *How to do things with words* (2nd ed.). Oxford, England: Clarendon Press.

Barton, S. (1994). Chaos, self-organization, and psychology. *American Psychologist, 49,* 5–14.

Baumeister, R. F. (1982). A self-presentational view of social phenomena. *Psychological Bulletin, 91,* 3–26.

Beck, A. T., Ward, C. H., Mendelson, M., Mock, J., & Erbaugh, J. (1961). An inventory for measuring depression. *Archives of General Psychiatry, 4,* 561–571.

Brown, P., & Levinson, S. (1978). Universals in language usage: Politeness phenomena. In E. N. Goody (Ed.), *Questions and politeness: Strategies in social interaction* (pp. 56–324). Cambridge, England: Cambridge University Press.

Burchill, S. A. L., & Stiles, W. B. (1988). Interactions of depressed college students with their roommates: Not necessarily negative. *Journal of Personality and Social Psychology, 55,* 410–419.

Chelune, G. (1976). The self-disclosure situations survey: A new approach to measuring self-disclosure. *JSAS Catalog of Selected Documents in Psychology, 6,* 111–112.

Coyne, J. C., Burchill, S. A. L., & Stiles, W. B. (1991). An interactional perspective on depression. In C. R. Snyder & D. O. Forsyth (Eds.), *Handbook of social and clinical psychology: The health perspective* (pp. 327–349). Elmsford, NY: Pergamon Press.

Derlega, V. J., & Grzelak, J. (1979). Appropriateness of self-disclosure. In G. Chelune (Ed.), *Self-disclosure* (pp. 151–176). San Francisco, CA: Jossey-Bass.

Derogatis, L. R., Lipman, R. S. & Covi, M. D. (1973). SCL-90, an outpatient rating scale: Preliminary report. *Psychopharmacology Bulletin, 9,* 13–20.

Elkin, I., Shea, T., Watkins, J. T., Imber, S. D., Sotsky, S. M., Collins, J. F., Glass, D. R., Pilkonis, P. A., Leber, W. R., Docherty, J. P., Fiester, S. J., & Parloff, M. B. (1989). National Institute of Mental Health Collaborative Research Program: General effectiveness of treatments. *Archives of General Psychiatry, 46,* 971–982.

Elliott, R. (1984). A discovery-oriented approach to significant change events in psychotherapy: Interpersonal process recall and comprehensive process analysis. In L. N. Rice & L. S. Greenberg (Eds.), *Patterns of change: Intensive analysis of psychotherapy process* (pp. 249–286). New York: Guilford Press.

Elliott, R., Shapiro, D. A., Firth-Cozens, J., Stiles, W. B., Hardy, G. E., Llewelyn, S. P., & Margison, F. R. (in press). Comprehensive process analysis of insight events in cognitive–behavioral and interpersonal–dynamic psychotherapies. *Journal of Counseling Psychology.*

Gleick, J. (1987). *Chaos: Making a new science.* New York: Penguin Books.

Goffman, E. (1959). *Presentation of self in everyday life.* New York: Doubleday.

Goodwin, C. (1981). *Conversational organization: Interaction between speakers and hearers.* San Diego, CA: Academic Press.

Grice, H. P. (1975). Logic and conversation. In P. Cole & J. L. Morgan (Eds.), *Syntax and semantics: Vol. 3. Speech acts.* San Diego, CA: Academic Press.

Harrigan, J. A., Lucic, K. S., & Rosenthal, R. (1991). Retelling anxious events: Effects on trait and state anxiety. *Personality and Individual Differences, 12,* 917–927.

Jacobson, N. S., & Anderson, E. A. (1982). Interpersonal skill and depression in college students: Analysis of the timing of self-disclosures. *Behavior Therapy, 13,* 271–282.

Jourard, S. M. (1958). Some factors in self-disclosure. *Journal of Abnormal and Social Psychology, 56,* 95–99.

Kent, G. S., Davis, J. D., & Shapiro, D. A. (1978). Resources required in the construction and reconstruction of conversation. *Journal of Personality and Social Psychology, 36,* 13–22.

Klein, M. H., Mathieu-Coughlan, P., & Kiesler, D. J. (1986). The experiencing scales. In L. S. Greenberg & W. M. Pinsof (Eds.), *The psychotherapeutic process: A research handbook* (pp. 21–71). New York: Guilford Press.

Labov, W., & Fanshel, D. (1977). *Therapeutic discourse.* San Diego, CA: Academic Press.

Laird, J. D., Wagener, J. J., Halal, M., & Szegda, M. (1982). Remembering what you feel: Effects of emotion on memory. *Journal of Personality and Social Psychology, 42,* 646–657.

Lambert, M. J., & Bergin, A. E. (1994). The effectiveness of psychotherapy. In A. E. Bergin & S. L. Garfield (Eds.), *Handbook of psychotherapy and behavior change* (4th ed., pp. 143–189). New York: Wiley.

Lang, P. J. (1985). The cognitive psychophysiology of emotion: Fear and anxiety. In

A. H. Tuma & J. Maser (Eds.), *Anxiety and the anxiety disorders* (pp. 131–170). Hillsdale, NJ: Erlbaum.

Mayo, P. R. (1968). Self-disclosure and neurosis. *British Journal of Social and Clinical Psychology, 7,* 140–148.

McDaniel, S. H., Stiles, W. B., & McGaughey, K. J. (1981). Correlations of male college students' verbal response mode use in psychotherapy with measures of psychological disturbance and psychotherapy outcome. *Journal of Consulting and Clinical Psychology, 49,* 571–582.

McGaughey, K. J., & Stiles, W. B. (1983). Courtroom interrogation of rape victims: Verbal response mode use by attorneys and witnesses during direct examination vs. cross-examination. *Journal of Applied Social Psychology, 13,* 78–87.

Miller, L. C., Berg, J. H., & Archer, R. L. (1983). Openers: Individuals who elicit intimate self-disclosure. *Journal of Personality and Social Psychology, 44,* 1234–1244.

Orlinsky, D. E., Grawe, K., & Parks, B. K. (1994). Process and outcome in psychotherapy—Noch einmal. In A. E. Bergin & S. L. Garfield (Eds.), *Handbook of psychotherapy and behavior change,* (4th ed., pp. 270–376). New York: Wiley.

Pegalis, L. J., Shaffer, D. R., Bazzini, D. G., & Greenier, K. (1994). On the ability to elicit self-disclosure: Are there gender-based and contextual limitations on the opener effects? *Personality and Social Psychology Bulletin, 20,* 412–420.

Post, A. L., Wittmaier, B. C., & Radin, M. E. (1978). Self-disclosure as a function of state and trait anxiety. *Journal of Consulting and Clinical Psychology, 46,* 12–19.

Premo, B. E., & Stiles, W. B. (1983). Familiarity in verbal interactions of married couples versus strangers. *Journal of Social and Clinical Psychology, 1,* 209–230.

Prigogene, I., & Stengers, I. (1984). *Order out of chaos: Man's new dialogue with nature.* New York: Bantam Books.

Rippere, V. (1977). "What's the thing to do when you're feeling depressed?"—A pilot study. *Behaviour Research and Therapy, 15,* 185–191.

Russell, R. L., & Stiles, W. B. (1979). Categories for classifying language in psychotherapy. *Psychological Bulletin, 86,* 404–419.

Salovey, P. (1992). Mood-induced self-focused attention. *Journal of Personality and Social Psychology, 62,* 699–707.

Schlenker, B. R. (1980). *Impression management: The self concept, social identity, and interpersonal relationships.* Monterey, CA: Brooks/Cole.

Searle, J. R. (1969). *Speech acts: An essay in philosophy of language.* Cambridge, England: Cambridge University Press.

Shapiro, D. A., & Firth, J. A. (1987). Prescriptive v. exploratory psychotherapy: Outcomes of the Sheffield Psychotherapy Project. *British Journal of Psychiatry, 151,* 790–799.

Sloan, W. W., Jr. (1990). *Development of a verbal coding system for measuring relational immediacy in psychotherapy.* Unpublished doctoral dissertation, Department of Psychology, Miami University, Oxford, Ohio.

Sloan, W. W., Jr., & Stiles, W. B. (1990, June). *Development of the Relational Immediacy Coding System: Correlations with the Experiencing Scale.* Paper presented at the meeting of the Society for Psychotherapy Research, Wintergreen, Virginia.

Sloan, W. W., Jr., & Stiles, W. B. (1994). *Client self-disclosure and psychotherapy outcome.* Manuscript submitted for publication.

Stiles, W. B. (1978). Verbal response modes and dimensions of interpersonal roles: A method of discourse analysis. *Journal of Personality and Social Psychology, 36,* 693–703.

Stiles, W. B. (1979). Verbal response modes and psychotherapeutic technique. *Psychiatry, 42,* 49–62.

Stiles, W. B. (1981). Classification of intersubjective illocutionary acts. *Language in Society, 10,* 227–249.

Stiles, W. B. (1984). Client disclosure and psychotherapy session evaluations. *British Journal of Clinical Psychology, 23,* 311–312.

Stiles, W. B. (1986). Levels of intended meaning of utterances. *British Journal of Clinical Psychology, 25,* 213–222.

Stiles, W. B. (1987). "I have to talk to somebody." A fever model of disclosure. In V. J. Derlega & J. H. Berg (Eds.), *Self-disclosure: Theory, research, and therapy* (pp. 257–282). New York: Plenum Press.

Stiles, W. B. (1988). Psychotherapy process-outcome correlations may be misleading. *Psychotherapy, 25,* 27–35.

Stiles, W. B. (1989). Evaluating medical interview process components: Null correlations with outcomes may be misleading. *Medical Care, 27,* 212–220.

Stiles, W. B. (1992). *Describing talk: A taxonomy of verbal response modes.* Newbury Park, CA: Sage.

Stiles, W. B. (1993). Quality control in qualitative research. *Clinical Psychology Review, 13,* 593–618.

Stiles, W. B. (1994a, June). Assimilation of very problematic experiences. In W. B. Stiles (Moderator), *Semiosis and assimilation of warded-off experiences: Theoretical developments.* Panel presented at the Society for Psychotherapy Research meeting, York, England.

Stiles, W. B. (in press 1994b). Drugs, recipes, babies, bathwater, and psychotherapy process-outcome relations. *Journal of Consulting and Clinical Psychology, 62,* 955–959.

Stiles, W. B., Elliott, R., Llewelyn, S. P., Firth-Cozens, J. A., Margison, F. R., Shapiro, D. A., & Hardy, G. (1990). Assimilation of problematic experiences by clients in psychotherapy. *Psychotherapy, 27,* 411–420.

Stiles, W. B., McDaniel, S. H., & McGaughey, K. (1979). Verbal response mode correlates of experiencing. *Journal of Consulting and Clinical Psychology, 47,* 795–797.

Stiles, W. B., Meshot, C. M., Anderson, T. M., & Sloan, W. W., Jr. (1992). Assimilation of problematic experiences: The case of John Jones. *Psychotherapy Research, 2,* 81–101.

Stiles, W. B., Morrison, L. A., Haw, S. K., Harper, H., Shapiro, D. A., & Firth-Cozens, J. (1991). Longitudinal study of assimilation in exploratory psychotherapy. *Psychotherapy, 28,* 195–206.

Stiles, W. B., & Putnam, S. M. (1989). Analysis of verbal and nonverbal behavior in doctor-patient encounters. In M. Stewart & D. Roter (Eds.), *Communicating with medical patients* (pp. 211–222). Newbury Park, CA: Sage.

Stiles, W. B., & Putnam, S. M. (1995). Categories for coding medical interviews: A metaclassification. In M. Lipkin, Jr., S. M. Putnam, & A. Lazare (Eds.), *The medical interview.* New York: Springer-Verlag.

Stiles, W. B., Putnam, S. M., & Jacob, M. C. (1982). Verbal exchange structure of initial medical interviews. *Health Psychology, 1,* 315–336.

Stiles, W. B., & Shapiro, D. A. (1989). Abuse of the drug metaphor in psychotherapy process-outcome research. *Clinical Psychology Review, 9,* 521–543.

Stiles, W. B., & Shapiro, D. A. (1994). Disabuse of the drug metaphor: Psychotherapy of process–outcome correlations. *Journal of Consulting and Clinical Psychology, 62,* 942–948.

Stiles, W. B., Shapiro, D. A., & Elliott, R. (1986). "Are all psychotherapies equivalent?" *American Psychologist, 41,* 165–180.

Stiles, W. B., Shapiro, D. A., & Harper, H. (1994). Finding the way from process to outcome: Blind alleys and unmarked trails. In R. L. Russell (Ed.), *Reassessing psychotherapy research* (pp. 36–64). New York: Guilford Press.

Stiles, W. B., Shuster, P. L., & Harrigan, J. A. (1992). Disclosure and anxiety: A test of the fever model. *Journal of Personality and Social Psychology, 63,* 980–988.

Stiles, W. B., & Sultan, F. E. (1979). Verbal response mode use by clients in psychotherapy. *Journal of Consulting and Clinical Psychology, 47,* 611–613.

Stiles, W. B., Walz, N. C., Boyd, M. A. B., Williams, L. L., & Ickes, W. (1995). *Attractiveness and disclosure in initial encounters of mixed-sex dyads.* Manuscript submitted for publication.

Strupp, H. H., & Hadley, S. W. (1979). Specific versus nonspecific factors in psychotherapy: A controlled study of outcome. *Archives of General Psychiatry, 36,* 1125–1136.

Suh, C. S., O'Malley, S. S., & Strupp, H. H. (1986). The Vanderbilt process measures: The Vanderbilt Psychotherapy Process Scale (VPPS) and the Vanderbilt Negative Indicators Scale (VNIS). In L. S. Greenberg & W. M. Pinsof (Eds.), *The psychotherapeutic process: A research handbook* (pp. 285–324). New York: Guilford Press.

Tomkins, S. S. (1962). *Affect, imagery, and consciousness, Vol. 1: The positive affects.* New York: Springer.

Tomkins, S. S. (1963). *Affect, imagery, and consciousness, Vol. 2: The negative affects.* New York: Springer.

Wegner, D. M., & Giuliano, T. (1980). Arousal-induced attention to self. *Journal of Personality and Social Psychology, 38,* 719–726.

Weintraub, W. (1981). *Verbal behavior: Adaptation and psychopathology.* New York: Springer-Verlag.

Wing, J. K., Cooper, J. E. & Sartorius, N. (1974). *The measurement and classification of psychiatric symptoms.* Cambridge, UK: Cambridge University Press.

Wood, J. V., Saltzberg, J. A., & Goldsamt, L. A. (1990). Does affect induce self-focused attention? *Journal of Personality and Social Psychology, 58,* 899–908.

Yeaton, W. H., & Sechrest, L. (1981). Critical dimensions in the choice and maintenance of successful treatments: Strength, integrity, and effectiveness. *Journal of Consulting and Clinical Psychology, 49,* 156–167.

6

The Power of the Narrative: A Multiple Code Account

Wilma Bucci

F reud was a pioneer in the use of language as a remedy for bodily ills. Psychoanalytic treatment is referred to as the "talking cure." Freud relied on the telling of stories to treat paralyses, convulsions, sleep disturbances, anorexia, vasomotor and respiratory ills, and many other physical and emotional conditions. Contemporary psychotherapists, within psychodynamic and other orientations, also rely primarily on talking to treat the broad range of disorders that are diagnosed today. The work of Pennebaker and his colleagues suggests that the effects of talking might be extended to a "writing cure." However, the question of accounting for the effects of verbalization, in any medium, remains for us, as for Freud:

> If we are asked by what methods and means this result is achieved, it is not easy to find an answer. We can only say: 'So muss denn doch die Hexe dran!—the Witch Metapsychology' [We must call the Witch to our help after all]. (from Goethe's Faust, quoted in Freud, 1937/1964, p. 225)

Freud's theory of the mental apparatus, the metapsychology, was his attempt to explain the process by which recall and verbalization of memories can eliminate symptoms and cure mental and physical disorders. The metapsychology was a model of the distribution of "psychic energy" in an enclosed apparatus, based on the principles of Newtonian mechanics. Mental representations that are unconscious and not verbalized, which constitute the primary process of thought, are characterized by psychic energy that is mobile and unbound. Unbound psychic energy seeks immediate release, and is likely to be discharged in the form of hallucinations, delusions, fantasies and dreams, or alternatively as somatic symptoms or uncontrolled behavior. Language—the secondary process—serves to bind the energy of the instincts, enabling delay of discharge and adaptive problem solving. Through verbalization, in psychoanalytic treatment, insight occurs; the unconscious becomes conscious (Freud, 1900/1953; 1915/1957); the ego subdues the forces of the id (Freud, 1923/1961).

Many of the concepts and methods introduced by Freud continue to exert their influence today, not only in psychoanalysis proper, but in most treatments in the United States and around the world. These basic psychoanalytic contributions include the fundamental notion of unconscious mental processes, the technique of free association in the context of the therapeutic relationship, and the curative effects of remembering and talking. Many of the approaches represented in this book, which are concerned with the effects of verbalization on physical and emotional health, may be seen as incorporating aspects of the psychodynamic approach, in new contexts and forms. In treating anxiety disorders using cognitive behavioral techniques, Borkovec (chapter 4, this volume) incorporates imaginal rehearsal of childhood and past trauma experiences, as well as current life events. Mahoney (chapter 12, this volume) stresses the role of unconscious processes in the experiencing and communication of therapist and client as a central aspect of the constructivist approach.

Whereas the psychoanalytic observations concerning the therapeutic functions of verbalization remain influential, Freud's metapsychology unfortunately does not help us to understand these effects in modern, scientific terms. This is not surprising for a theoretical model that has not changed in essential respects since its turn of the century formulation (Freud, 1900/1953), whose concepts have never been systematically defined, and that is based on principles of distribution of energy in a closed system, which the human information processor certainly is not (Berta-lanffy, 1950). In recent years, attempts were made by Rapaport and his colleagues to systematize the metapsychology and to formulate coherent propositions that could be tested empirically, in effect, taking seriously Freud's scientific claims. The general conclusion that was reached, after years of such effort, was that neither the structural organization nor the dynamic principles of the metapsychology survived this attempt at scientific cure: ". . . the operation was successful though the patient died" (Holt, 1989, p. 342).

THE MULTIPLE CODE THEORY

A new theoretical model is required to account for the effect of language, and in particular the effects of storytelling, on physical and emotional health. In my work over the past 10 years, I have been developing a theory of the interaction of language with other cognitive, emotional and physiological systems, and have applied this to the process of treatment in psychoanalysis. I originally called this a "dual code" theory of the psychoanalytic process, and have now elaborated it as a multiple code theory (Bucci, 1985, 1989, 1994, In press). The dual code theory (Bucci, 1985), based on the work of Paivio (1986) and others, emphasized the distinction between verbal and a wide range of nonverbal processing modes, including sensory representations in all modalities, as well as representations of motoric and visceral experience. The multiple code theory includes the verbal-nonverbal distinction, but incorporates this within a more basic distinction between symbolic and subsymbolic processing and accounts more fully for the heterogeneity of processing in the nonverbal domains. The theory is based on current research in cognitive science, along with work in the areas of emotion theory, developmental psychology, and neurophysiology.

Models based on symbolic processing have been dominant in cognitive science from its beginnings. Within the past decade a radically different format of human information processing has been proposed, termed connectionist, subsymbolic, or Parallel Distributed Processing (PDP) models, which do not assume this symbolic format (Rumelhart, McClelland, & the PDP Research Group, 1986). According to the new multiple code theory, information is represented in the mind in complex subsymbolic and symbolic nonverbal forms, which begin to develop early in infancy and continue throughout life. Subsymbolic information is registered in modality specific format in all sensory systems, as well as in visceral and motoric forms. The symbolic systems include nonverbal and verbal representations.

The multiple code theory and research supporting it have previously been presented in several publications cited above. Here, I will present a brief outline of the basic theory, including (a) a description of subsymbolic processing; (b) the symbolic processing systems, including nonverbal and verbal forms; (c) the referential process that connects the nonverbal to the verbal modes; (d) the central concepts of the emotion schemas, which constitute the organizing structures of emotional life; and (e) the operation of the referential cycle, by which emotional experience may be, at least partially, expressed in verbal form. I will then present several applications of this approach in psychotherapy and experimental research.

The Subsymbolic Processing Systems

In the current research on subsymbolic PDP formats (Rumelhart et al., 1986), complex constructs are being developed, really for the first time, that account systematically for the types of intuitive and implicit processing that analysts associate with unconscious and primary process functions, and that have eluded classical information processing models. Subsymbolic processing operates with rapid and complex computations on implicit continuous dimensions, based on principles that are analogic and global, without formation of discrete categories and without explicit metrics. Rather than being determined by formal, structural, or logical principles, applied across a range of contents, subsymbolic processing is content sensitive. The mode of operation is specific to modality and to contents within modalities. Particular types of visual processing occur in the formats of different visual systems; processing in other sensory systems takes place in the format of each modality; visceral and motoric processing each occur in its own format as well. Subsymbolic "computations" underlie the capacity to navigate a ship through a narrow channel, ski a slalom course, hit a tennis ball effectively, or distinguish the taste and aroma of burgundies from different hillsides or from different years. Such computations also serve to distinguish subtle shifts in facial expression, to identify changes in body movement or vocal qualities, and to recognize changes in one's own visceral state. The cat uses subsymbolic processing to program its leap onto a table full of objects; the creative mathematician or scientist uses visual–spatial analogic processing to find or generate the parameters of the problem space; the analyst to recognize his patient's subjective state, and to decide when and how to intervene.

The defining feature of subsymbolic processing is not that it is nonverbal rather than verbal; not that it is implicit or unconscious, rather than conscious, although it is likely to be all of those. The fundamental feature is that it can operate in contexts in which specific dimensions and discrete categories have not been identified. Thus it lays the groundwork for identification of the dimensions and formation of categories upon which symbolic processes may be based. In this sense, subsymbolic processing is an essentially creative (rather than generative) function, which may operate in emotional and physiological as well as intellectual domains (Bucci, 1993, 1994).

Symbolic Processes

In information processing terms, symbols are defined as discrete entities that refer to or represent other entities, and may be combined in rule-governed ways, so that a vast, essentially infinite set of meaningful combinations may be generated from a finite set of elements (Simon & Kaplan, 1989; Fodor & Pylyshyn, 1988). Symbols may be images or words; the major processing distinction within the symbolic formats is between nonverbal and verbal forms. We generate and process language and logic using symbolic systems, and carry out many imaging functions as well.

Symbolic Imagery

The work of Kosslyn (1987) and his colleagues, in the area of visual imagery, provides a basis for understanding the formation of symbolic imagery and its role in the organization of thought. The functions of vision include both recognizing changes in the location or form of an object, and recognizing objects as the same over such changes in location or form. We identify changes in the position or facial expression of the people we know or changes in the look of familiar places in different lights or different times of day; we also identify things or people as the same entities across such manifest transformations. The recognition of alterations involves analogic and parallel processing on continuous dimensions with implicit, modality-specific metrics. We can identify subtle shifts in our friend Jane's facial expression, or notice that her body appears tense. In the second function, recognition of identity, ranges of continuous variation, which are functionally equivalent, are chunked into visual "categories" or prototypes. We recognize Jane when she is happy, sad, sitting up, lying down, and also across a wide range of changes in other features. We also recognize expressions of happiness or tension as they may appear in different people; such expressions form an emotion category in a different sense. The categorical processor of the visual system ignores variation within a functionally equivalent class of representations, responding to this range of manifestations as if they were the same. The prototypic images—of Jane, a triangle, an apple, the living room couch, the physical features of tension—are stored in long-term memory and provide a basis for symbolic processing within the nonverbal system itself. Such images are organizing categories that operate within the visual system itself, providing discrete symbolic entities that may be named. An important point that emerges from Kosslyn's formulation, and that needs to be stressed for our purposes, is that the organization into prototypic imagery must occur within the sensory system itself, without intervention by language, to provide the basis for construction of the type of discrete symbolic representation that may be mapped into language. We do not have labels for the continuous variations within subsymbolic systems; verbal labels—*mother, Jane, the yellow house, tension*—cannot be applied until prototypic images of some sort are formed.

J. Mandler's (1992) theory of cognitive and linguistic development incorporates a similar mechanism by which experience that originates in early subsymbolic formats may eventually be connected to the categorical, prototypic symbols of the nonverbal imagery systems, and mapped, via that organization, onto verbal forms. Rosch's theories concerning the formation of prototypes and their role in the organization of mental representation, also provide a related account (1975). Rosch has extended this approach to a formulation of prototypic episodes, as well as images. The concept of prototypic episodes is central to the multiple code formulation of the emotion schemas.

The Verbal System

Language is primarily a symbolic format, and is the quintessential one. Words are entities that refer to other entities, and that have the capacity to be combined in rule governed ways. From a limited set of phonemes in each language, a virtually unlimited array of words are generated and meanings expressed. Words are organized *phonologically,* based on relationships between the sounds of speech; *syntactically,* in sequential strings, based on grammatical rules, and *semantically,* in categories of increasing abstractness and generality, within the logical hierarchies of verbal memory. Thus, *apples, bananas, grapes, oranges* are stored in semantic memory as members of the category *fruit; fruit* is a member of the category *food; food* may be classified within the category of *bodily needs* and so on, within the complex and interwoven hierarchies of verbal knowledge.

The verbal system is a single channel processor operating primarily within the focus of awareness. We can produce only one message at a time, and can listen to and understand only one. Language is the code of communication and reflection, in which private, subjective experience, including emotional experience, may be shared, and through which the knowledge of the culture and the constraints of logic may be brought to bear upon the contents of individual thought. It is also the code that we may call upon, explicitly and intentionally, to direct and regulate ourselves, to activate internal representations of imagery and emotion, to stimulate action, and to control it.

The Referential Process

The multiple nonverbal systems, with their diverse contents and formats, are connected to language via the referential links, which enable us to name what we experience, and to identify what we have named. Referential Activity (RA) is defined as activity of the referential connections, in both directions, between verbal and nonverbal systems. Level of RA, the degree to which an individual is able to connect nonverbal, including emotional experience to language, and to connect the words of others back to nonverbal representation in his or her own mind, varies among individuals as a matter of stable competence or trait. Level of RA also varies for each individual as a function of internal state or external context. The interpersonal context, in particular, plays a primary role.

The referential connections between the verbal and nonverbal system are most active and direct for concrete and specific entities, such as *apples, orange, figs*, and words referring to them; less direct for higher order category words, such as *fruit* or *food*, which do not have specific exemplars in imagery; still less direct for abstract concepts such as *beauty, truth, epistemology*. Such words may be represented in the nonverbal system—if at all—by working down the verbal hierarchies to specific exemplars (Bucci & Freedman, 1978; Bucci, 1984). From the converse direction, the referential connections from experience to words are least direct for the sensory, visceral, and motoric contents of the subsymbolic systems. These connect to words only indirectly through their organization in prototypic imagery, as discussed by Kosslyn and others. The referential process is necessarily partial and incomplete; much occurs in the nonverbal system that cannot be connected to words; much verbal processing occurs without reference to the nonverbal system. Individual differences in RA are not assessed by standard psychometric measures and have not generally been considered within the cognitive science perspective. Variation in RA—between and within individuals—and factors affecting this variation have been studied extensively in our own research (Bucci & Freedman, 1978; Bucci, 1984; Bucci & Miller, 1993).

The Emotion Schemas

Emotions are characterized as image–action schemas registered in memory, built up through repetitions of interactions with others—particularly the caretaker—that share a common affective core. The core affective state is defined here as a cluster of components that are primarily subsymbolic and that include motoric activity, facial and vocal expression, and somatic activity, particularly in autonomic and endocrine systems (Emde, 1983). Repetitions of episodes characterized by a core affective state form functionally equivalent classes, which are then represented as prototypes, and which provide the structure of the emotion schemas. The affective state is repeatedly associated with representations of people and places in these episodes. These are the type of prototypic memories that emerge as "screen memories," in psychoanalytic terms. This formulation builds on the concept of prototypic imagery as the basis for organization of the nonverbal system, as developed by Kosslyn, J. Mandler, and Rosch, and applied here to the construction of prototypic episodes.

Stern's (1985) concept of Representations of Interactions that have been Generalized (RIGs) refers to prototypic episodes of this nature. According to Stern, memory for repeated episodes provides the basis for the integration of features of experience into the organizing perspectives that are characterized as the sense of self, and complementarily, of others. As defined by Stern, episodes are small but coherent chunks of experience, which include "sensations, perceptions, actions, thoughts, affects and goals" and "which occur in some temporal, physical, and causal relationship." He gives the example of a "breast-milk" episode, with the following attributes: "being hungry, being positioned at the breast (with accompanying tactile, olfactory, and visual sensations and perceptions), rooting, opening mouth, beginning to suck, getting milk" (p. 95). As specific episodes repeat, the infant begins to form a generalized memory, which Stern characterizes as:

> ... an individualized, personal expectation of how things are likely to proceed on a moment-to-moment basis. The generalized breast-milk episode is not in itself a specific memory any more; it is an abstraction of many specific memories, all inevitably slightly different, that produces one generalized memory structure. It is, so to speak, average experience made prototypic. (pp. 95–96)

These prototypic memory structures, involving actions, sensations and affects, all occurring in a temporal, physical and causal relationship, in an interactive, interpersonal context, are the basis for the emotion schemas.

101

The emotion schemas begin to be formed from birth and continue to develop throughout life. The prototypic episodes that make up the emotion schemas are dominated by the subsymbolic components of the affective core, as in the "breast-milk" episode. They may be associated with satisfaction and soothing, with delay and anger, with arousal or pain or pleasure of various sorts. They also incorporate symbolic imagery and may become connected to language, to varying degrees. They constitute the sensory and bodily "knowledge" people have about each other, the wishes, fears, expectations, and beliefs that make up each individual's interpersonal world. They operate to give symbolic and interpersonal meaning and to determine an individual's reactions in situations where the core affective state is evoked.

The notions of emotion schemas and emotional information processing, which have been introduced here, are compatible with current work in emotion theory, in which cognition, emotion, and motivation are seen as interacting rather than independent domains (Scherer, 1984). Thus, according to Lang (1994)

> . . . a memory of an emotional episode can be seen as an information network that includes units representing emotional stimuli, somatic or visceral responses, and related semantic (interpretive) knowledge. The memory is activated by input that matches some of its representations. Because of the implicit connectivity, the other representations in the structure are also automatically engaged, and as the circuit is associative, any of the units might initiate or subsequently contribute to this process. (p. 218)

Information leading to activation of the emotional circuitry may originate in the external environment, within the body, or within the brain, in the form of thoughts and memories. Regardless of what initially arouses the emotion schemas, their activation may have physiological or motoric effects. They may be activated by language or images, by a sight or a sound, as well as by internally generated needs or desires. The capacity of language to activate the emotion schemas, with their physiological components, provides the central mechanism by which emotional disclosure has its cross-modal effects. The model of the multicomponent emotion schemas, and the understanding of motivation that has been proposed here is also compatible with what is known today concerning the neurophysiological substrate of emotion, the thalamo-cortico-amygdala circuitry, the feeding of this circuitry into the musculoskeletal, autonomic, and endocrine systems, and the bidirectional interaction of these systems with the cortex (LeDoux, 1989).

In their general structure or function, emotion schemas are memory schemas like any others, as defined initially by Bartlett (1932) and elaborated by many investigators since then. They differ from other types of memory schemas in their interpersonal contents and in their relative domination by the subsymbolic, including visceral processing systems. As for all memory schemas, new input in emotion schemas is perceived and encoded in the context of information already present, and is later retrieved as determined by this encoding. Components of the emotion schemas, like any mental representation or process, may occur within or outside of the focus of awareness. What is referred to in psychoanalytic theory as the dynamic unconscious, incorporating representations that are repressed or "warded off," is accounted for in terms of particular contents and particular forms of dissociation in the emotion schemas (Bucci, 1993, 1994).

Verbalization of Emotion and the Referential Cycle

The complex, multicomponent organization of the nonverbal information processing system operates primarily outside of language, and also outside of symbol processing systems. The problem of verbalizing emotional experience now becomes clear. To translate emotional experience into words, the massively parallel, analogic, subsymbolic contents of the nonverbal system must be connected to the single channel, symbolic format of the verbal code. Language is not the optimal mode of expressing emotion. For most people, it is extremely difficult to express strong emotion verbally. It is sometimes easier to talk instead about what cannot be expressed: "my heart is too full for speech"; "I was struck dumb with awe"; "My mouth hung open, I was absolutely speechless"; "My heart was in my mouth." Emotions are expressed most directly by gesture, facial expression, or vocalization, which are components of the emotion schemas themselves. The fundamental difficulty of representing emotion in words is greater than that of expressing other forms of nonverbal experience, because of the dominance of the subsymbolic contents in the emotion schemas. This difficulty exists over and above dynamic factors of resistance and defense, in the psychoanalytic sense, but is exacerbated for such contents.

Emotional experience may be captured most effectively in the verbal system by describing specific images and episodes, as poets know, and as the multiple code theory postulates. Such concrete and specific images constitute the type of material for which the referential connections are most active, and which are likely to activate referential connections in the listener. Images and their concatenations in episodes constitute the essential symbolic contents of the emotion schemas. In episodic form, the emotion schemas can be "told." In that sense, the telling of a story is precisely the expression of an emotion schema, or parts of a schema, in verbal form. The concept of the *referential cycle* (Bucci, 1993) provides a model of the process by which nonverbal, including emotional experience, is expressed, at least partially, in words. The cycle includes the following stages:

1. Subsymbolic Activation

The cycle begins with activation of emotional experience, dominated by subsymbolic nonverbal components, and including patterns of visceral and autonomic arousal as well as sensory experiences in all modalities. This may be more readily expressed by facial expression, gesture, emotive vocalization, and action, but may also be expressed directly in verbal form: "I feel tired"; "I feel angry"; "you look weird today." The subsymbolic components have been activated, but without retrieval, as yet, of specific images or other symbolic contents. The patient in the analytic situation is committed to saying whatever "comes to mind," no matter how trivial or irrelevant it may appear. In this phase, he may speak about staring at the ceiling, the smells of the room, feeling hungry, cold, or tired, having nothing to say, having impulses to act in a certain way.

The following example is taken from a verbatim transcript of a session in the middle phase of a tape-recorded analysis, which we are currently studying (Bucci, 1993, 1994). The patient, here called Mr. A., is a young man who is successful in his work, but has difficulties in establishing a relationship with a woman, and feels increasingly bereft as his circle of male friends is depleted by marriage. He opens the session with an immediate reference to bodily experience, dissociated from emotional state:

> Patient: *I see it's cold in here today. I guess it's the ah, yeah, I can feel the ah cold coming through the mattress. Ah, it's not my imagination. It's the temperature.*

He then goes on to tell how he was stood up by a date last night; he did not feel angry at this:

> Patient: *So, ah, what, what was I feeling then? Well, I tried to, at this point I tried to understand it right then and there. I didn't feel anything. I said, boy, am I taking this calm and cool, huh? Didn't (stutters) didn't, didn't get upset, didn't do anything. Took it real calm and cool.*

Later that evening, he "got very lonely, all of a sudden," and called some friends; his attention then turns back to aspects of somatic experience:

> Patient: . . . *and I called this one, and called that one, ok, just to touch base, to uh—I have a terrible itch here—just, just to call base, ah, call base, touch base.*

The theory postulates that the sensory and bodily experience, which is largely subsymbolic—itching, feeling cold—constitutes a component of emotional experience, which is accessible before the emotional contents themselves can be recognized or acknowledged in symbolic form. The fragmentary verbalization of sensory or somatic experience is an intermediate step, which contributes to the process of symbolizing and verbalizing the emotion itself.

2. Connecting: The Referential Phase

This includes two subphases:

(a) The speaker (or writer) retrieves concrete and specific prototypic images and episodes that represent these emotion schemas. This is the conversion of the subsymbolic to the symbolic format, operating first in the nonverbal system.

(b) The discrete images and episodes of the symbolic nonverbal system may then be mapped into language.

In this session, Mr. A. recalls a long and detailed dream from the previous night. First, he is riding a bicycle or unicycle with several of his male friends, in a village square with three movie theatres. He feels some responsibility for his friends that he has been unable to carry out adequately, and feels that he is blamed by his parents for this. The scene of the dream shifts, and he is in an upstairs apartment with his friends. He describes an image of a room seen through a door, in which there is a couch and a chair; all his friends are in the room; he is having a great time talking to them. Then he sees five good-looking girls in the doorway, who intrude on this. He first says that the dream ended there; then, as an afterthought, remembers another part. Going from downstairs to upstairs, he got quite upset. He had to go to the bathroom, but there was no toilet and he ended up holding his feces in toilet paper in his hand. He had no place to put it all. Then when he went upstairs, he found a wastepaper basket, under a table. He dumped the whole thing in there and then covered it up. He was hoping that it wouldn't smell, he was embarrassed; then, in the dream, he began to itch again.

The special function of the referential process is to provide a way to symbolize emotional experience while retaining access to the analogic components of the feeling state. The ongoing experiences and images link subsymbolic representations to symbolic images. In the initial phase, Mr. A. felt the cold coming through the mattress; he felt no emotion, took it all "calm and cool", but he had a terrible itch that recurs as he tells the story of his dream. The visceral experience of an emotion, which cannot be communicated in words, is represented in the images of the dream, and also activated by these. Mr. A.'s therapist suggests that the dream represents a retreat from the excitement and anxiety of the world to "this upstairs room, with the couch and with the man, holding all this dirty filthy stuff in your hand." The patient responds that yes, he has the dirty stuff and must "get rid of it", but he is retreating from getting rid of it with a woman; he is able to dump the feelings in the therapist's room.

3. Verbal Mediation and Emotional Insight

After telling the narrative of his dream, Mr. A. spends much of the remainder of the session associating further to this, moving back and forth between images and words. Additional connections within the verbal systems may be retrieved, permitting associated features, categories, and dimensions to be verbalized. Emotional categories that are defined in the verbal mode, and in the interpersonal context—feelings of rage, fear of loss of control, feelings of identification with his father—feed back to activate additional nonverbal elements, now seen for the first time as components of particular emotional schemas. This is a multidirectional interactive process, ongoing between therapist and patient, as well as among the multiple representational systems of each. Through the building of these multidirectional connections, emotional experience may be named.

> **Patient:** *I'm afraid of women, I tell you, I am. They scare me. They're not compassionate and not reasonable like men, ah. (Pause) ah, well, so I understand it and intellectualize. Still, the feelings, I don't know what the feelings were. Embarrassing with the feces, and annoyance with the women, frustration that I couldn't find the ah right movie. And I wasn't doing a good job. Ah, those were the feelings.*
> **Therapist:** *Suppose the bowel movement and the shit represented some kind of very violent feeling that is hidden behind that image, what would it be? If you suddenly blurted it out.*
> **Patient:** *Rage.*
> **Therapist:** *Yes?*
> **Patient:** *Rage, what right does that girl got to do to stand me up. That's it. I'm pretty important. I'm a pretty good guy. Rage, that would be the feeling.*

Here, with the help of the therapist, Mr. A. has done some new categorizing in his emotional systems; this is the process of emotional insight. He knows that he is not cool and calm; he knows that the set of feelings he experienced toward the woman the previous night, and is experiencing again towards her in the session, belong in the category of rage. He had not explicitly carried out this classification before.

The process of accessing and verbalizing subsymbolic experience and connecting this to specific imagery and to language—in some cases, re-defining the experience—is a fundamentally creative function, which may be traced in scientific work as well as in the interpersonal and emotional domain of psychoanalysis. Hadamard (1945) has identified stages in the process of inventive or creative mathematical thought, including prepara-tion, incubation, illumination, and verification, which parallel the stages of the referential cycle that have been outlined here. A progression of this nature may also be traced in the construction and interpretation of dreams. The latent contents emerge primarily in subsymbolic format; these are connected to the discrete specific images which make up the manifest contents of the dream, and are then verbalized in the dream narrative. Fi-nally, associations to the dream elements and reflections upon them may lead to a new formulation of the underlying contents of the dream, now in symbolic form (Bucci, 1993; Bucci, Severino, & Creelman, 1991).

Support for dual or multiple coding and the referential process has been developed in experimental cognitive psychology, and in my own ex-perimental and clinical research, as summarized elsewhere (Paivio, 1986; Bucci & Miller, 1993). Recent research on modularity of function supports the new multistage formulation of the referential cycle and goes well be-yond the simple bicameral left-brain right-brain dichotomy that was ini-tially postulated (Gazzaniga, 1985; Kosslyn, 1987; Farah, 1984). In my ther-apy process research, I have attempted to map the hypothetical constructs of the multiple code theory and the referential cycle onto operational in-dicators and to develop the construct validity of these measures. I have developed observable indicators of the three major phases of the cycle as these emerge in the free association; several of these are described in Bucci (1993) and Bucci and Miller (1993).

MEASURES OF REFERENTIAL ACTIVITY

The referential cycle is defined initially based on fluctuation in Referen-tial Activity (RA). The development of measures of Referential Activity was based on the premise, discussed above, that referential connections are most active and direct for specific and concrete images and words referring to them, less direct for abstract concepts and words (Paivio, 1986; Bucci, 1985; Bucci & Miller, 1993). Thus high RA is reflected in language that is concrete, specific and clear, that captures a quality of immediacy in the speaker's representations, and that is likely to evoke vivid and immediate experience in the listener as well, as in the following example:

> I can't stand fruit with bad spots in it. It gives me the creeps. So I picked up that pineapple and it looked so nice, and then my finger went right through inside it, into this brown, slimy, mushy stuff, and my stomach just turned over. (Bucci, Kabasakalian-McKay, the RA Research Group, 1992, p. 47)

The experience described in that passage is understood by most readers or listeners not in words only, but directly in the viscera—perhaps in a feeling of one's throat or stomach tightening, or sensations in one's skin. In contrast, low RA language is general, abstract, and vague. The speaker whose language is low in RA does not appear to be connecting to his or her own experience, and fails to arouse the listener. RA may be low where contents are abstract, and may also be low where emotions are talked about in general and abstract rather than concrete and specific ways:

> I love people and I like to be with people. And right now I feel very bad because I can't be with them and do the things I would like to do. But I'm looking forward to a happier and healthier future and— I don't know what else to say. What else can I talk about? Well—I've had a very eventful life, I think. I've worked practically all my life and I love people. (Bucci, Kabasakalian-McKay, & the RA Research Group, 1992, p. 54).

Here the speaker is talking about emotions, but she is unable to connect to nonverbal elements of the emotion schemas, and the passage does not reflect or activate visceral or emotional meanings. The following examples compare high and low RA speech focused on the same general topic, descriptions of the speakers' fathers:

> He was a hard-working man. He left home very early in the morning. I remember in the winter he left home while it was still dark,

and it was so cold. And he arrived home exhausted, haggard, sweaty, uncommunicative (Bucci, Kabasakalian-McKay, & the RA Research Group, 1992, p. 47)

I can't really think of too many times when he forced me to do something when I didn't want to. I mean, there's a lot of times he didn't do stuff that I wanted him to do. The other way around. He was; if I didn't understand something, he would tell me what was going on, stuff like that. (Bucci, Kabasakalian-McKay, & the RA Research Group, p. 46)

The subject of the first excerpt comes alive and evokes an emotional response; the subject of the second excerpt remains a blur for the listener (or reader) as he presumably also has been for the speaker.

In my research, I have developed systematic procedures for capturing the different qualities of language style illustrated in these excerpts. The methods for scoring RA include qualitative rating scales, and objective measures based on quantifiable linguistic features. These measures have been validated in the experimental and clinical work cited above. The RA rating scales measure the *Concreteness, Imagery, Specificity,* and *Clarity,* of speech. *Concreteness* is based on degree of perceptual or sensory quality, including references to all sensory modalities, action, and bodily experience.

The use of concrete language in this sense is not incompatible with a capacity for abstraction, and is to be distinguished from the type of cognitive concreteness that would be associated with regression, intellectual deficit, or thought disorder. Poetic metaphors rely on concrete images to express abstract ideas in precisely this sense.

Imagery refers to the degree to which the language evokes corresponding experience in the reader or hearer. These two scales are usually highly correlated, and their scores are combined to produce the composite scale *CONIM,* interpreted as measuring level of sensory imagery in a text. *Specificity* refers to amount of detail; a highly specific text involves explicit descriptions of persons, objects, places, or events. *Clarity* refers to clarity of an image as seen through the language; how well-focused is the linguistic image. These two scales are combined to yield the composite scale *CLASP,* defined as tapping the organizational quality of discourse.

The RA scales are scored reliably by raters after brief training, using a manual developed for this purpose (Bucci, Kabasakalian-McKay, & the RA Research Group, 1992).

Fluctuations in the RA Scales in the Referential Cycle

The *Subsymbolic Activation* phase is characterized by direct expression of emotional, somatic and sensory experience, with relatively low RA, and particularly low levels of the Specificity and Clarity (CLASP) scales. The patient may also express the activation of subsymbolic experience, which he is unable to verbalize, in the fragmentation of language and stammering of this phase, as in the example above from the session of Mr. A.

The verbalization of imagery and description of episodes in the *Referential* phase produces the RA peak, with all four scales converging at high levels. The connections between nonverbal and verbal systems are most active in this phase. In therapy sessions, this phase will usually be expressed in a narrative of a dream, a memory, or a recent event in the patient's life, as in the case of Mr. A. The major underlying theme of the session is likely to be expressed in the narratives of the RA peaks. Empirical measures developed by other researchers have confirmed this premise of the theory. Measures of emotion structures, and measures of the transference, such as the Core Conflictual Relationship Theme of Luborsky and Crits-Cristoph (1988) are concentrated in the high RA (or CRA) narrative phase (Bucci, 1993). The association of high RA with the narrative mode of discourse has been validated in several studies using a wide range of speech samples by many speakers (Mergenthaler & Bucci, 1993).

In the phase of *Verbal mediation*, Specificity and Clarity may remain relatively high, but Concreteness and Imagery are likely to decline, yielding overall lower RA scores. Here, the speaker or writer is focusing on building connections within the verbal system, as well as between imagery and words.

Computer Assisted Measures of the Referential Cycle

Computer assisted measures of Emotional Tone (ET) and Abstraction (AB) developed by Mergenthaler (1992) and computer assisted Referential Activity (CRA) procedures developed by Mergenthaler and Bucci (1993) have also been used to model phases of the cycle. In using computer assisted procedures, lists of words that have been identified as representing particular categories of contents are applied to texts, and proportions of matched words are computed.

The Emotional Tone (ET) word list consists of items that demonstrate an emotional or affective state of the speaker and are likely to cause emotion in the listener. High ET is generally characteristic of the initial phase of the cycle, in which information processing and language are driven by sensory and emotional concerns. These features are illustrated in the material from the Subsymbolic phase of Mr. A's session; he feels cool and calm, he itches, he says he did not feel angry, but later he felt very lonely.

The Abstraction (AB) dictionary consists of complex, abstract nouns that are understood as signs of logical reflection and evaluation. The AB word list as developed by Mergenthaler consists of abstract nouns constructed by adding suffixes such as *-ness, -ity, -ion* to words belonging to other parts of speech, for example, as in *tenderness, contrition, humility.* Abstract nouns constructed in this way usually distance the concrete nature of an experience, in comparison to the concepts that would be represented in the root words. Thus, to speak of "Paul's tenderness" is further from experience than to say that "Paul is a tender person." Reflection and verbal mediation are characterized by high proportions of AB words. High AB alone indicates intellectualization; however high AB with a concomitant increase in ET indicates emotional insight, not intellectual insight only. In the third phase of Mr. A.'s speech, he talks of 'ident*ity*' and 'one*ness*'. The analyst uses several emotion laden words—"violent and filthy and dirty and destructive"—which the patient then incorporates into his next utterance, increasing his expressive power. Scientific or other academic or technical writing usually contains relatively large proportions of words produced by such suffixes. (This paragraph, for example, contains eight different words ending in 'tion'; I could say it was designed to illustrate high AB.)

ET words are expected to be dominant in the initial subsymbolic phase of the cycle, while AB words are dominant in the third phase (verbal mediation and insight). These measures are not designed to capture the narrative phase of the cycle, which is reflected in high RA. While the ET and AB word lists were built conceptually, the computer Referential Activity (CRA) dictionary was formed empirically by modeling the RA measure as scored by expert judges. From large and diverse samples, texts belonging to the lowest and highest thirds of the range of RA scores were selected. Through a series of statistical procedures, applied in an iterative manner to several text samples, words were selected that differentiated the high and low RA texts. Words that were specific to special subject domains were eliminated, leaving only words that met the statistical criteria of differentiation across all speech samples. By this means, distinct characteristic vocabularies of the high and low RA texts were identified.

The CRA list now in use includes approximately one hundred each high and low RA words. The items in this list are primarily function words with high frequency in language use. While CRA is considerably smaller than most dictionaries used in computer assisted content analysis, it has considerably larger coverage, generally matching between 20% and 30% of words in a text. It is generally applicable across subjects regardless of the individual contents of speech, and allows for scoring speech segments as small as twenty words. It is of particular interest linguistically, as a computer assisted procedure, in that it reflects the style rather than contents of language. The high CRA list includes the kind of words that people tend to use when they describe images and events, such as prepositions and other words representing spatial relations, ('in', 'on', 'outside') and third person singular pronouns, referring to the specific individuals that figure in narrative episodes. In contrast, the low CRA list consists largely of words that are used primarily to represent logical relations and functions such as quantification, as well as nonspecific modifiers (e.g., 'or', 'although', 'but', 'more', 'something', 'sometimes'). The CRA measure represents overall RA, the average of the four individual scale scores. My colleagues and I are attempting to develop separate word lists that will model the individual RA scales, but at this point have completed only the overall CRA dictionary.

The three computer dictionaries, CRA, Emotional Tone, and Abstraction have been independently validated in research as representing the phases of the referential cycle. Optimally, the referential cycle, as this oc-

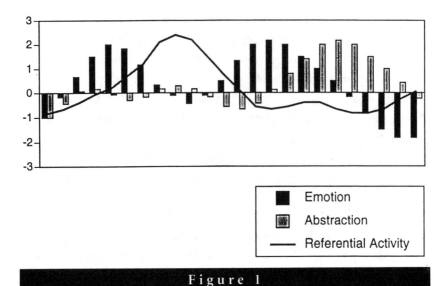

Figure 1

Cycles Model

curs in free association or other types of undirected verbalization, would begin with emotional arousal indicated by high ET, leading to a narrative of an incident, a memory, or a dream, which appears as an RA peak. This would then be followed by concomitant increases in ET and AB. The CRA peak is central and essential for the cycle. High ET and AB utterances without a CRA peak indicate activation of subsymbolic and verbal symbolic representations, but without connections between them; thus the dissociation that is the focus of treatment is allowed to continue unchanged. Figure 1, developed by Mergenthaler and Bucci (1993) shows the pattern of an optimal referential cycle, based on fluctuation of these three computer assisted measures.

In several ongoing projects, these computer assisted procedures are being applied to study the treatment process in psychoanalysis, using verbatim transcripts of psychoanalytic sessions, as in the example of Mr. A. In general, successful treatments, or phases of treatments, as well as storytelling that has a positive health effect, are marked by higher RA, and even more crucially, by playing out of the referential cycle. This finding has been supported in several studies (Hull, 1990; Bucci, 1993).

AN EXPERIMENTAL APPLICATION

I would expect the process embodied in the cycle to play out in story-telling that has a positive health effect. The CRA, ET, and AB measures have been applied to narratives produced by beginning college students who were subjects in a study by Pennebaker and Francis (1994). Subjects in the experimental group were assigned to write about their thoughts and feelings about coming to college, for three consecutive days, while a control group wrote about neutral topics. On average, the experimental subjects showed more positive effects, as indicated by fewer health center visits and improved grade point averages, compared with the control subjects. However, a range of effects was also found within the experimental group. I was interested in examining the variation within the experimental group, to differentiate ways in which subjects showing different levels of improvement used the writing experience and thus to begin to identify the potentially 'curative' factors in this writing task. The experimental subjects were classified into three subgroups, characterized as showing health improvement, unchanged and becoming worse. ET, CRA, and AB scores for the three groups, over the three sessions, are shown in Figure 2.

For the health improvement subjects, the initial writing session was characterized by ET and CRA peaks and low AB, indicating the telling of narratives with considerable emotional content, and with little abstract language. Subjects in this initial session were describing episodes representing emotion schemas, with both imagery and related emotional components. The second day is characterized by some decline in CRA and ET, and an increase in AB, as the subject begins to reflect on the stories and experiences he or she has reported. On the third day, these improved subjects show concomitant increases in all measures, indicating insights about emotional material expressed in concrete and specific form, not intellectual insight only. This pattern of peaks in ET and CRA, followed by fluc-

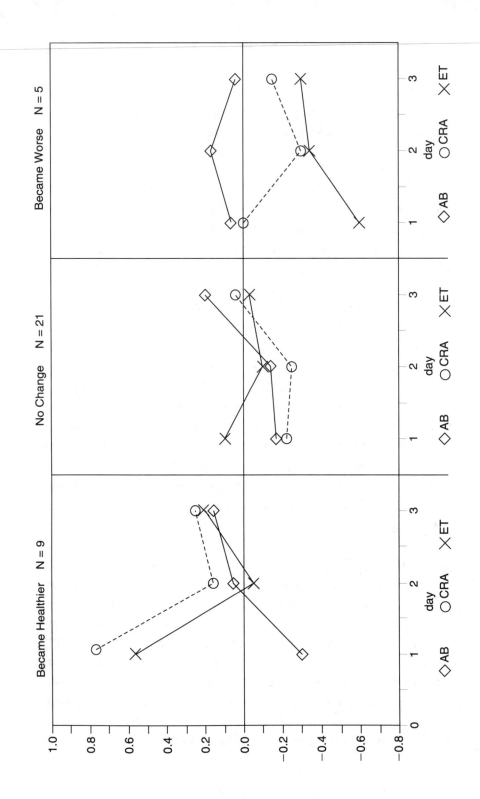

tuations in these measures and increases in AB, corresponds to the optimal pattern of a therapy session, as illustrated in Figure 1.

This pattern is not seen in the other groups. The unchanged group shows relatively low CRA and ET, while AB follows essentially the pattern of the health improvement subjects. In the first session, ET is above AB, but CRA is low. This indicates some attempt at connection to emotional experience, but without the narrative—the story—the connections to the nonverbal system are not made. The increase in AB across the three sessions occurs with little emotion and imagery to reflect upon.

The subjects who became worse are clearly differentiated from the other two groups by high AB across all three writing sessions, and by ET consistently below the levels of the other students, as well as by CRA that never rises above the standard score mean. The measures indicate that this group begins by warding off emotional experience to a considerably greater extent than the other two, and consistently remains within the abstract verbal mode, rather than using language first to access emotional experience and then to represent it in symbolic form. Very speculatively, I would also suggest that the fact that they became symptomatically worse, rather than remaining unchanged, may be accounted for by their increasing (although still quite low) ET. Emotion was aroused by the task, but they were unable to symbolize this adequately. This may account for the somatizing that is indicated by the increased health service visits in this group.

The results for the group who became worse in Pennebaker and Francis's study, as well as some unexpected results of my own work (Okie, 1991; Miller, 1994), suggests an additional point that I will not have time to explore, but that I would like to introduce here. The referential process, embodied in storytelling, is a powerful function that has potentially signifi-

Figure 2

How the Three Groups Used the Writing Experience. Means of Emotional Tone (ET), Abstraction (AB), and Computer-measured Referential Activity (CRA) for Three Writing Sessions.

cant emotional and also bodily impact. Any powerful treatment has its dangers. It is possible that under some circumstances, the attempt at verbalization—through its power to activate emotion schemas that have physiological components—may operate to increase symptoms rather than reduce them, and might endanger rather than enhance psychological and even physical health. Symptoms are symbols, as Freud knew, although he did not carry out the full implications of this. For some patients, physical symptoms may occur as a transitional phase constituting entry to the symbolic process, before images and words can be retrieved (Bucci, in press).

The power of the word, linking emotion to the verbal system, is not without its risks. If the speaker can bear the affect that is evoked, can retrieve memories and images stored in symbolic form, and can be supported in this by the therapist, he or she has a chance to bring the powers of the symbolizing process and the verbal system to bear in reorganizing emotion schemas and rendering them more veridical and adaptive in current life. If the speaker cannot retrieve such memories or if they evoke intolerable affect, he or she may respond by attempting to close down access to the emotion system. This may be accompanied by increased reliance on physical symptoms as symbols, with negative health effects. It might be interesting to look further at variability within the health research results from this perspective.

CONCLUSIONS

The multiple code theory builds on Freud's basic insights concerning mental representations and processes outside of the conscious verbal domain. However, the new theory differs from the metapsychology of psychoanalysis in recognizing the continuing importance of multiple forms of nonverbal processing, with their own contents and own organizing principles, which continue throughout normal, adult mental life, and connect to language to varying degrees. In Freud's formulation, the goal of psychotherapy is defined as domination of one system by another: the unconscious becoming conscious or placing ego where id has been. Within the multiple code theory, the goal of psychotherapy is defined instead as connection of systems that have been dissociated. The emotion schemas, with their multiple subsymbolic and symbolic nonverbal components, begin to develop in organized form from the beginning of life, long before the onset of language. In normal development, the sensory and somatic components of the emotion schemas are connected to symbolic imagery and to words; in pathology the schemas may become dissociated. The individual is particularly vulnerable to somatic expression in symptomatic form where dissociation and distortion of the emotion schemas have occurred.

The concept of the organized emotion schemas, with physiological, sensory, and cognitive components, and their capacity to activate and be activated by language, helps us to understand the relation between emotional disclosure and physical health that is shown in many of the chapters in this volume. Certain types and patterns of verbalization are valuable in facilitating the processes of integrating the emotion schemas; other types of verbalization insulate the emotion schemas and leave them disconnected and unchanged. As we have shown, concrete and specific language, and its organization in the patterning of the referential cycle, is particularly powerful in facilitating such symbolic integration. These factors seem to be sufficiently powerful to have measurable effects even in a series of brief written essays, in an experimental, nonclinical setting.

In these terms, a common ground may be seen among cognitive–behavioral, constructivist, and experiential as well as psychodynamic treatment forms. All recognize, in different ways, the importance of experience in the nonverbal realm, the power of language in connecting to and affecting nonverbal experience, and the adaptive effects of the symbolizing process. In collaborative research efforts, we could begin to examine how these processes play out in different therapeutic orientations, and to search for common curative factors shared by diverse treatment forms.

REFERENCES

Bartlett, F. C. (1932). *Remembering: A Study in Social Psychology.* Cambridge, England: Cambridge University Press.

Bertalanffy, L. von (1950). The theory of open systems in physics and psychology. *Science, III*, 23–29.

Bucci, W. (1984). Linking words and things: Basic processes and individual variation. *Cognition, 17*, 137–153.

Bucci, W. (1985). Dual Coding: A cognitive model for psychoanalytic research. *Journal of the American Psychoanalytic Association, 33*, 571–607.

Bucci, W. (1989). A reconstruction of Freud's tally argument: A program for psychoanalytic research. *Psychoanalytic Inquiry, 9*, 249–281.

Bucci, W. (1993). The development of emotional meaning in free association. In J. Gedo & A. Wilson (Eds.), *Hierarchical Conceptions in Psychoanalysis* (3–47). New York: Guilford Press.

Bucci, W. (1994). The multiple code theory and the psychoanalytic process: A framework for research. *Annals of Psychoanalysis*, 243–263.

Bucci, W. (1989). A reconstruction of Freud's tally argument: A program for psychoanalytic research. *Psychoanalytic Inquiry, 9*, 249–281.

Bucci, W. (In press). *Psychoanalysis and cognitive science: A multiple code theory.* NY: Guilford Press.

Bucci, W., & Freedman, N. (1978). Language and hand: The dimension of referential competence. *Journal of Personality, 46*, 594–622.

Bucci, W. and Kabasakalian, R. and the RA Research Group. (1992). *Instructions for scoring Referential Activity (RA) in transcripts of spoken narrative texts.* Ulm, Germany: Ulmer Textbank.

Bucci, W. & Miller, N. (1993). Primary process analogue: The Referential Activity (RA) Measure. In N. Miller, L. Luborsky, J. Barber, & J. Docherty (Eds.), *Psychodynamic Treatment Research* (387–406). New York: Basic Books.

Bucci, W., Severino, S. K. & Creelman, M. L. (1991). The effects of menstrual cycle hormones on dreams. *Dreaming, 1*, 263–275.

Emde, R. N. (1983, March). *The affective core.* Paper presented at the Second World Congress of Infant Psychiatry, Cannes, France.

Farah, M. J. (1984). The neurological basis of mental imagery: A componential analysis. *Cognition, 18*, 245–272.

Fodor, J. A. & Pylyshyn, Z. W. (1988). Connectionism and cognitive architecture: A critical analysis. *Cognition, 28*, 3–71.

Freud, S. (1953). The interpretation of dreams. In J. Strachney (Ed. and Trans.), *Standard edition* of the complete psychological works of Sigmund Freud (Vol. 4, pp. 1–310, & Vol. 5, pp. 339–610). London: Hogarth Press. (Original work published 1900)

Freud, S. (1957). The unconscious. In J. Strachney (Ed. and Trans.), *Standard edition* of the complete psychological works of Sigmund Freud (Vol. 14, 166–215). London: Hogarth Press. (Original work published in 1915)

Freud, S. (1961). The ego and the id. In J. Strachney (Ed. and Trans.), *Standard edition* of the complete psychological works of Sigmund Freud (Vol. 19, 3–66), London: Hogarth Press. (Original work published in 1923)

Freud, S. (1964). Analysis terminable and interminable. In J. Strachney (Ed. and Trans.), *Standard edition* of the complete psychological works of Sigmund Freud (Vol. 23, 216–253). London: Hogarth Press (Original work published in 1937)

Gazzaniga, M. S. (1985). *The Social Brain.* New York: Basic Books.

Hadamard, J. (1945). *The psychology of invention in the mathematical field.* New York: Dover.

Holt, R. (1989). The current status of psychoanalytic theory. In R. R. Holt (Ed.), *Freud reappraised: A fresh look at psychoanalytic theory* (pp. 324–344). New York: Guilford Press.

Hull, J. (1990). Attunement and the rhythm of dialogue in psychotherapy: I. Empirical findings. Paper presented at annual conference of the Society for Psychotherapy Research, Wintergreen, W.Va.

Kosslyn, S. M. (1987). Seeing and imagining in the cerebral hemi-spheres: A computational approach. *Psychological Review, 94,* 148–175.

Lang, P. J. (1994). The varieties of emotional experience: A meditation on James–Lange Theory. *Psychological Review 101,* 211–221.

LeDoux, J. E. (1989). Cognitive-emotional iteractions in the brain. *Cognition and Emotion, 3,* 267–289.

Luborsky, L. & Crits-Cristoph, P. (1988). The assessment of transference by the CCRT method. In H. Dahl, H. Kaechele, H. Thomae (Eds.), *Psychoanalytic Process Research Strategies* (pp. 99–108). New York: Springer-Verlag.

Mandler, J. (1992). How to build a baby: II. Conceptual primitives. *Psychological Review, 99,* 587–604.

Mergenthaler, E. (1992, June). Emotion/Abstractness as indicators of "hot spots" in psychotherapy transcripts. Paper presented at the Society for Psychotherapy Research 23rd Annual International Meeting, Berkeley, CA.

Mergenthaler, E., & Bucci, W. (1993). *Computer assisted procedures for analyzing verbal data in psychotherapy research.* Symposium presented at the Society for Psychotherapy Research 24th Annual International Meeting, Pittsburgh, PA.

Miller, S. (1994). The waking nightmare. (Doctoral dissertation, Adelphi University, 1994) *Dissertation Abstracts International,* 5502B.

Okie, J. E. (1991). Action, somatization and language in borderline inpatients. (Doctoral dissertation, Adelphi University, 1992) *Dissertation Abstracts International,* 5303A.

Paivio, A. (1986). *Mental representations: A dual coding approach.* New York: Oxford University Press.

Pennebaker, J. W. , & Francis, M. E. (1994). *Cognitive, emotional and language processes in writing: Health and adjustment to college.* Paper submitted for publication.

Rosch, E. (1975). Cognitive representations of semantic categories. *Journal of Experimental Psychology: General, 104,* 192–233.

Rumelhart, D. E., McClelland, J. L., & the PDP Research Group. (1986). *Parallel Distributed Processing: Explorations in the microstructure of cognition.* Cambridge, MA:MIT Press.

Scherer, K. R. (1984). On the nature and function of emotion: A component process approach. In K. R. Scherer & P. Ekman (Eds.), *Approaches to Emotion* (pp. 293–317). Hillsdale, NJ: Erlbaum.

Simon, H. A., & Kaplan, C. A. (1989). Foundations of cognitive science. In M. I. Posner (Ed.), *Foundations of cognitive science* (pp. 1–47). Cambridge, MA:MIT Press.

Stern, D. N. (1985). *The interpersonal world of the infant.* New York: Basic Books.

PART THREE

Emotions, Expressiveness, and Psychosomatics

7

Emotional Attention, Clarity, and Repair: Exploring Emotional Intelligence Using the Trait Meta-Mood Scale

Peter Salovey, John D. Mayer, Susan Lee Goldman,
Carolyn Turvey, and Tibor P. Palfai

I n differing ways, all of the contributors to this volume take it for granted that the disclosure of emotions can have positive consequences for individuals—that emotional disclosure is a Good Thing like democracy, mother, and an annual physical. But, although contemporary psychologists may view emotional disclosure as a Good Thing, this has not been the prevailing view in much of Western thought nor even in twentieth century psychology. For example, the psychologists who first studied human intelligence contrasted rational thought with emotional experience (Schaffer, Gilmer, & Schoen, 1940; Woodworth, 1940; Young, 1936). To

Some of the data in this chapter were also presented as "Emotional intelligence and emotional control" at the third annual Nags Head Conference on Self Control of Thought and Emotion, Highland Beach, FL, May 1991, and as "Emotional intelligence and the measurement of attention to, clarity, and regulation of mood" at the joint meeting of the European Association of Experimental Social Psychology and the Society for Experimental Social Psychology, Leuven/Louvain-la-Neuve, Belgium, July 1992.

Our thanks to Theresa Claire, who provided valuable feedback on earlier versions of this chapter, and to John Beauvais and Susan Greener for assisting in the preparation of this chapter. The research presented in this chapter was supported in part by an NSF Presidential Young Investigator Award (9058020) to the first author. We also wish to acknowledge the support provided by a grant from the National Cancer Institute (CA 42101) and from the MacArthur Foundation sponsored Program on Conscious and Unconscious Mental Processes. Susan Goldman was supported by a predoctoral minority fellowship from the National Science Foundation.

think clearly, they believed, one had to keep emotions in check. This idea resides in popular psychological theories about human nature even today; Elster (1985), for instance, wrote, "When emotions are directly involved in action, they tend to overwhelm or subvert rational mental processes, not to supplement them" (p. 379).

In recent years, however, there has been something of a backlash against the view that reason and passion are incompatible. Even cognitively oriented investigators recognize that emotions can serve as a source of information to individuals (cf. Schwarz, 1990), and that individuals may be more or less skilled at processing this kind of information. The ability to utilize information provided by emotions can be adaptive, and the relationship between emotion and thought need not be antagonistic. Many of the contributors to this volume also take this positive view of human emotions. For example, Rimé's view that most emotional experiences are socially shared suggests that emotions can serve social goals such as social comparison, clear communication, or the elicitation of assistance from others (chapter 14, this volume).

In considering individual differences in the ability to use the information conveyed by emotions adaptively, Gardner (1983) described what he called personal intelligence in part as "access to one's own feeling life— one's range of affects or emotions: the capacity instantly to effect discriminations among these feelings and, eventually, to label them, to enmesh them in symbolic codes, to draw upon them as a means of understanding and guiding one's behavior" (p. 239). We, too, believe that individuals differ in the skill with which they can identify their feelings and the feelings of others, regulate these feelings, and use the information provided by their feelings to motivate adaptive social behavior. These skills are likely related to the use of feelings to motivate, plan, and achieve in life. Elsewhere, we have organized these competencies into a framework termed *emotional intelligence* (Mayer & Salovey, 1993; Salovey & Mayer, 1990; Salovey, Hsee, & Mayer, 1993).

It is the purpose of this chapter first to describe a measure of individual differences in the ability to reflect upon and manage one's emotions. Our measure indexes the degree of attention that individuals devote to their feelings, the clarity of their experience of these feelings, and their beliefs about terminating negative mood states or prolonging positive ones. Many of the competencies described within the emotional intelligence framework as well as investigations of the value of emotional disclosure in writing or in psychotherapy take as a starting point the individual's willingness to attend to feelings and to experience these feelings clearly. Thus, although we have little interest in claiming that the measure discussed here is some kind of emotional intelligence test (or that individuals should even be differentiated according to some kind of emotional IQ), we do believe it has utility in helping us to identify core individual differences that may characterize emotionally intelligent individuals capable of disclosing their feelings to themselves and other people.

Our interest in attention to, clarity, and regulation of feelings grew out of earlier work on the reflective processes that accompany most mood states. Mayer and Gaschke (1988; see also Mayer, Salovey, Gomberg-Kaufman, & Blainey, 1991; Mayer & Stevens, 1994) demonstrated that there is an ongoing process associated with moods whereby individuals continually reflect upon their feelings, monitoring, evaluating, and regulating them. They termed this process the *meta-mood experience* and developed the Meta-Mood Experience Scale that measures an individual's thoughts about an ongoing mood state. This measure, because it emphasizes moment-by-moment changes in reflections about ongoing moods, is now termed the State Meta-Mood Scale (SMMS). Its factors include beliefs about the controllability of the mood, its clarity, acceptability, typicality, and changeability.

The SMMS focused primarily on thoughts about an ongoing mood experience. The scale did not address more stable attitudes about moods in general nor enduring strategies with which individuals deal with mood experiences. In this chapter, we first present a study of the factor structure and reliability of a scale that measures the more enduring qualities of the reflective experience of mood. The measure is called the Trait Meta-Mood Scale (TMMS) because it was designed to assess relatively stable individual differences in people's tendency to attend to their moods and emotions, discriminate clearly among them, and regulate them.

Studies presented subsequently provide data regarding both the concurrent and predictive validity of the TMMS. Its correlations with related personality constructs are examined, and associations between ruminative thought and attending to feelings, experiencing them clearly, and beliefs about regulating them are studied in a laboratory experiment in which subjects watched a distressing film and then provided ongoing reports of their thoughts and feelings.

DEVELOPMENT OF THE TRAIT
META-MOOD SCALE

We started our investigation of the trait meta-mood construct by asking nearly 200 individuals to respond to 48 items drawn from a larger item set employed by Mayer, Mamberg, and Volanth (1988) that divide into 5 item domains: clarity of emotional perception, strategies of emotional regulation, integration of feelings, attention to emotions, and attitudes about emotion. Half of the items in each domain were worded positively, and half were worded negatively. Items in the clarity of emotional perception domain referred to the ability to understand one's mood (e.g., "I always know exactly how I am feeling"). The items concerning the strategies of emotional regulation referred to the degree to which individuals moderate their moods (e.g., "When I become very upset, I remind myself of all the little pleasures in life"). The items concerning integration of feelings involved questions about correspondences between feelings and thoughts (e.g., "When I am in a good mood, I am optimistic about the future"). Attention to emotions conveyed the degree to which individuals notice and think about their feelings (e.g., "I pay a lot of attention to how I feel"). Finally, attitudes about emotions referred to subjects' perceptions of the importance of emotional experiences (e.g., "I believe in acting from the heart"). Subjects responded to randomly ordered items along a five-point scale anchored by 1 = strongly disagree and 5 = strongly agree. Our hope was that the factor structure of the measure would map onto the three primary domains of reflective mood experience described by Mayer and Gaschke (1988): monitoring moods, discriminating among moods, and regulating them.

Indeed, the three factor solution was clearly interpretable, and it presented the most optimal solution from the standpoint of the usual factor extraction criteria. Items loading on the three factors are illustrated in Table 1. We reversed the direction of scoring for all items loading on the first factor so that items phrased positively would have positive loadings and vice versa. Thus, the highest positively loading item was now "I pay a lot of attention to how I feel," and the highest negative item was now "I don't pay much attention to my feelings." This factor was thus labeled *Attention to Feelings*. The second factor was labeled *Clarity of Feelings* because its highest positive loading item was "I am usually very clear about my feelings," and its highest negative item was "I can't make sense out of my feelings." The final factor was labeled *Mood Repair*, because the items loading on to it primarily concerned attempts to repair unpleasant moods or maintain pleasant ones. Its highest positive loading item was "Although I am sometimes sad, I have a mostly optimistic outlook." The most highly negative loading item was "Although I am sometimes happy, I have a mostly pessimistic outlook." Additional items concerned descriptions of active strategies for improving mood (e.g., "When I become upset, I remind myself of all the pleasures in life").

Three scales were created based on the factor analysis. At first, we included all 48 items; 21 defined the first scale (Attention), 15 the second (Clarity), and 12 the third (Repair) with all negatively loading items reverse scored. The internal consistency of these three scales was evaluated by computing Cronbach's coefficient alpha for each scale (Attention: α = .86; Clarity: α = .87; Repair: α = .82). Intercorrelations among the three factors are provided in Table 2. The only significant interscale correlation was that between Clarity and Repair. These two scales seem to have about 19% overlapping variance in this data set.

We next tried to evaluate whether a shorter version of each scale could be derived by dropping items with low loadings. Three scales were con-

Table 1

Maximum Likelihood Factor Analysis for 48 TMMS Items

	Factor I	Factor II	Factor III
Factor 1: Attention to Feelings			
I don't pay much attention to my feelings.	0.75	−0.13	0.03
I never give in to my emotions.	0.65	−0.30	−0.30
I don't usually care much about what I'm feeling.	0.63	0.01	0.01
One should never be guided by emotions.	0.62	−0.13	−0.08
It is usually a waste of time to think about your emotions.	0.58	−0.11	−0.11
People would be better off if they felt less and thought more.	0.52	0.05	−0.13
Feelings are a weakness humans have.	0.49	−0.18	−0.10
I don't think it's worth paying attention to your emotions or moods.	0.46	−0.00	−0.21
I don't let my feelings interfere with what I am thinking.	0.39	0.25	0.20
When I am happy I sometimes remind myself of everything that could go wrong.	0.36	−0.14	−0.33
It's important to block out some feelings in order to preserve your sanity.	0.16	−0.14	0.05
When I am happy I realize how foolish most of my worries are.	−0.12	−0.11	0.07
I think about my mood constantly.	−0.31	−0.30	−0.28
I usually have lots of energy when I'm happy.	−0.34	−0.04	0.30
I believe it's healthy to feel whatever emotion you feel.	−0.36	0.28	0.06
Feelings give direction to life.	−0.40	−0.06	−0.19
The best way for me to handle my feelings is to experience them to the fullest.	−0.40	0.15	0.05
When I'm in a good mood, I'm optimistic about the future.	−0.43	−0.02	0.37
I believe in acting from the heart.	−0.44	−0.18	−0.01

(*continues*)

Table 1 (cont.)

	Factor I	Factor II	Factor III
I often think about my feelings.	−0.69	−0.08	−0.23
I pay a lot of attention to how I feel.	−0.76	0.02	0.00
Factor 2: Clarity of Feelings			
I am usually very clear about my feelings.	−0.09	0.77	0.15
I am rarely confused about how I feel.	0.28	0.66	0.09
I almost always know exactly how I am feeling.	0.07	0.65	0.00
I feel at ease about my emotions.	−0.10	0.58	0.29
I usually know my feelings about a matter.	−0.11	0.58	0.22
I am often aware of my feelings on a matter.	−0.25	0.44	0.20
I have lots of energy when I feel sad.	0.05	0.29	−0.09
The variety of human feelings makes life more interesting.	−0.20	0.20	−0.07
When I'm depressed, I can't help but think of bad thoughts.	−0.01	−0.32	−0.22
I usually don't have much energy when I'm sad.	0.02	−0.42	0.03
My belief and opinions always seem to change depending on how I feel.	0.08	−0.45	−0.22
I can never tell how I feel.	0.21	−0.50	−0.12
Sometimes I can't tell what my feelings are.	−0.06	−0.64	−0.07
I am usually confused about how I feel.	0.06	−0.68	−0.11
I can't make sense out of my feelings.	0.10	−0.70	−0.11
Factor 3: Mood Repair			
Although I am sometimes sad, I have a mostly optimistic outlook.	−0.09	0.20	0.72
No matter how badly I feel, I try to think about pleasant things.	0.04	0.17	0.57
When I become upset I remind myself of all the pleasures in life.	0.08	0.19	0.56
I try to think good thoughts no matter how badly I feel.	0.04	0.16	0.56

(*continues*)

Table 1 (cont.)

	Factor I	Factor II	Factor III
If I find myself getting mad, I try to calm myself down.	−0.01	−0.10	0.35
I never worry about being in too good a mood.	−0.23	0.13	0.34
I don't have much energy when I am happy.	−0.02	0.01	−0.19
When I'm angry, I usually let myself feel that way.	−0.22	0.12	−0.32
Whenever I'm in a bad mood, I'm pessimistic about the future.	0.12	−0.33	−0.34
If I'm in too good a mood, I remind myself of reality to bring myself down.	0.32	−0.15	−0.37
When I am upset I realize that the "good things in life" are illusions.	0.05	−0.29	−0.49
Although I am sometimes happy, I have a mostly pessimistic outlook.	0.29	−0.15	−0.74

structed for each of the three factors by including items with loadings ≥ .40. Those items with loadings on a factor other than the one they defined within .20 of their highest loading were also eliminated from the scale.[1] This procedure yielded 30 items that could be assigned to one of the three scales. Internal consistencies remained as high as those for the scales created from all 48 items (Coefficient α = .86, .88, .82, respectively) and, as expected, interscale correlations were comparable, as depicted in Table 2. We especially recommend the use of this more efficient 30-item version of the scale.

---

[1]Two items did load on factors at ≥ .40, but contained content that was not consonant with the conceptual basis of the subscale. The item "I usually don't have much energy when I am sad" was the lowest loading factor on the clarity subscale (−.42) and "When I'm in a good mood, I'm optimistic about the future" loaded on the attention subscale (−.43). Because these items were not theoretically consistent with the subscales they were supposed to define, they were not included in subsequent confirmatory analyses.

Table 2

Scale Statistics and Intercorrelations Among Scales

	Items	Alpha	Attention	Clarity	Repair
Full Scales Created From All 48 Items					
Attention	21	.86	1.00		
Clarity	15	.87	−.11	1.00	
Repair	12	.82	−.12	.44**	1.00
30-Item Form Created From Items with Loadings > .40 and Deletion of 2 Other Improperly Assigned Items					
Attention	13	.86	1.00		
Clarity	11	.88	−.13	1.00	
Repair	6	.82	−.12	.39**	1.00

In order to confirm the factor structure of the TMMS, a second sample of subjects was recruited from 152 students enrolled in an undergraduate psychology course. Of these students, 148 consented to participate in a four phase longitudinal study of psychological stress and health–illness behavior (Goldman, Kraemer, & Salovey, submitted for publication). These students were administered the 48-item TMMS as part of a battery of measures that was collected during the second week of regular classes.

To test the theoretical structure of the TMMS, we performed a confirmatory factor analysis (CFA) using LISREL VI (Jöreskög & Sörbom, 1986). The chi-square significance test of global fit suggested that our three factor model fits the data generated by this second sample (χ^2 (48) = 49.56, $ns.$). The goodness-of-fit index (GFI) provided by the LISREL program was .94 (adjusted GFI was .91), indicating that the three-factor structure of the TMMS accounted for a large proportion of the total covariation. The root mean square residual was .05, also suggesting that there was a relatively small discrepancy between the predicted and the actual covariance matrix. Examination of the final factor loadings demonstrated the conceptual distinctiveness of the Attention, Clarity, and Repair subscales of the TMMS.

CONVERGENT AND DISCRIMINANT VALIDITY

Given the stability of the three-factor structure of the TMMS, it is important to determine (a) the extent to which these subscales are related to other measures of mood and mood management and (b) whether these subscales predict the actual regulation and control of mood. A number of measures related to the meta-experience of mood have been described in the literature. A specific sort of evaluation is measured by the Ambivalence Over Emotional Expressiveness Questionnaire (AEQ; King & Emmons, 1990, 1991), for example, which taps, among other thoughts, dissatisfaction with one's emotional expression. Participants who are high on the scale may want to, but fail to, express a feeling and subsequently regret it. The AEQ is related to self-reported and peer-rated emotional expressiveness and to daily negative moods. Catanzaro and Mearns (1990) have developed an instrument called Expectancies for Negative Mood Regulation (NMR). This construct concerns beliefs about the changeability of negative moods. High scorers are less likely to be depressed than those individuals lacking in such expectancies (Kirsch, Mearns, & Catanzaro, 1990). Similarly, the Life Orientation Test (LOT) was developed to measure the tendency to have optimistic expectancies about future events (Scheier & Carver, 1985). Finally, the Self-Consciousness Scale (SCS) measures the tendency to attend to aspects of ongoing consciousness including mood (Fenigstein, Scheier, & Buss, 1975). Each of these scales is reliable and provides a valid index of what it purports to measure. In general, however, they are not based on a singular theoretical perspective. The result has been more of a bottom-up approach to the issue of emotion evaluation and regulation. We have argued elsewhere that the meta-mood experience and emotional intelligence concepts can be employed to organize such constructs (Mayer & Salovey, 1993; Mayer & Gaschke, 1988; Salovey,

Hsee, & Mayer, 1993; Salovey & Mayer, 1990). We would expect that the TMMS scale may capture in the domain of feelings the variance accounted for by this large collection of measures.

Correlations Among Measures

We asked 86 undergraduates to complete the TMMS, all of the measures described above, as well as a measure of depression (the Center for Epidemiological Studies Depression Scale [CES-D]; Radloff, 1977). The correlations among the TMMS subscales and the other measures included in this study are presented in Table 3. In this sample, the Repair scale was correlated positively with both Attention and Clarity, although the magnitude of these correlations was not large. We should also mention that in this sample, the internal consistency of the Repair scale was a bit lower than in previous studies. More importantly, the three TMMS subscales were associated with other measures in the literature with which we would expect them to be correlated (convergent validity) but not with others (discriminant validity). For example, Attention to feelings was associated with private and public self-consciousness. People who attend to their feelings also, to some extent, attend to other aspects of their conscious experience. Clarity was negatively associated with ambivalence over emotional expression and with depression. Individuals who experience their feelings clearly tend not to be depressed and are less likely to experience ambivalence over the amount and quality of the emotions they display to others. These associations of other measures with Attention and Clarity were moderate, suggesting that these two TMMS subscales do account for emotion-related variance not measured by self-consciousness, ambivalence, or depression. Finally, Repair was negatively associated with depression and positively associated with optimism and beliefs about negative mood regulation. These latter two correlations are the highest among those generated in this study, and the discriminant validity of beliefs about the repairability of moods from optimism and other similar constructs will need to be demonstrated in future work.

Table 3

Correlations Among TMMS Subscales and With Other Measures

	Alpha	Attention	Clarity	Repair
Attention	.78	1.00		
Clarity	.80	.11	1.00	
Repair	.62	.32**	.26*	1.00
Private Self-Consciousness		.42**	.09	.18
Public Self-Consciousness		.36**	.01	.14
Ambivalence Over Emotional Expression		−.04	−.25*	−.17
CES-Depression		−.08	−.27*	−.37**
Optimism (LOT)		.09	.12	.57**
Negative Mood Regulation (NMR)		.17	.12	.53**

Principal Components Analysis on Scale Scores

	I	II	III
Attention (TMMS)	.21	**.75**	.06
Clarity (TMMS)	.05	.15	**.81**
Repair (TMMS)	**.76**	.33	.11
Private Self-Consciousness	−.13	**.78**	.11
Public Self-Consciousness	.00	**.71**	−.15
Ambivalence Over Emotional Expression	−.25	.15	**−.70**
CES-Depression	**−.65**	.06	−.37
Optimism (LOT)	**.82**	−.13	.00
Negative Mood Regulation (NMR)	**.81**	.04	.14

Note.
*$p < .05$
**$p < .01$

The Creation of Higher Order Factors

The creation of the TMMS was in part based on our belief that meta-mood experiences could be understood as falling in three primary domains: attending to moods, experiencing them clearly, and trying to regulate them. If this is so, the collection of measures that have proliferated in this general area should cluster along these three themes as well. We conducted a principal components analysis in which scores on the three TMMS subscales and on the other measures collected in this study served as "items." Three factors had eigenvalues greater than one and accounted for 63% of the total variance.

The factor loadings following varimax rotation are presented in Table 3. The three TMMS subscales defined the three different factors. The first factor was defined by the TMMS-Repair subscale and included as well Optimism (LOT), Negative Mood Regulation (NMR), and Depression (CES-D), which loaded negatively. The second factor loaded TMMS-Attention highly and also included the two Self-Consciousness Scales (SCS). And the third factor was defined by TMMS-Clarity on one end and Ambivalence About Emotional Expression (AEQ) on the other. Thus, this analysis suggests that the TMMS taps into three fundamental domains of meta-mood experience that are also represented in a more piecemeal way by other measures of affective style and processes.

The TMMS subscales, Attention, Clarity, and Repair, seem efficiently to represent several existing measures concerned with the processing of affect. The measures included in this study could be organized empirically around the themes of attending to feelings, experiencing them clearly, and trying to regulate them. Of the many relationships uncovered in this study, one is particularly interesting to us and that concerns the placement of Clarity and Ambivalence About Emotional Expression on opposite ends of the same dimension. Similar data have been reported by Emmons (1992), who calls this factor *emotional complexity.*

This study assessed the convergent validity of the TMMS with only a few of the measures that can be found in the meta-mood literature. In future work, we would like to examine relationships between the TMMS subscales and other measures. Some ideal candidates include Levels of Emotional Awareness (Lane, Quinlan, Schwartz, Walker, & Zeitlin, 1990; Lane & Schwartz, 1987), the Mood Awareness Scale (Giuliano & Swinkels, 1992, 1993), Constructive Thinking—especially the CTI subscales of emotional coping, naive optimism, negative thinking, and superstitiousness (Epstein, 1990; Epstein & Meier, 1989; Katz & Epstein, 1991)—and alexithymia, the inability to use words to describe feelings (Apfel & Sifneos, 1979; Krystal, Giller, & Cicchetti, 1986; Sifneos, 1972, 1973; Taylor, 1984; Thayler-Singer, 1977). The relations among attention, clarity, and a measure of emotional disclosure would be interesting to explore as well.

TRAIT META-MOOD AND SUSCEPTIBILITY TO NEGATIVE RUMINATIVE THOUGHT AFTER A STRESSFUL EVENT

The importance of meta-mood skills and processes perhaps becomes most apparent under conditions of stress. In another study, we investigated the hypothesis that adapting successfully to a stressful experience would depend, in part, on the capacity to attend to, discriminate among, and regulate feelings. The relation between negative mood and intense, involuntary, and persistent cognitions following stressful life events has been demonstrated rather consistently (Horowitz, 1975; Parkinson & Rachman, 1981a, 1981b; Rachman,1980; Silver, Boon, & Stones, 1983; Tait & Silver, 1987). However, this coupling of ruminative thought and negative affect is not a consequence specific to major life events. It is a general response to a wide range of stressful events that occur in a large portion of the nonclinical population and has been successfully documented in the laboratory (Horowitz, 1975; Rachman, 1980). As Borkovec describes in the present volume (chapter 4), it is possible that rumination (or, in his model, worrying) prevents more complex emotional engagement with the stressful material; worry and rumination, paradoxically, may be avoidance strategies similar to the alexithymic style described in Paez's chapter (chapter 10, this volume).

Many investigators have explained the reduction in ruminative thoughts and accompanying negative affect associated with recovery from stressful experiences in cognitive processing terms (e.g., Antrobus, Singer, & Greenberg, 1966; Horowitz, 1975). Aversive, intrusive thinking is believed to subside because the individual assimilates the stressful information into existing cognitive schemata or accommodates schemata accordingly (Horowitz, 1976). Immediately following the stressful event, the new information may be too discrepant from existing representations and too overwhelming to be integrated adequately. The individual is motivated to reduce such discrepancies in order to regain a coherent set of representations about the self and the environment and regain a sense of mastery. This process may require repeated experiencing of the negative material in the form of ruminative thought until such processing is complete. This chain of events is quite similar to the distress, disclosure, relief model described by Stiles in this volume.

Research on the treatment of fear and anxiety with exposure-based therapies suggests that other features of the stress reaction require processing in a similar manner (see Foa & Kozak, 1986; Rachman, 1980). Affect, behavior, and cognition are part of an interrelated response structure to the stressful event. Though each component is partially independent from the others in the way that it is processed, they are all related to one another as part of an affective memory structure for the negative event. In other words, the stress-response consists of multiple features that follow different processing patterns but are mutually interdependent (see Barlow, 1988, for a review of this literature).

Central to the emotional processing approach is the notion that complete adjustment to a stressor is facilitated by simultaneous activation of the various components of the affective memory structure that underlie the stress reaction. Fear, for example, is represented as (a) information about the feared event, (b) verbal (e.g., reported emotion, cognitions), physiological, and behavioral responses, and (c) interpretive information about the stimulus and the response (Foa & Kozak, 1986). Modification of a fear response requires that the fear structure be activated and then incompatible elements be incorporated within it, otherwise the likely reaction is persistent negative mood, ruminative thought, or fearful images (Rachman, 1980).

In line with this view, we suggest that successful processing of intrusive thoughts may depend on skills related to the activation, experience, and modification of feelings. We examined the relation of individual differences in attention to, clarity, and regulation of feelings to sustained negative affect and the intensity, insistency, controllability, and negativity of ruminative thoughts that followed a distressing stimulus. Subjects were first exposed to distressing video footage after which measures of mood and quality of thought were obtained. No differences in affective response or quality of thoughts were expected among subjects immediately after the distressing stimulus. However, subscales of the TMMS were expected to predict recovery of positive mood and improvement in the quality of thought across the time period that followed. Specifically, we hypothesized that individuals who reported greater clarity in discriminating mood and who considered negative mood to be repairable would (a) have fewer, less negative thoughts in general, (b) report more positive thoughts over time, (c) display a decline in intrusiveness and uncontrollability of negative thoughts, and (d) report more positive mood at the conclusion of the experimental session. Attention was not expected to be a predictor because instructions for the thought-sampling procedure explicitly required subjects to pay attention to their thoughts and feelings.

We asked 78 student volunteers to come to the laboratory, where we told them that they would be participating in two studies, one involving watching television and a second one on the stream of consciousness. First, these participants completed a battery of measures that included (a) the Eysenck Personality Inventory (EPI; Eysenck, 1973), (b) the Center for Epidemiological Studies Depression Scale (CES-D Radloff, 1977), (c) the Trait Meta-Mood Scale (TMMS), (d) the Affect Grid (Russell, Weiss, & Mendelsohn, 1989), and (e) the Weinberger Adjustment Inventory (WAI; Weinberger, 1989, 1990).

Next, when all of the subjects in a group completed the battery, a film clip was presented. The video clip was a 12 min segment of a documentary on drunk driving. The film contained graphic footage of serious automobile accidents and the emergency room and hospital sequences that followed. Victims also described the nature of their traumatic experience. This theme was chosen for its relevance to individuals of this age group. After the film, subjects were asked to complete another mood measure. This ostensibly marked the conclusion of the "first experiment."

At this point, the experimenter redescribed the supposed purpose of the "second experiment" and the rationale of the thought sampling procedure. The instructions asked subjects to: (a) focus on whatever thoughts, feelings, and images they were experiencing at the time of a prearranged signal, (b) jot down a few select words to describe the thought on a page in a thought sampling record, and (c) answer the questions that appeared on the bottom of each page with regard to the recorded thought. Four Likert-scale items were included at the bottom of each page that asked subjects to rate the positiveness, intensity, insistency, and controllability of their recorded thoughts. Subjects were then given a practice thought sampling page and participated in a trial run. The actual thought listing session began after subjects had a chance to ask questions and felt comfortable with the procedure. The thought sampling procedure followed a designated protocol. Subjects were signaled with a tone to report a thought every 60–120 s. This procedure was repeated 12 times. After the last of the thought samples was elicited, subjects were requested to complete another mood measure.

TMMS and Associations With Other Mood-Relevant Measures

The intercorrelations among the TMMS subscales and their correlations with the CES-D and WAI subscales are presented in Table 4. In this study, there were no significant correlations among the three subscales of the TMMS, and the internal consistency of all three scales was satisfactory. When we examined the relation of the TMMS with other measures of emotionality and negative affectivity, there was an interesting pattern of correlations with depression. Depression was associated with low Clarity in discriminating feelings, high Attention to emotions, and beliefs that one cannot Repair negative moods. Low Clarity was also associated with neuroticism. In other words, greater mood lability is associated with a lack of clarity about mood. Also worth noting is the coherent pattern of relations between the TMMS subscales and the WAI. Clarity and Repair were negatively related to WAI distress. Clarity in discriminating emotions, as well as the belief that one can regulate emotional experience were associated with lower vulnerability to distress reactions. Moreover, repressive-defensiveness was associated with low attention to moods, as it should be.

Table 4

Correlations Among TMMS Subscales and With Other
Measures in Rumination Study

	Alpha	Attention	Clarity	Repair
Attention	.78	1.00		
Clarity	.87	.13	1.00	
Repair	.76	−.02	.12	1.00
CES-Depression		.25*	−.25*	−.26*
EPI-Neuroticism		.22*	−.40**	−.20
WAI				
Distress		.12	−.44**	−.44**
Self-Restraint		−.09	−.14	.19
Repressive-Defensiveness		−.22*	.08	.07

Note.
*$p < .05$
**$p < .01$

Changes in Mood

There was no doubt that watching the drunk driving film had a powerful impact on mood. Our participants reported relatively high levels of positive mood before the film (Time 1). However, mood reports just after the film dropped significantly (Time 2). Finally, there was a significant recovery of positive mood by the very end of the experiment (after the thought sampling task; Time 3).

A hierarchical regression analysis was used to determine the effects of Attention, Clarity, and Repair on mood at each of the three time points. Analysis proceeded in the following manner: Scores on the CES-D, EPI neurosis subscale, and WAI were entered first to account for any variance explained by depression, neuroticism, or socio-emotional adjustment. Baseline measures of mood were entered next. This strategy allowed for predictions of change in mood by removing from it all variance shared with the earlier measurement. For mood at the beginning of the experi-

Table 5

Regression Analysis for Rumination Study

DV = Affect Time 3	Beta	t	p
CES-Depression	.30	2.33	<.05
EPI-Neuroticism	.21	1.66	<.10
WAI-S			
Distress	−.25	1.71	<.10
Restraint	−.03	0.28	n.s.
Defensiveness	−.03	0.26	n.s.
Affect Time 1	.55	4.75	<.001
Affect Time 2	.20	1.82	<.10
Clarity (TMMS)	.25	2.05	<.05

Model: $R^2 = .38$, $F(8,62) = 4.73$, $p = .0001$ (Addition of Clarity: $\Delta R^2 = .04$, $p < .05$)

ment, there were no antecedent mood measures. As a result, the TMMS subscales were included in the analysis directly following the CES-D and WAI scores. The same regression technique was employed for mood measured at Time 2 and Time 3, with the exception that prior mood ratings were entered in the regression equation before the TMMS subscales were stepped into the model. For each equation, the subscales of the TMMS were allowed to enter based on the magnitude of their contribution in accounting for the remaining variance.

In the analysis that included the CES-D and the WAI, none of the TMMS subscales predicted initial mood (Time 1) or the decline in mood directly following the video (Time 2). Moreover, mood at Time 1 was not a significant predictor of mood at Time 2. Thus, it appears that the film had a negative effect on mood that was not mediated by baseline mood (the mood in which subjects walked into the laboratory). Mood recovery (positive mood at Time 3), however, was predicted by Clarity, over and above that accounted for by time. In other words, those individuals who reported that they were "usually very clear about [their] feelings" were more likely to rebound from induced negative mood. The results of these regression analyses are presented in Table 5.

In order to look at the associations between the TMMS scales and mood without worrying about overlap between the TMMS and the other dispositional measures collected, we also calculated a series of regression equations in which we regressed mood at each of the three points during the experiment on just the three TMMS subscales. At the beginning of the experimental session, positive mood was significantly associated with high Repair ($\beta = .34$, $p < .01$) and low Attention ($\beta = -.28$, $p < .05$). Following the film about drunken driving, subjects who scored high on Repair were the least distressed ($\beta = .26$, $p < .05$), even if mood at the beginning of the experiment was included in the model ($\beta = .30$, $p < .05$).

Thought Quality

Four characteristics of ruminative thought were examined in this study: intensity, insistency, controllability, and positiveness of thoughts that followed a distressing stimulus. Preliminary bivariate analysis of these thought quality dimensions revealed a strong relationship between intensity and insistency of thought. Due to the high correlation, r (72) $= .74$, $p = .0001$, and conceptual relatedness of these two variables, they were combined into an index of the intrusiveness of the thought. Thus, positiveness, intrusiveness, and controllability were used as the primary measures of thought quality.

Repeated measures analysis of covariance (ANCOVA) was used to test hypotheses pertaining to the ability of the TMMS subscales to predict improvement in the dimensions of thought quality over time. Because depression is associated with persistent negative cognitive patterns (e.g., Metalsky, Abramson, Seligman, Semmel, & Peterson, 1982), we felt it necessary to control for (i.e., covary) the influence of depression on thought patterns.

For purposes of analysis, subjects were divided into three groups based on their scores on each of the subscales of the TMMS. Those subjects whose score on a particular subscale fell into the upper quartile were considered to possess high ability with respect to that subscale. Those who scored in the lower quartile were considered to possess low ability. Scores for the remaining subjects were classified in the average range. This resulted in three grouping levels (High, Average, and Low) for each of the TMMS subscales: Attention, Clarity, and Repair. The three measures of thought quality (positiveness, intrusiveness, and controllability) were assessed across 10 points in time. Thus, three repeated measures ANCOVAs with one between subjects factor (group) and four within subjects factors (time and the three thought quality ratings) were performed, covarying any possible effect of depression. The only significant effect that emerged was a Time × Group interaction for Clarity, $F(18,567) = 1.92, p = .05$. To examine this interaction, we collapsed across the three dimensions of thought quality by taking the mean of standardized scores at each time point. The collapsed scores were scaled such that higher numbers indicated more negative, intrusive, uncontrollable thoughts—more ruminative thought. The Time × Group interaction for Clarity indicated that the effect of time on ruminative thought was different in at least one group. Because we were specifically interested in the improvement over time, regression lines were plotted for ruminative thought for each of the three groups. The High Clarity group had a significant negative slope ($b = -.66$, $p = .05$), indicating a significant decline in ruminative thought, as compared with a near zero slope for those in the Low Clarity group ($b = -.06$, ns). The slope difference between High and Low Clarity was significant ($z = 1.67$, $p < .05$; one-tailed). The slope coefficient for Average Clarity was not significantly different from the slope coefficients for either the Low or High Clarity groups. Thus, it appears that individuals who report being very clear about their feelings experienced a significant decline in ruminative thought over time when compared with individuals who report being unclear about their moods. These results support our hypothesis that clarity in discriminating feelings is important in the recovery from ruminative thought following a negative or stressful event.

This study investigated individual differences in the persistence of negative mood and ruminative thought. Because affect plays a critical role in ruminations, we believed that individuals who possess some of the skills measured by the TMMS would be less prone to continued negative mood and ruminative thought. We were able to demonstrate the importance of

Clarity in buffering the impact of a stressful event on subsequent mood and quality of thought. Recovery of positive mood following a stressful event was predicted by Clarity, over and above that accounted for by time or earlier mood states. Those individuals who reported experiencing feelings clearly were more likely to rebound from induced negative mood; they also tended to show a decline in ruminative thought across time following a distressing event.

Although Clarity was associated with the affective quality of ruminations, Attention to feelings was not. The differential predictive validity of these constructs deserves further comment. Clarity is the tendency to be able to distinguish among feelings. Individuals who experienced feelings clearly were more likely to feel positive at the experiment's end and to show a decline in troubling ruminations after stressful events. Perhaps emotional clarity is a required precondition for effective mood management. Individuals who experience affect clearly—who know what they feel—may be able to terminate aversive ruminative processes quickly simply because their feelings are clear. They know how they feel; they do not need to engage in prolonged rumination in order to figure it out. Rather, they can turn their attentional resources toward coping and minimizing the impact of the stressful event.

In part, the lack of an effect for Attention may be due to the methodology of this study. Subjects were asked explicitly to attend to their thoughts and, perhaps, implicitly to their feelings as well. As such, individual differences in the tendency to attend to feelings may not have been provided an opportunity to emerge. Moreover, merely attending to feelings may not change their experience. Feelings may arise with minimal higher order cognitive processing (cf. Zajonc, 1980) regardless of whether attention is focused explicitly on them. If anything, attending to feelings may intensify them (Scheier & Carver, 1977; Scheier, Carver, & Gibbons, 1981), regardless of valence. There was some evidence, however, that negative moods at the start of the experience were associated with Attention. Perhaps apart from stressful experiences, we are more likely to attend to our feelings when they are negative.

Finally, although Repair was unrelated to mood improvement or the attenuation of intrusive thoughts when other measures were included in the regression models, when the TMMS scales were examined alone, Repair was associated with the intensity of negative feelings immediately after viewing the distressing film. Individuals who seem to be good at repairing negative moods reported lower levels of negative affect in this context.

WHAT HAVE WE LEARNED?

This chapter described the development of the Trait Meta-Mood Scale (TMMS) and the extraction and confirmation of its three factors: Attention to Feelings, Clarity in Discrimination of Feelings, and Mood Repair. Scales based on these factors appear to be reliable as well as sufficiently differentiated from related constructs such as neuroticism and repression. Moreover, the Clarity scale in particular demonstrated validity in predicting the unpleasant quality of ruminations after a stressful experience.

More important, perhaps, than the reliability and validity of the TMMS is its utility. Is the trait meta-mood construct helpful in understanding individual differences in people's reactions to changes in their feeling states? We believe that the TMMS is a reasonable operationalization of aspects of *emotional intelligence* (Mayer & Salovey, 1993; Mayer, DiPaolo, & Salovey, 1990; Salovey et al., 1993; Salovey & Mayer, 1990). Individuals differ in their understanding of and ability to articulate their affective states (and those of others as well). And they vary in their ability to regulate such feelings and use them adaptively to motivate behavior. Attention to, Clarity, and Repair of feelings seem fundamental to the self-regulatory domain of emotional intelligence.

We believe that in this chapter, we have introduced a construct and a measure that will be of use to investigators interested in emotional disclosure. Certainly, however, future research needs to be focused on the discriminant validity of the TMMS vis-à-vis the constructs noted (but not measured) earlier in this chapter. Moreover, we need to explore whether the TMMS can predict emotional adjustment in other domains. In recent work with the TMMS, Emmons (1992) has reported that among a sample of individuals who reported their moods daily for three weeks, positive and negative moods were associated with Attention, Clarity, and

Repair, and, moreover, Repair was associated with the tendency to over-estimate levels of positive affect at the end of the study. In another set of studies (Goldman et al., submitted for publication), we have gathered data suggesting that Attention and Repair influence the reporting of physical symptoms and illnesses in the face of stressful conditions such as midterm and final examinations. Such findings may prove useful in understanding the role of emotional intelligence in psychosomatic disorders. Research efforts in the health domain and in other fields (close relationships may be a good place to look as well) should clarify the psychological importance of relatively stable thoughts about one's feeling life.

REFERENCES

Antrobus, J. S., Singer, J. L., & Greenberg, S. (1966). Studies in the stream of consciousness: Experimental enhancement and suppression of spontaneous cognitive processes. *Perceptual and Motor Skills, 23,* 399–417.

Apfel, R. J., & Sifneos, P. E. (1979). Alexithymia: Concept and measurement. *Psychotherapy and Psychosomatics, 32,* 180–190.

Barlow, D. H. (1988). *Anxiety and its disorders: The Nature and treatment of anxiety and panic.* New York: Guilford Press.

Catanzaro, S. J., & Mearns, J. (1990). Measuring generalized expectancies for negative mood regulation: Initial scale development and implications. *Journal of Personality Assessment, 54,* 546–563.

Elster, J. (1985). *The multiple self.* New York: Cambridge University Press.

Emmons, R. A. (1992, June). *Styles of emotion regulation and the experience of mood.* Paper presented at the Tenth Nags Head Conference on Affect and Cognition, Highland Beach, FL.

Epstein, S. (1990). Cognitive-experiential self-theory. In L. Pervin (Ed.), *Handbook of personality theory and research* (pp. 165–191). New York: Guilford Press.

Epstein, S., & Meier, P. (1989). Constructive thinking: A broad coping variable with specific components. *Journal of Personality and Social Psychology, 57,* 332–350.

Eysenck, H. J. (1973). *On extroversion.* New York: Wiley.

Fenigstein, A., Scheier, M. F., & Buss, A. H. (1975). Public and private self-consciousness: Assessment and theory. *Journal of Consulting and Clinical Psychology, 43,* 522–527.

Foa, E. B., & Kozak, M. J. (1986). Emotional processing of fear: Exposure to corrective information. *Psychological Bulletin, 99,* 20–35.

Gardner, H. (1983). *Frames of mind.* New York: Basic Books.

Giuliano, T. A., & Swinkels, A. (1992, August). *Development and validation of the mood awareness scale.* Paper presented at the annual convention of the American Psychological Association, Washington, DC.

Giuliano, T. A., & Swinkels, A. (1993, August). *Exploring the role of mood awareness in mood regulation.* Paper presented at the annual convention of the American Psychological Association, Toronto, Ontario.

Goldman, S. L., Kraemer, D., & Salovey, P. (1995). *Beliefs about mood as a moderator of the relationship between distress, illness, and symptom reporting.* Manuscript submitted for publication.

Horowitz, M. J. (1975). Intrusive and repetitive thoughts after experimental stress. *Archives of General Psychiatry, 32,* 1427–1463.

Horowitz, M. J. (1976). *Stress response syndromes.* New York: Jason Aronson.

Jöreskög, K. G., & Sörbom, D. (1986). *LISREL VI: Analysis of linear structural relationships by maximum likelihood, instrumental variables, and least squares methods.* Mooresville, IN: Scientific Software, Inc.

Katz, L., & Epstein, S. (1991). Constructive thinking and coping with laboratory-induced stress. *Journal of Personality and Social Psychology, 61,* 789–800.

King, L. A., & Emmons, R. A. (1990). Conflict over emotional expression: Psychological and physical correlates. *Journal of Personality and Social Psychology, 58,* 864–877.

King, L. A., & Emmons, R. A. (1991). Psychological, physical, and interpersonal correlates of emotional expressiveness, conflict, and control. *European Journal of Personality, 5,* 131–150.

Kirsch, I., Mearns, J., & Catanzaro, S. J. (1990). Mood regulation expectancies as determinants of depression in college students. *Journal of Counseling Psychology, 37,* 306–312.

Krystal, J. H., Giller, E. L., & Cicchetti, D. V. (1986). Assessment of alexithymia in post-traumatic stress disorder and somatic illness: Introduction of a reliable measure. *Psychosomatic Medicine, 48,* 84–94.

Lane, R. D., Quinlan, D. M., Schwartz, G. E., Walker, P. A., & Zeitlin, S. B. (1990). The levels of emotional awareness scale: A cognitive-developmental measure of emotion. *Journal of Personality Assessment, 55,* 124–134.

Lane, R. D., & Schwartz, G. E. (1987). Levels of emotional awareness: A cognitive-developmental theory and its application to psychopathology. *American Journal of Psychiatry, 144,* 133–143.

Mayer, J. D., DiPaolo, M., & Salovey, P. (1990). Perceiving the affective content in ambiguous visual stimuli: A component of emotional intelligence. *Journal of Personality Assessment, 50,* 772–781.

Mayer, J. D., & Gaschke, Y. N. (1988). The experience and meta-experience of mood. *Journal of Personality and Social Psychology, 55,* 102–111.

Mayer, J. D., Mamberg, M., & Volanth, A. J. (1988). Cognitive domains of the mood system. *Journal of Personality, 56,* 453–486.

Mayer, J. D., & Salovey, P. (1993). The intelligence of emotional intelligence. *Intelligence, 17,* 433–442.

Mayer, J. D., Salovey, P., Gomberg-Kaufman, S., & Blainey, K. (1991). A broader conception of mood experience. *Journal of Personality and Social Psychology, 60,* 100–111.

Mayer, J. D., & Stevens, A. A. (1994). An emerging understanding of the reflective (meta-) experience of mood. *Journal of Research in Personality, 28,* 351–373.

Metalsky, G. I., Abramson, L. Y., Seligman, M. E. P., Semmel, A., & Peterson, C. (1982). Attributional styles and life events in the classroom: Vulnerability and invulnerability to depressive mood reactions. *Journal of Personality and Social Psychology, 43,* 612–617.

Parkinson, L., & Rachman, S. (1981a). The nature of intrusive thoughts. *Advances in Behavioral Research and Therapy, 3,* 101–110.

Parkinson, L., & Rachman, S. (1981b). Intrusive thoughts: The effects of an uncontrived stress. *Advances in Behavioral Research and Therapy, 3,* 111–118.

Rachman, S. (1980). Emotional processing. *Behavioral Research and Therapy, 18,* 51–61.

Radloff, L. S. (1977). The CES-D scale: A self-report depression scale for research in the general population. *Applied Psychological Measurement, 1,* 385–401.

Russell, J. A., Weiss, A., & Mendelsohn, G. A. (1989). Affect grid: A single-item scale of pleasure and arousal. *Journal of Personality and Social Psychology, 57,* 493–502.

Salovey, P., Hsee, C., & Mayer, J. D. (1993). Emotional intelligence and the regulation of affect. In D. M. Wegner & J. W. Pennebaker (Eds.), *Handbook of mental control* (pp. 258–277). Englewood Cliffs, NJ: Prentice Hall.

Salovey, P., & Mayer, J. D. (1990). Emotional intelligence. *Imagination, Cognition, and Personality, 9,* 185–211.

Schaffer, L. F., Gilmer, B., & Schoen, M. (1940). *Psychology.* New York: Harper & Brothers.

Scheier, M. F., & Carver, C. S. (1977). Self-focused attention and the experience of emotion: Attraction, repulsion, elation, and depression. *Journal of Personality and Social Psychology, 35,* 625–636.

Scheier, M. F., & Carver, C. S. (1985). Optimism, coping, and health: Assessment and implications of generalized outcome expectancies. *Health Psychology, 4,* 219–247.

Scheier, M. F., Carver, C. S., & Gibbons, F. X. (1981). Self-focused attention and reactions to fear. *Journal of Research in Personality, 15,* 1–15.

Schwarz, N. (1990). Feelings as information: Informational and motivational functions of affective states. In E. T. Higgins & R. M. Sorrentino (Eds.), *Handbook of motivation and cognition: Foundations of social behavior* (Vol. 2, pp. 527–561). New York: Guilford Press.

Sifneos, P. E. (1972). *Short-term psychotherapy and emotional crisis.* Cambridge: Harvard University Press.

Sifneos, P. E. (1973). The presence of "alexithymic" characteristics in psychosomatic patients. *Psychotherapy and Psychosomatics, 22,* 225–262.

Silver, R. L., Boon, C., & Stones, M. H. (1983). Searching for meaning in misfortune: Making sense of incest. *Journal of Social Issues, 39,* 81–102.

Tait, R., & Silver, R. C. (1987). *The long-term psychological impact of major life events.* Unpublished manuscript, University of Waterloo, Ontario, Canada.

Taylor, G. J. (1984). Alexithymia: Concept, measurement and implications for treatment. *American Journal of Psychiatry, 141,* 725–732.

Thayler-Singer, M. (1977). Psychological dimensions in psychosomatic patients. *Psychotherapy and Psychosomatics, 28,* 13–27.

Weinberger, D. A. (1989). *Social-emotional adjustment in older children and adults. I. Psychometric properties of the Weinberger Adjustment Inventory.* Unpublished manuscript, Stanford University.

Weinberger, D. A. (1990). The construct validity of repressive coping style. In J. L. Singer (Ed.), *Repression and dissociation* (pp. 337–386). Chicago: University of Chicago Press.

Woodworth, R. S. (1940). *Psychology* (4th Ed.). New York: Henry Holt.

Young, P. T. (1936). *Motivation of behavior.* New York: John Wiley & Sons.

Zajonc, R. B. (1980). Feeling and thinking: Preferences need no inferences. *American Psychologist, 35,* 151–175.

APPENDIX: TRAIT META-MOOD SCALE

Please read each statement and decide whether or not you agree with it. Place a number in the blank line next to each statement using the following scale:

5 = strongly agree
4 = somewhat agree
3 = neither agree nor disagree
2 = somewhat disagree
1 = strongly disagree

_____ 1. The variety of human feelings makes life more interesting.

_____ 2. **I try to think good thoughts no matter how badly I feel.** [Repair]

_____ 3. I don't have much energy when I am happy.

_____ 4. **People would be better off if they felt less and thought more.** [Attention (R)]

_____ 5. I usually don't have much energy when I'm sad.

_____ 6. When I'm angry, I usually let myself feel that way.

_____ 7. **I don't think it's worth paying attention to your emotions or moods.** [Attention (R)]

_____ 8. **I don't usually care much about what I'm feeling.** [Attention (R)]

_____ 9. **Sometimes I can't tell what my feelings are.** [Clarity (R)]

_____10. If I find myself getting mad, I try to calm myself down.

_____11. I have lots of energy when I feel sad.

_____12. **I am rarely confused about how I feel.** [Clarity]

_____13. I think about my mood constantly.

_____14. I don't let my feelings interfere with what I am thinking.

_____15. **Feelings give direction to life.** [Attention]

Note. Items in bold face refer to those items included on the recommended 30-item short-form of the scale. The subscale on which these items are assigned is indicated after them. R indicates that the item is reversed scored.

_____16. Although I am sometimes sad, I have a mostly optimistic outlook. [Repair]

_____17. When I am upset I realize that the "good things in life" are illusions. [Repair (R)]

_____18. I believe in acting from the heart. [Attention]

_____19. I can never tell how I feel. [Clarity (R)]

_____20. When I am happy I realize how foolish most of my worries are.

_____21. I believe it's healthy to feel whatever emotion you feel.

_____22. The best way for me to handle my feelings is to experience them to the fullest. [Attention]

_____23. When I become upset I remind myself of all the pleasures in life. [Repair]

_____24. My belief and opinions always seem to change depending on how I feel. [Clarity (R)]

_____25. I usually have lots of energy when I'm happy.

_____26. I am often aware of my feelings on a matter. [Clarity]

_____27. When I'm depressed, I can't help but think of bad thoughts.

_____28. I am usually confused about how I feel. [Clarity (R)]

_____29. One should never be guided by emotions. [Attention (R)]

_____30. If I'm in too good a mood, I remind myself of reality to bring myself down.

_____31. I never give into my emotions. [Attention (R)]

_____32. Although I am sometimes happy, I have a mostly pessimistic outlook. [Repair (R)]

_____33. I feel at ease about my emotions. [Clarity]

_____34. It's important to block out some feelings in order to preserve your sanity.

_____35. I pay a lot of attention to how I feel. [Attention]

_____36. When I'm in a good mood, I'm optimistic about the future.

_____37. I can't make sense out of my feelings. [Clarity (R)]

_____38. I don't pay much attention to my feelings. [Attention (R)]

_____39. Whenever I'm in a bad mood, I'm pessimistic about the future.

_____40. I never worry about being in too good a mood.

_____41. I often think about my feelings. [Attention]

_____42. I am usually very clear about my feelings. [Clarity]

_____43. No matter how badly I feel, I try to think about pleasant things. [Repair]

_____44. Feelings are a weakness humans have. [Attention (R)]

_____45. I usually know my feelings about a matter. [Clarity]

_____46. It is usually a waste of time to think about your emotions. [Attention (R)]

_____47. When I am happy I sometimes remind myself of everything that could go wrong.

_____48. I almost always know exactly how I am feeling. [Clarity]

8

Inhibition and Muscle Tension in Myogenic Pain

Harald C. Traue

In the early days of my work with pain patients more than fifteen years ago, I was puzzled by some enigmatic findings. Rather clinically inexperienced, I could not fit my notions about the patients' personalities into the stereotypes proposed by the existing literature on pain personality. There was nothing remarkable about the patients. Family life was normal, job situation was normal, intimate life was normal; every part of their life and their personality seemed to be normal. The patients simply loved the word *normal,* and, indeed, a kind of supernormality seemed to be their salient personality feature. The personality data from tests were not out of the ordinary either. The one exception, however, was the pain problem. Without the pain problem, everything would be fine again.

Some time later, in one of the early studies of the Ulm headache project employing ambulatory muscle activity measures, Barbara Schlote let the headache patients estimate their daily stress level. Contrary to expectations, the headache group reported significantly lower stress levels than

This chapter has been supported by DFG-grants (SFB 129 & Tr233/4-1,2,3) from the German Research Foundation given to the author. Many thanks to Hannelore Kelley and Boris C. Traue for their help on an earlier draft of this chapter.

the control group, but showed nearly twice as much neck muscle tension as the controls. Although still short of an explanation, we were uncovering consistent discrepancies between the report of problems, troubles, emotions, and stress on the one hand and, on the other, the activity of the physiological system in terms of pain symptoms or muscle tension or both (Schlote, 1989; Traue, Bischoff, & Zenz, 1994).

These discrepancies fueled the interest in the role of emotional behavior in the etiology and the maintenance of pain, particularly of muscular origin. Wilhelm Reich's idea from the 1940s about "muscular armoring" in connection with inhibited expressiveness had to be reconsidered. "Tension and cramps of muscle are the bodily realization of suppression and both are the basis for the maintenance of disorders," he assumed (Reich, 1969, p. 260). Pioneering beyond this heritage of thought, new tools and investigative concepts had to be developed. The theoretical foundation, the course of these inquiries, and their results shall be elaborated in this chapter.

INHIBITION AND EMOTION

Conceptualized as a process of appraisal of transactions with the social environment of a person, emotions comprise several components: cognitive interpretation of intero- and exteroceptive stimuli, physiological patterning of arousal, motoric mobilization, and affective expressions. These different components are mediated by the central nervous system as a result of the interaction between the individual and the social and physical environment. The emotion can be considered as a response to environmental stimuli or as an act to control the environment (Traue, 1989a). From a system regulation point of view, emotional expressiveness has two important functions: First, as a communicative function, it facilitates regulation of person–environment transactions; and second, the feedback function of behavioral expression controls the internal (intraindividual) regulation of emotion. Active responding may influence the experienced demand from the environment indirectly through the attenuation of the stressful agents controlling the environment, or directly through self-regulation. Thus, expressive behavior is simultaneously part of emotional processes and a coping response. Inhibition of emotional expressiveness as part of emotional behavior overall becomes relevant to these regulation processes (Traue & Pennebaker, 1993).

For quite some time, inhibition of emotional expressiveness has been considered to be significant in the etiology and maintenance of psycho-somatic disorders. As early as 1920, Prideaux described an inverse rela-tionship between mimical expression and autonomic activity. In 1935, Jones pointed out that voluntary suppression of expressive behavior co-incided with physiological activation. He assumed that physiological acti-vation and expression were alternative means of reducing psychic tension. These early studies led toward the concept of internalization and exter-nalization, where two behavioral coping styles for dealing with psychic tension are discerned: either physiological within the individual or out-wardly directed. Following this concept, internalizers are persons with a high level of physiological excitation and a low level of expressiveness un-der stress, and externalizers are characterized by a low physiological level of excitation and high expressiveness in social situations.

It can be assumed that behavioral style in the direction toward inter-nalization or externalization is strongly neurobiologically based. As pos-sible neurobiological structures, the behavioral inhibition system and the behavioral activation system have been discussed (Gray, 1976; Traue & Pennebaker, 1993). This neurobiological genetic factor is superimposed by socialization or even reinforced. For example, introverts are more easily conditioned than extraverts. To the degree that introversion is the basis for externalization or internalization, the process of socialization is of greater importance for them than it is for extraverts (Traue, 1989b).

Facial muscles, muscles of the nape, of the back and the arms take part in expressive–emotional behavior through posture and communica-tion movements. In psychosomatics a lack of emotional experience and behavior is looked upon as a typical personality indicator for persons with psychosomatic disturbances (Pennebaker & Traue, 1993). Following this tradition, female patients with rheumatoid arthritis participated in a struc-tured interview by Moos and Salomon (1965). The patients described themselves as definitely more shy and more inhibited compared with their healthy sisters. Different groups of psychosomatic patients were exposed to physical and mental stress by Anderson (1981). After the experiment, patients were interviewed regarding the extent of tension experienced. Patients with the strongest physiological responses reported lesser stress. Other studies show that differences between patients and controls with respect to expressive inhibition cannot be demonstrated by questionnaire scores, but rather through overt behavior; that is, it is not represented by the patient's self concept (Traue & Michael, 1993).

This paper focuses on the role of behavioral inhibition in relation to muscular activity as a part of maladaptation of the interaction between individuals and their social environment. Although reduced expressiveness and heightened bodily reactions may be adaptive when one is faced with a social stress situation, in the long run these behaviors can take a harmful toll on the organism.

Inhibition in Pain Patients

The hypothesis of pain patients being emotionally inhibited has a long medical tradition. A personality description based on clinically orientated observations with patients originated with Wolff (1937). According to his studies, migraine and other headache patients were found to be rigid and to suppress their emotions. They were characterized by "a quality of studied poise, most often accompanied with tense facial expression with furrowed forehead, contractions between the eye brows, etc." (p. 905). However, the idea of inhibited aggressiveness as a feature of headache is much older, dating back to the late Middle Ages. Later, in a document from 1734, patients were said to be "*ira, imprimis tacita et supressa*" (when in a rage, they are particularly calm and restrained, cited from Jonckheere, 1971, p. 53). Since Engel (1959) described the "pain-prone patient," the hypothesis of suppressed anger and aggression as the personality characteristic of pain patients has been a consistent thread extending through the pain literature; yet a differentiation between headache patients and other psychosomatic patients has not been demonstrated (Henryk-Cutt & Rees, 1973).

From a psychometric point of view, the emotion suppression hypothesis has not been substantiated. Indeed, we feel that most studies are insufficient because self-report scales mirror mental attitudes rather than true behaviors. It follows that one's own suppressed behavior does not automatically reflect an attitude toward emotional expression. In addition, the need to conform to others, which has been claimed to be frequent in some pain sufferers, might be reflected in subjective statements and misconceptions that may well skew the results.

If pain patients are prone to a general suppression of emotions or otherwise less able to recognize their emotions than pain-free individuals, then these patients could scarcely report repressed anger, anxiety and aggression, as they would not be experiencing these emotions as strongly as other people do. Further scrutiny of the hypothesis must therefore focus on the observed behavior of patients, or rather attend to the question of impaired self-perception of emotions.

BEHAVIORAL INHIBITION AND MUSCLE
ACTIVITY IN HEADACHE

As a biologically oriented psychodynamic clinician, Reich considered socially punishing environmental conditions the cause of active emotional restraint in headache patients: "Our patients report without exception on childhood periods in their life, when they learned by means of physiological activity to suppress their feelings of anger, anxiety and love" (1969, p. 258).

Emotional and communicative expression of behavior is associated among other things with motor activity, which is a quality of emotional expressiveness, a component of complex behavioral processes, and is subject to classic and operant conditioning. As the head and neck musculature is of undeniable importance in the origin and maintenance of tension headaches—under the assumption that this musculature is a main source for this type of pain—motor behavior and, in particular, expressive behavior in headache sufferers is also of significance. It is conceivable that, under unfavorable circumstances, expressive behavior for mainly negative emotions like anger and aggressiveness is punished socially and thus justifiably avoided. Such avoidance behavior or inhibition is very adaptive in the short term, and it helps to modify a socially stressful situation. Simultaneously, though, a reduction of emotional expressiveness is conditioned by the learning mechanism of negative reinforcement (Bischoff & Traue, 1983; Traue & Kessler, 1992).

In order to examine the inhibition hypothesis for tension headache, we experimentally worked with a social stressor as a triggering condition for inhibited expression. The study compared nonverbal expressiveness in a symptom-free state, during a situational stressor in tension headache and nonheadache controls. Subjects were individuals with a history of tension headaches or with no such history. For the headache group, the mean reported duration of a headache problem was about two years. This was a group of headache patients without a long and thereby problematic pain history (Traue, Gottwald, Henderson, & Bakal 1985).

The following experimental phases were then presented. During relaxation, the subjects were guided through a series of Jacobson progressive relaxation and breathing exercises designed to relax the head and upper body musculature. Subjects were then presented with a picture from the Thematic Apperception Test (TAT) and were instructed to prepare a "good" story about the picture. Next, subjects delivered their TAT-Story while overt behavior was monitored on video. Then followed a phase of critique. Subjects were told in a standardized text that "a good short story should arouse your curiosity about something," that "the story should move along fast enough to keep your interest alive to the end," and so forth. Finally, subjects were required to react to the critique.

For behavioral rating, three raters, naive to the experimental hypotheses, rated the videos from the four experimental phases: TAT-Anticipation, TAT-Story, Critique, and Response. Each tape was viewed twice without sound and rated first for head and hand gestures and then a second time for facial behavior in terms of tension, communicative activity, and mimical expressiveness.

Inspection of the group values indicated that the headache group displayed less head and hand movement during each experimental phase.

Analysis of these differences with nonparametric tests indicated that statistically significant group differences in head movement were restricted to the TAT-Anticipation phase. The results of the analysis for expressiveness, tension, and facial activity ratings revealed that the headache subjects displayed significantly higher levels of facial tension. A comparison of group expressiveness ratings indicated that, overall, the headache group was significantly less expressive. Facial activity ratings were consistent with the expressiveness findings; the headache group exhibited less facial activity. This investigation confirms the claim that tension headache patients are less expressive overall compared to pain-free controls, communicate less, and show fewer communicative movements of the head and arms.

In the same experimental stress situation, muscle activity of the left and right frontalis as well as the trapezius muscle were recorded. The electromyographical (EMG) values were higher in the forehead and neck regions for tension headaches than for the pain-free controls in the social stress situation. As the investigation dealt with pain-free intervals, it is not concerned with the pain as a reason for the elevated tension values. These values, however, must be considered as a specific response by tension headache patients to social stress.

In order to verify the global relationship between expressiveness and muscle tension, correlations were computed between behavioral expression and EMG scores and vice versa. The correlations between facial expressiveness, head and hand movements, and EMG values were consistently negative and significant (see Figure 1). The expressiveness scales, which discriminated most strongly between the experimental groups, had the greatest negative correlations with EMG activity. It was also found that those individuals with the least movement and expression simultaneously displayed the greatest muscle tension in stressful social situations.

EMOTION REGULATION AND THE BACK

In colloquial speech, one can find examples for the symbolic significance of the back in social behavior: for instance "having backbone," "being spineless," "carrying a heavy load on one's back," or "stabbing someone in

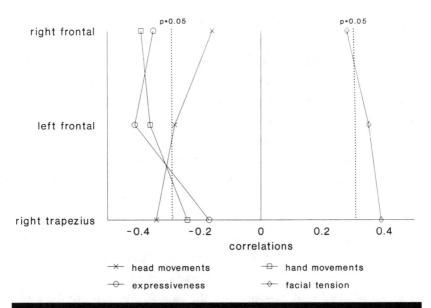

Figure 1

Correlations between head muscle activity and ratings of nonverbal behaviors in a stress situation ($n = 36$, threshold of 5% significance is marked by the dotted lines)

the back." Weintraub (1976) even associates low back-pain syndromes with certain problems according to pain location. For example, patients with cervical pain show little self-assertiveness; patients with thoracic pain of the spine are characterized by depression, despair, and discouragement; patients with lumbar pain are understood to be psychologically over-stressed and frustrated. Even if one does not agree with the hypothesis of a specific pain personality, the question remains as to specific behaviors that are not independent of the patient's personality, and that may play a role in the development or persistence of pain.

Clinical research concerning back-pain patients has revealed a number of psychological factors. Partnership and marital relations of patients with chronic pain problems are disturbed. Both partners often report less fulfillment in their relationship (Flor, Turk, & Scholz, 1987b; Schwartz et al., 1991). Quite often clinicians report that patients cannot accept emotional problems as the cause of pain. Rather, they communicate a dramatic picture of their suffering without exact location of pain to emphasize the organic nature of their illness. Even in regard to success or failure of surgical treatment, psychological factors appear to be important. According to Järvikowski and colleagues (1986), surgical treatment is more successful if patients show more self-assertiveness and less neurotic behavior.

Although the literature on personality structure of pain patients must be regarded very critically, especially owing to its strict separation of organic and psychic pain, the observations are nevertheless of heuristic value. The crucial point lies in the question of how psychic factors interact with arousal and muscular activity in order to make back pain probable.

Resulting from humanity's evolution to a two-legged creature, the human back is in an upright walking position. Therefore continued ineffective body posture especially predisposed to overburdening may cause muscle tension in the back muscles. This can lead to joint abrasion, mechanical irritation, infection, and neurological symptoms. In addition, back muscles are especially affected by the autonomic reaction of the central nervous system. In 1952, Holmes and Wolff described increase of lower back muscle activity during a conflict-centered interview. Increased muscle activity of back muscles has since been demonstrated in a number of studies (Kessler, Cram, & Traue, 1993; Traue & Kessler, 1992). What could be the causes for such an increase in muscle tension? A possible theoretical concept is supplied by the diathesis-stress model. According to this model, specific muscular tension of back muscles in patients under stress—especially socially caused stress—will occur when their stress control is deficient or takes the direction of internalization.

Nonverbal Expressiveness and Back Muscle Activity

The object of the back pain study was to examine the interrelationships among muscular activity, expressiveness, and coping. First, the nonverbal expressiveness of back-pain patients was compared to that of a control group. Subsequently, the measures of nonverbal expressiveness were correlated with EMG activity. Finally, the effects of inhibited expressiveness on the social network were analyzed.

The experimental group involved patients with nonspecific back pain and a pain-free control group matched according to age and gender. The back-pain patients were given an orthopedic diagnosis. Conditions for admission of back-pain patients to the project were the following: low back pain, which began at least 2 months before and 6 months at the most, still continuing at the time of admissions. By that procedure we provided for a clinically interesting group with a pain problem in a "chronification" period (i.e., between its being labeling acute and chronic).

A short form clinical interview was used with the back-pain patients and with the control group. It contained pain symptoms, social status and life satisfaction (work, family, partnership, sexuality, and leisure time). The interview was videotaped by a visible camera in the interview room. From each interview, two 3-min excerpts were recorded on a master tape. The evaluation of the video sequences was randomized in order to control for time-dependent effects.

The nonverbal expressive behavior was determined with the help of a coding and rating system (Traue, 1989b) from videotapes. The following nonverbal motor behavior items were coded: head nods, head shakes, other head movements, mimical behavior, smiling, different gestures (particularly body-focused movements), object focused movements, parallel-movement, shrugging, posture shifts, gaze, and speech activity.

Several differences of expressive behavior between back-pain patients and controls emerged. Back-pain patients showed less and shorter head nods, less and shorter head shakes, more and longer head movements, shorter mouth movements, less smiling, more often and longer hand-to-mouth contact, longer hand-to-hand contact, longer but more seldom speech activity, and less speech activity of the interviewer.

These differences concern mainly the variables of head movement. The significantly higher scores of back-pain patients in "miscellaneous head movements" and the strong reduction of the variables "head nods" and "head shakes" give reason to presume that many of the miscellaneous head movements were indistinct movements of head nods or head shakes. The patients did not seem to signal nonverbally as clearly as did the controls. An increase of hand-to-head contacts and hand-to-hand contacts in back pain patients indicates a reduction of expressiveness according to Friedman et al. (1985).

Patients with back pain showed more speech activity than controls. On the surface, this would not be expected because back pain patients supposedly show inhibited expressiveness. However, pain patients may be more willing to talk than to express nonverbally how they feel. The results are difficult to interpret because varying verbal behavior of the interviewers may be a systematic error, especially if the interviewer's speech activity is decreased. The duration of gaze while listening is reduced in back pain patients, an indication of an introvert personality (Argyle & Cook, 1976).

It is assumed that while back-pain patients show less expressiveness in essential variables (fewer head nods and head shakes, less smiling, shorter duration of gaze while listening), other behaviors such as head movements, hand-to-mouth contacts and hand-to-hand contacts are more often practiced. Head movements are to be interpreted as inaccurately transmitted head nods or head shake-movements and may in this sense be regarded as variables measuring inhibited expressive behavior. Hand-to-mouth contacts and hand-to-hand contacts are also identified as variables of low expressiveness. These results coincide with the theoretical assumptions concerning body focused behavior and with the results of comparable studies (Riggio & Friedman, 1983).

Factors of Expressiveness

The factor analysis of the expressiveness variables with sufficient interrater reliability resulted in a factor structure of six factors, which systematizes the variables meaningfully and compares well with other studies (Riggio & Friedman, 1983). The names given to the factors are based on the variables with the highest factor loadings. The results of factor analysis and the group differences indicate the multidimensional nature of expressiveness. Whereas some modes of behavior speak for expressiveness, others—among them overt behaviors—seem to be indices for inhibited

Table 1

Expressiveness Factor Score Differences Between Pain Patients and Controls

Factor	t-test		Pain group		Control group	
	t	p	M	SD	M	SD
1. Speech activity	2.23	0.03*	0.24	0.8	−0.3	1.1
2. Open gestures	0.65	0.52	0.07	1.1	−0.09	0.8
3. Inhibited gestures	2.25	0.03*	0.24	1.1	−0.29	0.7
4. Smiling	0.69	0.49	0.08	1.0	−0.09	0.9
5. Body shifts	−3.69	0.00**	−0.38	0.8	0.46	0.9
6. Head movements	−4.48	0.00**	−0.45	0.9	0.54	0.8

* = $p < 0.05$; ** = $p < 0.01$

emotional expressiveness: (a) speech activity (with speech time and gaze), (b) open gestures (with object focused movements and parallel movements), (c) inhibited gestures (with hand-head-contact, self-manipulation and body contact, negative loading of gaze), (d) smiling (with smiling frequency and duration, other head movements, and interviewer's speech behavior), (e) body shifts (with change of position and head nods), and (f) head movements (with head shakes, head nods and negative loadings on other head movements and hand-to-hand-contacts).

As can be seen in Table 1, back pain and control subjects evidenced significant differences for four of the six factors. For example, back pain patients showed higher speech activity, more inhibited gestures, fewer body movements, and fewer head movements than controls.

Back Pain Muscle Activity and Expressiveness

The relationship between muscle activity and expressive behavior was also examined. The factors of the factor analysis and the muscle activity along the back were correlated. The number of participating subjects was 59, collapsed across group assignment. Muscle activity was measured using an

EMG-Scanning technique. By scanning, EMG-measures were taken at 11 locations, on the left and on the right while standing and sitting upright. Kessler et al. (1993) describes methods and results of EMG-scannings in detail. The stronger the bracing of the back muscles, the more smiling is shown; the less speech activity practiced, the more inhibited gestures are shown; and the less the test persons move, the less open gestures and head movements are shown (see Table 2).

If factors of expressiveness are combined and correlated with the topographical structure of the back, one finds an interesting relationship. The general factor *positive expressiveness* shows slightly positive correlations with the upper part of the back, downwardly increasingly negative correlations with the tension schemes. The factor *inhibited gestures,* to be considered as negative expressiveness, shows no correlations for the upper part of the back, and positive correlations for the lower parts of the back with tension values. The factor smiling holds a special position here as well. The correlation for the upper part of the back is positive and drops to zero values for the lower back. It may therefore be theorized that tensions of the upper back correlate with smiling behavior and miscellaneous head

Table 2

Product–moment Correlations Between Muscle Activity and Expressiveness Factor Scores

EMG	Expressiveness factors	r	p
C4	4 Smiling	0.35	.003**
Th6	1 Speech activity	−0.22	.048*
Th10	3 Inhibited gestures	0.29	.011*
Th10	5 Body movements	−0.23	.037*
L3	2 Open gestures	−0.32	.007*
L3	6 Head movements	−0.19	.076+

(EMG data were averaged for each spine level from left and right as well as sitting and standing)
+ = $p < 0.10$; * = $p < 0.05$; ** = $p < 0.01$

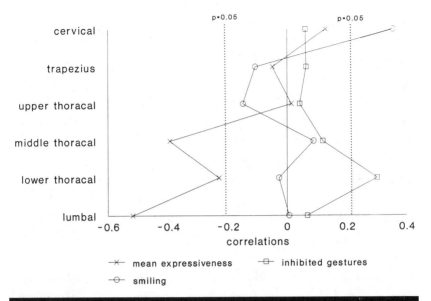

p•0.05   p•0.05

F i g u r e   2

Correlations between back muscle activity and factors of nonverbal behavior ($n = 58$, threshold of 5% significance is marked by the dotted lines)

movements. These may have to do with "keeping up one's face" in the form of "masked smiling;" on the other hand, the topographic proximity to neck and throat muscles may be the reason for head movements, in the sense of indistinct movements. As expected, tensions of the lower back correlate with inhibited expressiveness. Considering these findings according to which tensions in the lower back are connected with pain, the hypothesis of a correlation between tension, pain, and inhibited expressiveness in the case of back pain becomes more probable. Figure 2 shows the data of the combined factors of expressiveness.

PSYCHOBIOLOGICAL LINKS BETWEEN MUSCLE ACTIVITY, PAIN, AND INHIBITION

The reported data from myogenic headache and backache studies have shown that reduced expressiveness is related to physiological parameters that are also related to pain processes. Inhibition can thus influence physiological reactions under stress so that dysfunctional muscle activity is likely. Deriving from this psychobiological connection, inhibition has further consequences for the regulation of emotions and social behavior.

First, people normally react to emotion releasing stimuli, and such reactive expression is realized through facial muscle activity and movements with reafferent neuronal signals in the central nervous system (CNS), which contribute to individuals' emotional experience. In fact, subjective emotional experience does not depend exclusively on the nervous input as claimed in the facial feedback hypothesis. Feedback does, however, contribute positively to sensitivity toward the physiological aspects of emotion. If this sensitivity is disrupted, an individual will not adequately perceive increased muscle tension or other autonomic nervous system (ANS) reactions caused by stress, and consequently does not initiate healthy relaxing behavior. Indeed, Bischoff and Sauermann (1989) were able to demonstrate, in a signal detection design, that the hypothesis of deficient perception of muscle tension holds for tension headaches. These patients were less reliably able to judge the extent of their muscle strain than controls.

Alternatively, inhibited expression as seen with the suppression of feelings might be viewed as an active process that operates as a stressor in the individual (Pennebaker, 1985). When stress situations are frequent and inhibition habitual, a patient's sensitive physiological system becomes the weak link and symptoms in the form of myogenic pain can develop or be maintained.

Second, when the expressive components of emotional reactions are systematically repressed, the individual "unlearns" an accurate assessment of stressful circumstances. This learning mechanism occurs because the estimated load of a stress situation is not only dependent on external features of the situation but also on the subjective experience of stress-conditioned reactions as well.

When inhibited individuals take bodily reactions into account in the evaluation of a situation, their judgment will be impaired when the original physiological correlates of mainly negative emotions are confused and subsequently superimposed by tense muscle states. In fact people with chronic headaches and with tension headaches are inclined to underestimate situational stress. If one also considers muscle activity as part of a more general pattern of human motor activity in emotional processes, it is evident that muscle tension may be controlled by learning mechanisms. Classical or operant conditioning of motor behavior may lead to hyperactivity in a particular muscle system. Expressive behavior is prone to be punished under certain conditions of socialization starting with an individual history of increased tension and reduced expressiveness. With increased straining of head muscles, facial expression is suppressed so as to avoid facing up to the unpleasant consequences of self-expression of anger or annoyance. This suppression engenders the limitation of the duration of social stress. In the long run, though, this behavior does not serve to alleviate the strain of social conflicts: the inhibited individual avoids an active and stressful dispute that would otherwise help to resolve a difficult social situation (Bischoff & Traue, 1983).

Third, inhibited expressiveness under socially stressful encounters can be interpreted as a deficit in coping behavior. Such a deficit during social stress hampers the affected person's ability to influence a stressful environment actively, for example by confronting directly with a social stressor. These so-called social or natural stressors are encountered at work, or with family or peer group members. They relate to interpersonal problems and are integrated into one's lifestyle, and they tend to exert their influence over long time periods ranging from hours to weeks, or even to months. Furthermore, stressors like one's boss or partner frequently do not change. As a result, one's social control mechanism is affected in the area of human relations (Traue, 1991).

Finally, inhibited expressiveness exerts an influence on social relations and therefore on the social support network. Along with the ability to cope, a stable social system is both useful and helpful in mastering the strains of stress. For that reason the social support system is also considered as a stress buffer. Behavioral deficits in communicative and emotional areas can only adversely affect the relations between individuals and their immediate environment, thus also impairing the social network.

INHIBITION, MUSCLE TENSION, AND EMOTION THEORY

From a general perspective, inhibition of expression has a twofold meaning for the origin and maintenance of myogenic pain. On the one hand, inhibition works to the short-term benefit of the individual, but is accompanied by increased muscular activity. On the other hand, inhibited expressiveness is an overt display in the social environment of deficits in emotions and communication. This double problem is related to contemporary emotional concepts. The question of the specific role of motor mechanisms in emotional processes and inhibition is broadly discussed in Leventhal's perception–motor theory of emotional processes (Leventhal & Mosbach, 1983). According to this theory, there are three simultaneous levels of emotional processes: the expressive motor level, the schematic level, and the conceptual level. According to Leventhal and Mosbach, emotional behavior is directed on the conceptual level by rules on how to handle emotional episodes and on arbitrary reactions to emotional releasing stimuli. It is important, however, that the three levels of mastering the emotional processing mutually coincide, so that spontaneous motor reactions and arbitrary motor reactions can be superimposed or concealed and vice versa.

Accordingly, paradoxical effects can occur through control over automatic expressive movements. The suppression of spontaneous expression of feelings leads to an intensified experience of these feelings and an increased physiological response. This theory also explicitly describes a mechanism that assumes that the inhibition of affect leads to a rise in intense feeling and, associated with this, to increased motor activity (e.g., tensed-up muscles). Besides this, Leventhal's theory also explains the suppression of expressive motor behavior as an active process with concomitant stress induced through the effort and strain of suppressing the emotional impulse. This is in agreement with Pennebaker (1985), who understood the inhibition of feelings as active stress, with self-disclosure therefore allowing for a release of these stressors and thus leading to an improvement of health.

An explicit social–psychological and psychophysiological theory forms the basis of the illness model of Temoshok (1983). According to this model, the development of illness in the direction of psychic or psychosomatic disturbances depends on three dimensions: severity of stressors, coping style, and coping abilities. Whether a person under stressful conditions with a given lack in coping abilities develops a mental or psychosomatic disorder depends on whether he or she tends to internalize or externalize. Internalizing is understood as "the representation of aspects of the environment in the organism as perceptions" and an externalizing coping style denotes the "manifestation in the environment of some aspects of an organism's informational state and terms or as an expression of a thought or an emotion" (p. 217). This theory is concerned with internalizing and in particular externalizing as coping styles, and purports to describe finally whether a psychopathological or a psychosomatic disturbance will arise.

Moreover, in this multidimensional illness theory, the stress concept is bonded into the coping concept. "It is hypothesized that for situations of chronic stress, the nature of the expressed symptom is a function of three factors: coping style (internalizing or externalizing), severity of the stressor (slight or extreme), and coping abilities (including intelligence, education, flexibility, experience, psychological and physical health, social support, money, and so forth). These three factors are thought to determine the transformational level at which stressful information can be accommodated" (Temoshok, 1983, p. 221).

The findings on the myogenic pain syndromes fit well into this illness concept. On the one hand, pain patients are depicted as inhibited in their expressiveness. They fulfill the features of internalization and so, accordingly, they externalize their emotions and needs insufficiently in the form of actions and expressions in their social environment. Their impulsiveness and inner emotions remain activated together with their underlying motor and autonomic correlates, which in the long term may manifest themselves as a pain syndrome. In addition, an impairment of the social support system corresponds with inhibited expression, and thus with the internalized coping style. As a result, patients are more susceptible to being stressed. Thus it is necessary to regard inhibited expressiveness as a risk factor that can be altered through timely primary prevention (Traue & Kraus, 1988).

REFERENCES

Anderson, C. D. (1981). Expression of affect and physiological response in psychosomatic patients. *Journal of Psychosomatic Research, 25,* 143–149.

Argyle, M. & Cook, M.(1976). *Gaze and mutual gaze.* London: Cambridge University Press.

Bischoff, C. & Sauermann, G. (1989). Perception of muscle tension and myogenic headache: A signal detection analysis. In C. Bischoff, H. C. Traue, & H. Zenz (Eds.), *Clinical perspectives on headache and low back pain* (pp. 93–111). Toronto: Hogrefe & Huber Publishers.

Bischoff, C. & Traue, H. C. (1983). Myogenic headache. In K. A. Holroyd, B. Schlote, & H. Zenz (Eds.), *Perspectives in research on headache* (pp. 66–90). Kirkland, WA: Hogrefe & Huber Publishers.

Engel, G. (1959). "Psychogenic" pain and the pain prone patient. *American Journal of Medicine, 26,* 899–918.

Flor, H., Turk, D. C., & Scholz, O. B. (1987). Impact of chronic pain on the spouse: Marital, emotional and physical consequences. *Journal of Psychosomatic Research, 31,* 63–71.

Friedman, H. S., Hall, J. A., & Harris, M. J. (1985). Type A behavior, nonverbal expressive style, and health. *Journal of Personality and Social Psychology, 48,* 1299–1315.

Gray, J. A. (1976). The behavioral inhibition system: A possible substrate for anxiety. In M. P. Feldman & A. M. Brodhurst (Eds.), *Theoretical and experimental base of behavior modification.* New York: Wiley.

Henryk-Gutt, R. & Rees, W. L. (1973). Psychological aspects of migraine. *Journal of Psychosomatic Research, 17,* 141–153.

Holmes, T. H. & Wolff H. G. (1952). Life situations, emotions, and backache. *Psychosomatic Medicine, 14,* 18–33.

Järvikowski, A., Härkapaak, & Mellin, G. (1988). Symptoms of psychological distress and treatment effects with low-back-pain patients. *Pain, 25,* 345–355.

Jones, H. E. (1935). The galvanic skin reflex as related to overt emotional expression. *American Journal of Psychology, 47,* 241–251.

Jonkheere, P. (1971). The chronic headache patient: A psychodynamic study of 30 cases compared with cardiovascular patients. *Psychotherapy and Psychosomatics, 19,* 53–61.

Kessler, M., Cram, J., & Traue, H. C. (1993). EMG muscle scanning in pain patients and controls: A replication and new data. *American Journal of Pain Management, 3,* 10–18.

Leventhal, H., & Mosbach, P. A. (1983). The perceptual-motor theory of emotion. In J. T. Cacioppo, R. E. Petty, and D. Shapiro (Eds.), *Social psychophysiology* (pp. 353–390). New York: Guilford Press.

Moos, R. H., & Salomon, G. F. (1965). Psychological comparisons between women with rheumatoid arthritis and their nonarthritis sisters: I. Personality test and interview rating data. *Psychosomatic Medicine, 27,* 135–149.

Pennebaker, J. W. (1985). Traumatic experience and psychosomatic disease: Exploring the roles of behavioral inhibition, obsession and confiding. *Canadian Psychology, 26,* 82–94.

Pennebaker, J. W., & Traue, H. C. (1993). Inhibition and psychosomatic processes. In H. C. Traue, J. W. Pennebaker (Eds.), *Emotion, inhibition, and health* (pp. 146–163). Kirkland, WA: Hogrefe & Huber Publishers.

Prideaux, E. (1920). The psychogalvanic reflex: A review. *Brain, 43,* 50–73.

Reich, W. (1969). *Die Funktion des Orgasmus* [The function of the orgasm]. Köln: Kiepenheuer & Witsch.

Riggio, R. E., & Friedman, H. S. (1983). Individual differences and cues to deception. *Journal of Personality and Social Psychology, 45,* 899–915.

Schwartz, L., Slater, M. A., Birchler, G. R., & Atkinson, J. H. (1991). Depression in spouses of chronic pain patients: The role of patient pain and anger, and marital satisfaction. *Pain, 44,* 61–67.

Schlote, B. (1989). Longterm registration of muscle tension among office workers suffering from headache. In C. Bischoff, H. C. Traue, and H. Zenz (Eds.), *Clinical perspectives on headache and low back pain* (pp. 46–63). Kirkland, WA: Hogrefe & Huber Publishers.

Temoshok, L. (1983). Emotion, adaptation, and disease: A multidimensional theory. In L. Temoshok, C. v. Dyke, & L. S. Zegans (Eds.), *Emotions in health and illness* (pp. 207–234). New York: Grune & Stratton.

Traue, H. C. (1989a). Behavioral inhibition in stress disorders and myogenic pain. In C. Bischoff, H. C. Traue, & H. Zenz (Eds.), *Clinical perspectives on headache and low back pain* (pp. 29–46). Kirkland, WA: Hogrefe & Huber Publishers.

Traue, H. C. (1989b). *Gefühlsausdruck, Hemmung und Muskelspannung unter sozialem Stress: Verhaltensmedizin myogener Kopfschmerzen* [Emotional expression, inhibition, and muscle tension under social stress: Behavioral medicine of headaches]. Göttingen: Verlag für Psychologie.

Traue, H. C. (1991). Gehemmte Expressivität, Arousal und soziale Unterstützung [Inhibited expression, arousal, and social support]. In J. Haisch, & H. P. Zeitler (Eds.), *Gesundheitspsychologie: Zur Sozialpsychologie der Prävention und Krankheitsbewältigung* [Psychology of health: The social psychology of prevention and coping]. (pp. 345–360). Heidelberg: Asanger.

Traue, H. C., Bischoff, C., & Zenz, H. (1994). Zur Verhaltensmedizin myogener Kopfschmerzen: Ergebnisse der Ulm Kopfschmerzforschung [The behavioral medicine of myogenic headaches: Results of the Ulm headache research]. In R. Wahl & M. Hautzinger (Eds.), Psychotherapeutische Medizin bei chronischem Schmerz [Psychotherapeutic medicine of chronic pain]. Köln: Deutscher Ärzte Verlag.

Traue, H. C., & Kessler, M. (1992). Myogene Schmerzen [Myogenic pain]. *Zeitschrift für Medizinische Psychologie, 1*, 10–22.

Traue, H. C., & Kraus, W. (1988). Ausdruckshemmung als Risikofaktor: Eine verhaltensmedizinische Analyse [Expressive inhibition as risk factor: A behavioral medicine analysis]. *Praxis der klinischen Verhaltensmedizin und Rehabilitation, 2*, 89–94.

Traue, H. C., & Michael, A. (1993). Behavioral and emotional inhibition in head pain. In H. C. Traue, & J. W. Pennebaker (Eds.), *Emotion, inhibition and health* (pp. 226–246). Kirkland, WA: Hogrefe & Huber Publishers.

Traue, H. C., & Pennebaker, J. W. (1993). Inhibition and arousal. In H. C. Traue, & J. W. Pennebaker (Eds.), *Emotion, inhibition and health* (pp. 10–31). Kirkland, WA: Hogrefe & Huber Publishers.

Traue, H. C., Gottwald, A., Henderson, P. R., & Bakal, D. A. (1985). Nonverbal expressiveness and EMG activity in tension headache sufferers and controls. *Journal of Psychosomatic Research, 29*, 375–381.

Weintraub, A. (1976). Die Psychosomatik des Rheumakranken [The Psychosomatics of Rheumatic Illness]. In A. Jores (Ed.), *Praktische Psychosomatik* [Psychosomatic Practice]. Göttingen, Federal Republic of Germany: Huber.

Wolff, H. G. (1937). Personality features and reactions of subject with migraine. *Archives of Neurology and Psychiatry, 37*, 895–921.

9

Repression, Emotional Disclosure, and Health: Theoretical, Empirical, and Clinical Considerations

Gary E. Schwartz and John P. Kline

The potential benefits of emotional disclosure for mental and physical health presume not only that people are motivated to disclose but also that they are able to disclose. If a person (a) has a limited vocabulary for expressing emotional feelings as in alexithymia (Kleiger & Kinsman, 1980), (b) has a low level of emotional awareness (Lane and Schwartz, 1987, 1992), or (c) is repressive or defensive about emotional feelings and experiences (Weinberger, Schwartz & Davidson, 1979), not only will the person's capacity for disclosure be limited, but any potentially beneficial effects may be limited as well. Systematic research on individual differences in openness to emotional experience and on emotional expressiveness as moderator variables of emotional disclosure is just beginning (Esterling, Antoni, Kumar, & Schneiderman, 1990). The purpose of this chapter is to review current research on defensiveness and repressive coping and to consider theoretical, empirical, and clinical implications of the findings for emotional disclosure and health.

The chapter is divided into four parts. The first part considers the meaning of repression from a systems perspective, and suggests that active inhibition is involved in both healthy and unhealthy repressive processes. The second part discusses the operationalization of repressive coping and briefly reviews some of the earlier research. The third part presents recent research from our laboratory and others that is consistent with the hypothesis that repression involves active inhibition of sensory information. The final part considers some implications of these findings for research on emotional disclosure and health.

REPRESSION FROM A SYSTEMS PERSPECTIVE

Sigmund Freud originally used *repression* and *suppression* interchangeably, and held that the process could be unconscious. Later conceptualizations of repression, namely those of Anna Freud, distinguished it from conscious suppression and gave rise to the current definition of the term (Erdelyi, 1990). Thus repression typically refers to an unconscious process wherein aspects of undesirable content are excluded from awareness. Furthermore, repression involves no awareness that exclusion from awareness has taken place. This inhibition of information is an active, energy consuming process.

Repression comes from the Latin word *reprimere*, which roughly translates into "to hold back." Generically, this means "to check," or "to restrain." It is only in the context of psychological defenses that repression takes on the specific meaning of keeping painful ideas and impulses out of conscious awareness (Schwartz, 1990). In its broad sense, it might be considered synonymous with *inhibition.*

The concept of repression is not unique to psychoanalytic theory or cognitive psychology. From a systems perspective, repression is a process by which information is inhibited so that specific goals can be reached. From this perspective, affect and cognition are viewed as being in a cybernetic, mutually regulating feedback loop. When affect is disconnected from cognition (i.e., painful content is excluded from awareness), the two processes are no longer mutually regulating, and a state of "disorder" or "disease" may develop (Schwartz, 1990).

The proposition that repression can lead to disconnection of affect and cognition should not be viewed as necessarily maladaptive. To the contrary, the capacity to inhibit information is ubiquitous, and is a pre-requisite for goal directed behavior, and hence survival and health. This was made clear to the first author in the early 1970s when he was attempting to learn how neurologists interpret changes in reflexes and behavior in disease and injury.

After completing his teaching on Wednesdays at Harvard University, he went on all night rounds at the Massachusetts General Hospital (MGH) with his friend, Dr. Fernandez, who was then a neurology resident. One evening at approximately 2:00 a.m. a man in his late sixties was admitted to the Emergency Room at MGH with symptoms of confusion, dizziness, and partial paralysis. Dr. Fernandez completed a neurological exam. While stroking the bottom of the patient's foot, Dr. Fernandez observed that the patient appeared to show a Babinski reflex, a reflex of the toes that is found in newborn infants but rapidly "disappears" in a few weeks. Dr. Fernandez hypothesized that the man had a frontal stroke, which lead to disinhibition of previously inhibited reflexes. He then tested his hypothesis by stroking the corners of the patient's lips and discovered that the man showed a sucking reflex, a reflex that also is found in infants and "disappears" with development.

Dr. Fernandez's observation raises the following question: Where do these reflexes go when they "disappear" in infancy, and how can they "reappear" with a frontal stroke? Dr. Fernandez said that these reflexes are inhibited by the frontal cortex as part of normal development. The reflexes are not gone, they are simply inhibited. The reflexes can be disinhibited by damage to the frontal cortex (e.g., by a stroke), through inhibition of the frontal cortex by drugs (it has been reported that in some people, drinking alcohol can lead to the reexpression of the Babinski reflex), and by hypnosis (it has also been reported that in some highly susceptible subjects, age regression under hypnosis may be accompanied by reexpression of the Babinski reflex).

Obviously, people are not consciously aware that their Babinksi reflexes are being actively inhibited in order for them to be able to walk successfully. Similarly, people are not typically consciously aware that cognitions and memories are being actively inhibited, and hence repressed, in order for them to be able to think and talk successfully. It follows that repression defined as "keeping painful stimuli or memories out of awareness" is a special case of the active inhibition of information.

As will be seen below, just as it may inhibit the expression of primitive reflexes such as the Babinski reflex, the frontal cortex may also play a role in the repression of sensory stimuli in repressive coping.

OPERATIONALIZING REPRESSIVE COPING

If a person reports experiencing low levels of negative emotions such as anxiety, depression, or hostility, it is often assumed that these reports represent accurate self-presentations. It is this assumption that is used to justify assigning all low-scoring subjects into a single control group. However, if a subset of these subjects is actually engaged in (a) conscious deception of others (impression management) or (b) unconscious deception of self (repression), the "control" group may contain subjects who in actuality have high levels of negative emotions.

Weinberger, Schwartz, and Davidson (1979) revitalized research on repressive coping by proposing that certain social desirability scales (e.g., the Marlowe-Crowne Social Desirability Scale [MCSD]) and lie scales (e.g., the Lie scale from the Eysenck Personality Inventory) might reflect a defensive or deceptive orientation. Subjects scoring high on such scales and low on scales measuring negative emotions were classified as being high in repressive coping, whereas subjects scoring low on such scales and low on scales measuring negative emotions were classified as being *true low anxious*. The remaining two cells of the 2×2 table comprised subjects scoring low on such scales and high on scales measuring negative emotions (classified as *true high anxious* subjects), and subjects scoring high on such scales and high on scales measuring negative emotions (classified as *defensive high anxious* subjects). The term *defensive* refers to people with high scores on such scales in general, where the term *repression* is used to refer to the subset of subjects scoring high on such scales (defensive subjects) and low on scales measuring negative emotions.

Weinberger et al. (1979) documented that subjects who claimed to be low anxious as measured by the Taylor Manifest Anxiety scale (short form), but who scored high on the Marlowe-Crowne scale (i.e., repressive coping subjects), showed behavioral and physiological responses to a phrase association task that are equal or greater than those of subjects who were high anxious. Subjects who claimed to be low anxious and scored low on the Marlowe-Crowne scale (i.e., true low anxious subjects) showed behavioral and physiological responses suggesting that they were indeed less stressed by the task than the high anxious scoring subjects. These group differences would have been missed had the two low anxious subgroups been analyzed as a single, undifferentiated low anxious control group. The utility of this procedure for operationalizing defensive and repressive coping has been documented in substantial basic and clinical research (e.g., see Singer, 1990).

RESEARCH ON REPRESSION AS INHIBITION

Jamner and Schwartz (1986) found that high-defensive subjects as measured by the Lie Scale of the Eysenck Personality Inventory had higher pain thresholds and were more pain tolerant than low- and medium-defensive subjects. The high-defensive subjects did not have higher sensory thresholds, however. This and subsequent findings (e.g., Jamner, Schwartz, & Leigh, 1988) suggest that defensive individuals attenuate their awareness of intense, painful stimulation.

The possibility that defensive and repressive coping involves the inhibition of intense or painful sensory stimuli led Kline, Schwartz, Fitzpatrick, and Hendricks (1993) to hypothesize that high-defensive subjects should show decreased amplitude–intensity functions of auditory-evoked potentials compared to nondefensive subjects. Specifically, they reasoned that high-defensive subjects should attenuate evoked potential magnitudes to high-intensity stimuli, but not to low-intensity stimuli. Kline, Schwartz, Fitzpatrick, et al. (1993) drew their paradigm from the controversial augmentation–reduction literature (Buchsbaum, 1976; Connolly, 1986).

Though criticisms had been raised with regard to modality specificity, temporal instability, and nonstandardized methods for stimulus presentation, Kline, Schwartz, Fitzpatrick, et al. (1993) reasoned that when appropriate controls and stimulus intensities are used, reliable and theoretically relevant amplitude–intensity slopes could be obtained.

Undergraduate subjects at the University of Nebraska were classified into high- and low-defensive subjects as measured by the L scale of the Eysenck Personality Questionnaire. A total of 256 auditory stimuli of 74, 84, 94, and 104 dB Sound Pressure Level (SPL) intensities were presented to subjects in a counterbalanced order with random and variable interstimulus intervals while EEG was continuously recorded from Fz, Cz, Pz, T3, C3, T4 and C4 sites. Figure 1 shows averaged evoked potentials recorded from the vertex (Cz) separately for low- and high-defensive subjects. It can be seen that the P2 potential was diminished to the high intensity tones in the high-defensive subjects compared with the low-defensive subjects. Figure 2 shows the P2 values for the seven sites in the low- and high-defensive subjects. It can be seen that the P2 slopes were lower in the high-defensive subjects, especially in the central and frontal (Cz and Fz) regions. The frontal effects could be relevant to the association between frontal inhibition and the repression of reflexes, pain, and stimulus intensity.

Because the effects for defensiveness occurred so quickly in the averaged evoked potential (i.e., about 200 ms poststimulus) and because the effects occurred only to the high-intensity tones, it seems unlikely that the defensiveness effect is due to conscious response suppression. This would seem especially true, because the order of stimulus delivery was counterbalanced for intensity and interstimulus intervals were variable and random, which would make predicting stimulus intensity unlikely.

The finding that N1 amplitude–intensity slopes were similar for the two groups is potentially important. Kline, Schwartz, Fitzpatrick, et al. (1993) reasoned that N1 amplitude–intensity relationships may have reflected cortical registration of the more sensory and physical (exogenous) parameters of the stimulus, where P2 amplitude may have been responsive to a postsensory, but preconscious, affective appraisal of the stimulus. In

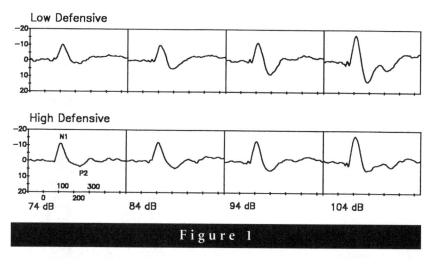

Figure 1

Averaged waveform from the vertex (CZ) for high- and low-defensive subjects in response to the four tone intensities. Of note is the diminished P2 amplitude to the 84 and 94 dB tones for high-defensive subjects. (From Kline et al., 1993.)

other words, high-defensive subjects may automatically and preconsciously attenuate the affective significance of stimuli that were rapidly, automatically, and unconsciously judged to be too intense. Therefore, high-defensive subjects may register the full sensory impact of high-intensity stimuli, as reflected in the lack of a defensiveness effect at N1, but attenuate the affective significance of the stimulus, hence the observed effect at P2.

These findings are consistent with the hypothesis that defensiveness, as measured by instruments such as the L scale, may reflect the active inhibition (repression) of high-intensity, and thus emotionally relevant, information. A surprising finding that provides curious and compelling support for this hypothesis emerged unexpectedly from research on subliminal registration of olfactory stimuli.

In a series of studies, we have found that low-intensity olfactory stimuli that cannot be detected (e.g., using a forced-choice, two bottle paradigm, subjects' accuracy in detecting the odor is 50% chance) can nonetheless be reliably registered in the EEG (reviewed in Schwartz et al., 1994). The EEG effects are typically observed in central and posterior regions, more so on the right side.

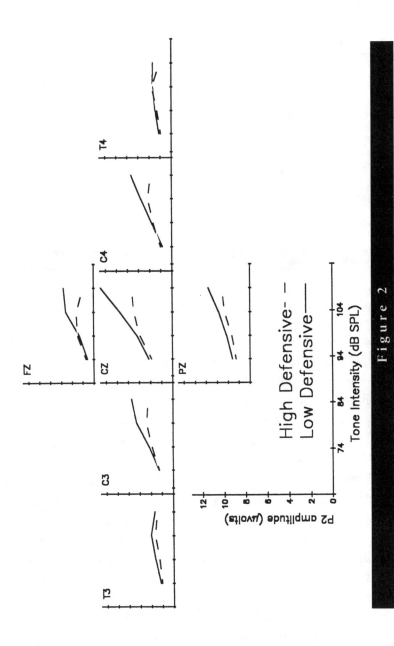

Figure 2

P2 amplitudes for the low- and high-defensive subjects, showing lower P2 amplitudes in response to the 84 and 94 dB tones for the high-defensive subjects. (From Kline et al., 1993.)

This research has been extended to the study of selective anosmia for 5-α-androst-16-en-3-one (androstenone). Androstenone is a putative human sex pheromone, which has an offensive urinous, sweaty odor for many who are osmic for it (Cowley & Brooksbank, 1991; Wysocki & Beauchamp, 1984). Roughly 50% of adults are specifically anosmic to androstenone, 15% detect a subtle odor and are not offended by it, and the remaining 35% are highly sensitive to it, detecting less than 200 parts per trillion in the air (Wysocki & Beauchamp, 1984). Another point of interest is that anosmia for androstenone seems to have a developmental component (Dorries, Schmidt, Beauchamp, & Wysocki, 1989; Schmidt & Beauchamp, 1988). Specifically, it appears that on the average children are more sensitive than adults to androstenone, sensitivity for it decreases during adolescence especially for males, and children are very unlikely to show a specific anosmia for it (Dorries et al., 1989).

At least two possible mechanisms have been proposed to explain this loss. One mechanism is that olfactory receptors in the nose may lose their ability to register these molecules. A second mechanism is that the olfactory receptors continue to detect the molecules, but the brain selectively inhibits the conversion of this information into a conscious experience. EEG recordings indicate that subjects anosmic for androstenone still reliably register the presence of androstenone compared to solvent alone (Schwartz, Kline, Dikman, Wright, & Polak, 1992; Schwartz, Kline, Dikman, & Polak, 1993). The EEG pattern for androstenone registration in androstenone anosmia turns out to be curiously similar to the EEG pattern observed to low intensity, subliminal odors.

On the basis of earlier research linking perceptual defense phenomena to the defensiveness dimension (e.g., Holroyd, 1972), Kline, Schwartz, and Dikman (1993; 1994) wondered whether one predictor of this selective anosmia for androstenone might be defensiveness. The L scale was used to split subjects into high- and low-defensive groups. Hit rates, ratings of confidence, and ratings of intensity, were obtained to androstenone and to iso-amyl acetate, a molecule that most people can readily smell. Figure 3 displays the findings separately for males and females. It can be seen that the two groups were virtually identical when smelling iso-amyl

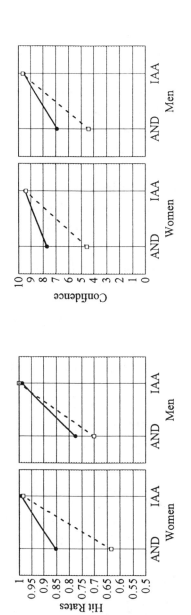
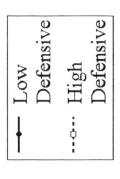
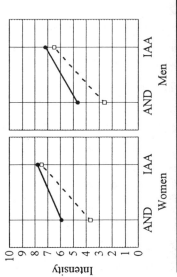

Figure 3

Hit rates, Confidence, and Intensity ratings for Androstenone (AND) and Iso Amyl Acetate (IAA; control) for High- and Low-Defensive Men and Women. (From Kline et al., 1994.)

acetate (IAA). However, the high-defensive subjects showed lower hit rates, lower confidence ratings, and lower intensity ratings when smelling the androstenone (AND). In other words, defensiveness predicted the selective anosmia for androstenone.

If androstenone anosmia involves an active inhibitory–repressive mechanism, then theoretically if this mechanism were somehow disinhibited, the capacity to smell androstenone should return. It is possible that in the same way that frontal strokes can result in the reexpression of the Babinski reflex, frontal strokes may also result in the reexpression of the smell of androstenone in anosmic subjects. Unfortunately, it is virtually impossible to know in a given stroke patient whether she or he could smell androstenone before suffering the stroke. On the other hand, if the percentage of androstenone anosmics was significantly reduced in a group of patients having frontal strokes compared to appropriate control groups, the findings would be consistent with the hypothesis.

Using similar logic, Pennebaker (personal communication, 1993) asked the first author if highly hypnotically susceptible, androstenone anosmic subjects were age regressed under hypnosis, would they regain some capacity to smell androstenone? Research is currently underway to address this intriguing question.

IMPLICATIONS FOR EMOTIONAL DISCLOSURE AND HEALTH

If repression involves an active inhibitory mechanism, and if the motivation for this mechanism is self-protection, then the effectiveness of emotional disclosure in defensive individuals, especially repressors, may well be limited. Schwartz (1990) has proposed that people develop defensive emotional styles as an adaptive mechanism that supports mental, physical, and social health, at least in the short run.

In the long run, however, it appears that defensiveness is associated with potentially deleterious consequences, for example, decreased immune efficiency (e.g., see Schwartz, 1990 for a review). For instance, Jamner, Schwartz, and Leigh (1988) found that high-defensive subjects showed decreased monocytes, and increased eosinophile and serum glucose levels. Because the findings generalized to the defensive high anxious group as well as the repressor group, these findings leave the role of emotional disclosure in producing these results unclear.

Esterling et al. (1990) conducted a study of direct relevance to the relationship of emotional disclosure to repression and health. They hypothesized that subjects who abstained from disclosing emotional material would have poorer control of latent Epstein-Barr virus and subjects with psychometrically derived repressive interpersonal styles would show the highest Epstein-Barr viral capsid antigen (EBV-VCA) titers. Undergraduates at the University of Miami completed a personality inventory and wrote an essay or letter for 30 minutes about a stressful event in their life. Blood was collected immediately after completing the essay. Repressors who were either high or low disclosers (based on ratings of the letters) had high levels of antibody titer to EBV-VCA, whereas only those nondefensive subjects who did not disclose had high antibody titers to EBV-VCA. In other words, emotional disclosure was associated with improved immune function in nondefensive subjects only. Esterling et al. (1990) highlighted the importance of obtaining behavioral and psychometric assessments in psychoimmunologic investigations of repression and emotional disclosure.

In a subsequent study, Esterling, Antoni, Kumar, and Schneiderman (1993) examined the relationship between defensiveness, trait anxiety, and EBV-VCA in healthy college students at the University of Miami. They found that subjects reporting high and medium levels of anxiety had higher antibody titers to EBV, suggesting poorer immune control over the latent virus, as compared with the low-anxious group. Similarly, high-defensive subjects, as measured by the Marlowe-Crowne scale, had higher antibody titers than low-defensive subjects.

Together, the Esterling et al. (1990; 1993) studies replicate and extend the Jamner et al. (1988) findings in patients in the Yale Behavioral Medicine Clinic, suggesting poorer immune function in high-defensive subjects. They further suggest that emotional nondisclosure may be an important variable in moderating these results.

The Marlowe-Crowne scale typically shows mild correlations (in the

−0.30 range) with scales related to psychopathology. The magnitude of these correlations suggests at least two possibilities: (a) the dimensions are psychometrically related, due to the statistically imprecise method for derivation of the MCSD (see Crowne & Marlowe, 1964), or (b) defensiveness serves the function of decreasing distress, but is not completely effective in doing so. Evidence for the first proposition comes from research with the Eysenck Personality Questionnaire, which reports relative orthogonality between the L scale of the EPQ and negative emotionality scales (Eysenck & Eysenck, 1987; Kline, Schwartz, Fitzpatrick, et al., 1993; Schalling, Edman, & Asberg, 1983). Although of potential psychometric importance, the first proposition is of little relevance to the present chapter. The second proposition poses some intriguing questions about the role of defensiveness in moderating emotional disclosure and maintaining emotional health.

Lane, Merikangas, Schwartz, Huang, and Prusoff (1990) conducted a family study of depression in which they interviewed depressed patients as well as with the patients' family members. The familial ratings were of interest because they provided a measure of functioning that was independent of the patients' self assessments. They reported that according to both self-report and relatives' reports, defensiveness and lifetime prevalence of psychiatric disorder were inversely related. In other words, it appears that not only do high-defensive subjects report being less distressed than low-defensive subjects, but they also appear less distressed to people who know them.

Tomarkin and Davidson, (1994) have reported relative left frontal activation (i.e. decreased log-transformed alpha power) in defensive subjects. Further, the interaction of anxiety and defensiveness contributed no unique variance to anterior asymmetry scores, so defensiveness, and not repressiveness, was the key factor. Considered along with results linking left frontal hypoactivation to depression (e.g., Henriques & Davidson, 1991), these results are also consistent with the hypothesis that defensiveness serves a protective function from psychopathology.

The findings presented thus far in this chapter raise the intriguing possibility that defensiveness, and thus inhibition, is a prerequisite for the appearance of mental and emotional health. However, it would also seem that this increased mental health may take a physical toll in the form of increased susceptibility to disease. The Marlowe-Crowne scale was originally intended to assess "need for approval," and the social desirability response set. Similarly, the L scale was intended to measure the tendency to "fake good." It would follow that anyone who was judged by others to possess the attributes that these scales represent would also be judged to be emotionally more healthy.

The literature on repressive coping suggests that future research on emotional disclosure should pay special attention to individual differences in defensiveness. Text analysis of self-reports of emotional disclosure in defensive subjects should reveal relatively impoverished emotional expression. As repressed individuals develop the comfort and then the skill to explore and communicate their feelings, they should show corresponding changes in self-reports, and possibly in physiology. Changes in frontal EEG may accompany decreases in defensiveness with psychotherapy.

Consistent with this hypothesis, we have found increased frontal activation (i.e., decreased frontal EEG alpha activity) in high-defensive subjects (Schwartz, Schwartz, Kline, & Eichling, 1992). Further, the between-group differences in alpha activity appear to decrease from the beginning to the end of a testing session, as subjects become more at ease with the experimental setting and the experimenter (Schwartz, Schwartz, Kline, & Eichling, 1992). Thus, increases in frontal alpha activity (decreased frontal activation) may appear in an environment that fosters emotional disclosure (e.g., during psychotherapy).

Frontal alpha activity has been correlated with increased natural killer cell activity (Schwartz, Schwartz, Eichling, & Yokum, 1992), so it might be expected that with psychotherapy, high-defensive individuals will show enhanced immune functioning as well as increased frontal alpha and disclosure. Improvements in emotional expression and immune function may come at a cost, however. If high-defensive subjects can somehow learn not to repress, and their defensiveness has served the purpose of warding off emotional illness, improved expression of emotion, especially negative emotion, could make them vulnerable to emotional illness.

If the frontal inhibition hypothesis is correct, frontal EEG should predict openness to emotional expression and show changes in brain function accompanying the improved capacity to experience and express emotion. It is possible that other side effects of reducing defensiveness may be increased awareness of the smell of androstenone, and increased auditory evoked potential amplitude–intensity slopes.

Future research needs to improve upon measurement of defensiveness and repression (Paulhus & Reid, 1991), and clarify hypotheses of defensiveness and repression (see Singer, 1990). Findings in the repression and defensiveness literature need to be related to alexithymia (Kleiger & Kinsman, 1980) and levels of emotional awareness (Lane & Schwartz, 1987; 1992). The role of emotional disclosure as a moderator variable for effects of repression and defensiveness on health should be explored. Finally, researchers and clinicians should explore ways to improve emotional openness in defensive persons without compromising their mental health. Hopefully, as defensiveness is considered in future research on emotional disclosure, psychologists will learn more about the role of emotional disclosure in health and illness.

REFERENCES

Buchsbaum, M. S. (1976). Self-regulation of stimulus intensity: Augmenting/reducing and the average evoked response. In G. E. Schwartz & D. Shapiro (Eds.), *Consciousness and self-regulation* (pp. 101–135). Plenum Press: New York.

Connolly, J. F. (1986). Evoked potential augmenting-reducing: A weak link in the biology-personality chain. *Behavioral and Brain Sciences, 9*(4), 746–747.

Cowley, J. J. & Brooksbank, B. W. (1991). Human Exposure to Putative Pheromones and Changes in Aspects of Social Behaviour. *Journal of Steroid Biochemistry and Molecular Biology, 39* (4b), 647–659.

Crowne, D. & Marlowe, D. (1964). *The approval motive: Studies in evaluative dependence.* New York: Wiley.

Dorries, K. M., Schmidt, H. J., Beauchamp, G. K., & Wysocki, C. J. (1989). Changes in sensitivity to the odor of androstenone during adolescence. *Developmental Psychobiology, 22*(5), 423–435.

Erdelyi, M. H. (1990). Repression, reconstruction, and defense: History and integration of the psychoanalytic and experimental frameworks. In J. L. Singer (Ed.), *Repression and Dissociation,* (pp. 1–31) Chicago: University of Chicago Press.

Esterling, B. A., Antoni, M. H., Kumar, M., & Schneiderman, N. (1990). Emotional repression, stress disclosure responses, and Epstein-Barr viral capsid antigen titers. *Psychosomatic Medicine, 52,* 397–410.

Esterling, B. A., Antoni, M. H., Kumar, M., & Schneiderman, N. (1993). Defensiveness, trait anxiety, and Epstein-Barr viral capsid antigen titers in healthy college students. *Health Psychology, 12*(2), 132–139.

Eysenck, H. J., & Eysenck, S. B. G. (1987). *Manual of the Eysenck Personality Questionnaire.* London: Hodder and Stoughton.

Henriques, J. B., & Davidson, R. J. (1991). Left frontal hypoactivation in depression. *Journal of Abnormal Psychology, 100,* 535–545.

Holroyd, K. (1972). Repression-sensitization, Marlowe-Crowne defensiveness, and perceptual defense. *Proceedings of the 80th Annual Convention of the American Psychological Association, 81,* 401–402.

Jamner, L. D. & Schwartz, G. E. (1986). Self-deception predicts self report and endurance of pain. *Psychosomatic Medicine, 48*(3/4), 211–223.

Jamner, L. D., Schwartz, G. E. & Leigh, H. (1988). The relationship between repressive and defensive coping styles and monocyte, eosinophile, and serum glucose levels: Support for the opioid peptide hypothesis of repression. *Psychosomatic Medicine, 50*(6), 567–575.

Kleiger, J. H., & Kinsman, R. A. (1980). The development of an MMPI alexithymia scale. *Psychotherapy and Psychosomatics, 34,* 17–24.

Kline, J. P., Schwartz, G. E., & Dikman, Z. V. (1994). *Defensiveness Predicts Olfactory Sensitivity for Androstenone, a Putative Human Sex Pheromone: Olfactory Perceptual Defense?.* Manuscript submitted for publication.

Kline, J. P., Schwartz, G. E., & Dikman, Z. V. (1993). Repressive and defensive subjects show selective anosmia for androstenone. *Chemical Senses, 18*(5), 581.

Kline, J. P., Schwartz, G. E., Fitzpatrick, D. F., & Hendricks, S. E. (1993). Defensiveness, anxiety, and the amplitude/intensity function of auditory evoked potentials. *International Journal of Psychophysiology 15,* 7–14.

Lane, R. D., Merikangas, K. R., Schwartz, G. E., Huang, S. S., & Prusoff, B. A. (1990). Inverse relationship between defensiveness and lifetime prevalence of psychiatric disorder. *American Journal of Psychiatry, 147,* 573–578.

Lane, R. D., & Schwartz, G. E. (1987). Levels of emotional awareness: A cognitive-developmental theory and its application to psychopathology. *American Journal of Psychiatry, 144,* 133–143.

Lane, R. D., & Schwartz, G. E. (1992). Levels of emotional awareness: Implications for psychotherapeutic integration. *Journal of Psychotherapy Integration, 2*(1), 1–18.

Paulhus, D. L., & Reid, D. B. (1991). Enhancement and denial in socially desirable responding. *Journal of Personality and Social Psychology, 60*(2), 307–317.

Schalling, D., Edman, G., & Asberg, M. (1983). Impulsive cognitive style and inability to tolerate boredom: Psychobiological studies of temperamental vulnerability. In M. Zuckerman (Ed.), *Biological bases of sensation seeking, impulsivity, and anxiety* (pp. 123–145). Hillsdale, NJ: Erlbaum.

Schmidt, H. J., & Beauchamp, G. K. (1988). Adult-like odor preferences and aversions in three-year-old children. *Child Development, 59*, 1136–1143.

Schwartz, G. E. (1990). Psychobiology of repression and health: A systems approach. In J. L. Singer (Ed.), *Repression and dissociation* (pp. 405–434). Chicago: University of Chicago Press.

Schwartz, G. E., Bell, I. R., Dikman, Z. V., Fernandez, M., Kline, J. P., Peterson, J. M., & Wright, K. P. (1994). EEG responses to low level chemicals in normals and cacosmics. *Journal of Toxicology and Industrial Health, 10*(4/5), 633–644.

Schwartz, G. E., Kline, J. P., Dikman, Z. V., & Polak, E. H. (1993). EEG registration of conscious and unconscious concentrations of isoamyl acetate and androstenone. *Chemical Senses, 18*(5), 625.

Schwartz, G. E., Kline, J. P., Dikman, Z. V., Wright, K. P., & Polak, E. H. (1992). EEG registration of androstenone in androstenone anosmic subjects. *Chemical Senses, 17*(5), 694.

Schwartz, G. E., Schwartz, J. I., Eichling, P. S., & Yokum, D. (1992). EEG alpha is correlated with natural killer cell activity. *Psychophysiology, 29* (suppl. 4A), 63.

Schwartz, G. E., Schwartz, J. I., Kline, J. P., & Eichling, P. (1992). Topographic EEG maps of defensiveness and repressive coping. *Psychophysiology, 29* (suppl. 4A), 63.

Singer, J. L. (1990). *Repression and dissociation: Implications for personality theory, psychopathology, and health.* Chicago: University of Chicago Press.

Tomarkin, A. J., & Davidson, R. J. (1994). Frontal brain activation in repressors and nonrepressors. *Journal of Abnormal Psychology, 103*(2), 339–349.

Weinberger, D. A., Schwartz, G. E., & Davidson, R. J. (1979). Low-anxious, high-anxious, and repressive coping styles: Psychometric patterns and behavioral and physiological responses to stress. *Journal of Abnormal Psychology, 88*, 369–380.

Wysocki, C. J., & Beauchamp, G. K. (1984). Ability to smell androstenone is genetically determined. *Proceedings of the National Academy of Sciences, 81*, 4899–4902.

10

Confrontation: Inhibition, Alexithymia, and Health

Dario Paez, Nekane Basabe, Maite Valdoseda,
Carmen Velasco, and Ioseba Iraurgi

This chapter presents our team's research into alexithymia, emotional coping, and health. First of all, we will briefly review the literature on the positive effect of confrontation on physical and mental health. We will then set out the basic elements of the alexithymia concept and scale (inability to identify and express emotions). The data on factorial, concurrent, and content validity of the Spanish version of Taylor et al.'s (1988) alexithymia scale will be presented. Next, we will also present data that confirm the association between alexithymia and inhibitory or avoiding styles of coping with emotions, as well as data on the predictive validity of alexithymia and inhibitory coping styles with regard to affective distress and health problems. Finally, we will show quasi-experimental data pertaining to the positive effect of participation in groups oriented toward improving affective coping, social sharing, and direct confrontation of stress, in the particular case of women with breast cancer. In this way we

The writing of this chapter and some of the research reported herein was supported by Grant UPV 109.230-H177/90 from the Basque Country University. We wish to thank the participants in the Taos Conference on Emotion, Disclosure and Health for their comments and suggestions. The authors would especially like to thank J. Pennebaker, G. Schwartz, W. Bucci, G. Bellelli, and the anonymous reviewer for their constructive comments on this chapter.

hope to present an overall picture of the research being carried out by our team and other scholars in Spain on the relation between emotional inhibition, as a personal characteristic and as a coping form, and affective distress and adjustment to serious diseases. We will also show the heuristic value of the alexithymia construct, and the relevance of the Pennebaker et al.'s program on the negative effect that emotional inhibition has on health (Pennebaker, 1989a, 1989b).

SOCIAL SUPPORT, EMOTIONAL COPING, SOCIAL SHARING, AND EMOTIONAL RECOVERY

Folkman and Lazarus (1988) viewed coping as a mediator of emotional reactions to stressful life events. Historically, coping has been seen primarily as a response to emotion. These responses are usually conscious strategies used by the individual (Endler & Parker, 1990).

Social support can be conceived of as a coping assistance: For instance, emotional support is seen as an aid to cope with emotions (Thoits, 1986). Coping functions refer to the goal, or purpose, that is assigned to a coping reaction. Any type of coping reaction can serve different functions (Folkman & Lazarus, 1988). The main coping functions are (a) problem-solving ("I wanted to solve the problem"); (b) regulating emotions—lessening emotional distress or amplifying emotional relations (in order to feel better); (c) protecting self-esteem (". . . to justify myself"); and (d) managing and shaping social interactions (". . . I wanted to make my partner feel better or get involved") (Laux & Weber, 1991). For example, social sharing or talking about feelings after a stressful event might be aimed toward solving problems (e.g., to be viewed as weak, so that others feel compelled to help), to lessen emotional distress (in order to vent and organize emotions), to protect self-esteem (e.g., to manage self-presentation by justifying an action: "I was very upset . . .") or it might aim at managing interactions (e.g., to show intimacy and self-disclosure, getting the partner to become more involved—see Ríme, chapter 14, this book). In this chapter we will focus on emotional coping and socioemotional aids to cope with emotions.

Types and Dimensions of Coping: Theoretical and Empirical Dimensions

Two general categories of coping are those of problem- and emotion-focused coping. Problem-focused coping includes information-seeking and problem-solving; emotion-focused coping is composed of affect regulation and emotional discharge. This latter class of behavior includes hostile confrontation, emotional discharge, and seeking emotional support (Barnett & Gottlib, 1988; Folkman & Lazarus, 1986). A distinction that must be made, and which although it does not perfectly correspond to the problem-solving and emotional regulation distinction does overlap with this one, is that between active coping (behavioral or cognitive efforts to manage a stressful event directly) and avoidance (attempts to avoid dealing with the problem or reduce tension through escapist behavior ; Taylor, 1990). People who rely more heavily on cognitive avoidance, emotional discharge, and resigned acceptance tended to report increases in depression, physical symptoms, and drinking problems. In contrast, reliance on active coping responses, such as cognitive redefinition and problem-solving, is associated with high self-esteem (Moos, 1988). In fact, viewed as coping reactions, emotional discharge, seeking emotional support, and cognitive and behavioral avoidance or inhibition are all moderately intercorrelated and are positively correlated with the trait of anxiety. This group of coping strategies tended to be inversely correlated with theoretically more positive strategies, that is, active coping and planning (Carver, Scheier, & Weintraub, 1989). Empirically, in Spanish research with a random sample of young adolescents, we found six dimensions of coping. We performed a factor analysis on a questionnaire with 17 items representing active direct coping, planning, reevaluation, suppression, seeking instrumental social support, seeking cognitive social support, seeking emotional support, venting or discharging emotions, denial, cognitive avoidance, behavioral avoidance, and disengagement by means of alcohol or other activities. Subjects stated how often they coped with the most important life event of the last year, using the reactions listed above. (1 = *never* to 4 = *often;* Basabe, Valdoseda, & Paez, 1993).

We found the following dimensions of coping: (a) *Confrontation Coping:* defined by planning, active coping, focusing on the problem, restraining, self-blaming, and positive reappraisal coping; (b) *Cognitive and Behavioral Avoidance:* disengagement through alcohol or by means of other activities, feeling unable to solve the problem, denial, and confrontive anger; (c) *Inhibition and Self-Blame:* fantasizing, repressing feelings, and self-blaming; (d) *Social Sharing and Social Support:* social sharing, seeking informative social support, and seeking emotional support; (e) *Internal Rehearsal:* rumination and reappraisal; and (f) *Discharge–Passive Coping:* venting and discharging emotions and passiveness. In a second study, with adult subjects and using a similar instrument and procedure, we found four factors. The first factor included three items: "I talked to someone about how I felt, I discussed my feelings with someone;" "I tried to get emotional support from friends or relatives, I sought sympathy and understanding," and "I felt very emotionally moved and I found myself expressing those feelings to many other people." This factor may be interpreted as the Social Sharing and Discharging dimension, confirming that sharing and venting emotions are related. The second factor included four items: "I hid from other people how I felt," "I avoided being with people," "I refused to believe that it had happened," and "I drank alcohol or took drugs in order to think less about it." This factor may be interpreted as an Emotional Inhibition and Avoidance dimension. The third factor included five items: "I thought about how I could modify the problem," "I talked to someone to find out more about the situation and I asked for other people's opinions," "I concentrated my efforts on doing something about it," "I voluntarily thought about what had happened in order to understand and explain what had happened," and "I tried to see it in a different light." This factor may be interpreted as the Cognitive–Active Confrontation coping strategy, including reappraisal. The fourth factor included two items: "I made a plan of action to solve the problem and I followed it" and "I concentrated my efforts on doing something about it." This factor may be interpreted as a Planning and Confrontation coping strategy.

To conclude, empirical results suggest that direct confrontation and cognitive confrontation are dimensions that are different from inhibition and avoidance coping. The inhibition and avoidance coping reactions were independent of each other in one study, but they formed part of a common dimension in a second sample.

SOCIAL SUPPORT, SITUATIONAL CONSTRAINT, AND COPING STRATEGIES

Consistent with Thoits's (1986) concept of social support as a source of coping assistance, individuals who enjoyed more social resources, especially from friends, relied more heavily on logical analyses and cognitive redefinition, sought more information and support, and engaged in more active problem solving. Respondents who had fewer social resources tended to rely more heavily on passive forms of coping: cognitive and behavioral avoidance, resigned acceptance, and emotional discharge (Moos, 1988). Consistent with literature in English, subjects who enjoyed less subjective social support relied more on negative forms of coping (cognitive and behavioral avoidance in the research with young adolescents and inhibition in the research with adults). The research with young adolescents confirm that negative affect increases with higher stress and inhibition. If the variables of objective and subjective social support are included in the regression analysis, the influence of coping styles on affect balance disappears (Basabe, Valdoseda, & Paez, 1993). Social support may act in this case as a source of external help in developing coping with stressful occurrences. Specifically, objective support facilitates the search for social support and affect regulation and diminishes cognitive avoidance. Subjective support acts on coping by impeding cognitive and behavioral avoidance.

In a longitudinal study with 43 Spanish breast cancer patients (see below), objective and subjective social support indicated some coherent tendencies of association with coping and affect. The mean of these correlations was between .15 and .20 (e.g., the predictive mean for objective support with positive affect was .16). Even though the association of these variables can be considered as medium, they were not thought to be significant because of the low number of subjects. Objective and subjective support coherently predicted direct coping and appraisal. Moreover, after 14 months these were positive affect predictors (Gabaldón, Mayoral, & Paez, 1993).

Research on the relation between situational constraints and coping (Folkman & Lazarus, 1988; Mattlin, Wethington, & Kessler, 1990) found that subjects used more problem-focused forms of coping in encounters they appraised as changeable, and more emotion-focused forms of coping in situations where they saw few, if any, options for affecting the outcome. These results were replicated in Spain (Calvete & Sampedro, 1990). Finally, some events cannot be changed and in these cases discharge–passive coping may be adaptive. What type of affective and cognitive coping can improve emotional recovery in these cases? We will review when and why inhibitory coping is dysfunctional for affect regulation and recovery.

EMOTIONAL INHIBITION AS PERSONAL DISPOSITION AND COPING STYLE

Inhibition has four defining features: a lower level of thinking about emotions, a dissociation between subjective and somatic emotional reactions, deficit of communication about emotions, and a conflict between tendency to confide and repression of this tendency. Inhibition is conceived of as a coping style, including cognitive–behavioral avoidance and emotional repression. An inhibitory coping style is related to a personal disposition (repression and alexithymia), to extreme stress (i.e., traumatic events), and to fewer social resources and lower social support (Pennebaker, 1989b). Inhibition is similar to extreme suppression, or rigid avoidance of internal and external emotional cues. Inhibition is different from voluntary suppression of emotional activation (counting to 10 before exploding in anger), "normal" illusions, and minimizing negative life aspects. Finally, what is distressing is not the absence of self-disclosure of emotions, but the concealment of a tendency toward self-disclosure (Derlega, Metts, Petronio & Pennebaker, 1989b; Margulis, 1993; Traue & Pennebaker, 1993; Vaillant, 1990).

Alexithymia: Definition and Measurement

The alexithymia construct focuses on the relationship between levels of emotional awareness and communication, and susceptibility to somatic illness. Individuals with alexithymia are often unable to produce vivid images in their minds, have difficulty juggling complex thoughts, and are low in creativity. This is derived from psychoanalysts' earlier observations that many patients suffering from posttraumatic syndromes, psychosomatic diseases, or other chronic diseases manifest difficulties in the verbal and symbolic expression of emotion. Alexithymia is a multidimensional construct defined by difficulty in identifying and describing feelings, difficulty in distinguishing between feelings and bodily sensations, paucity of fantasies, and a concern with external events (Pedinielli, 1992; Taylor et al., 1988). Pennebaker suggests that alexithymia stems from active attempts to exclude from one's consciousness upsetting thoughts about emotional experiences. Alexithymia is particularly relevant to the lack of ability to be self-reflective, and the inhibition of emotion. It has been hypothesized that the limited emotional awareness and cognitive processing of affects leads to a focusing on, and amplification of, the somatic component of emotional arousal (Pennebaker, 1989a). This tendency might explain the proneness towards "functional" somatic complaints of individuals described as alexithymic, and an increased susceptibility to physical disease (Taylor, 1984).

The Toronto Alexithymia Scale (TAS) is a 26-item self-report measure developed by Taylor et al. (1988), composed of a five-point Likert scale (ranging from "strongly disagree" to "strongly agree"), with 42% of items negatively keyed to control for acquiescence responses. This 26-item scale demonstrated a high level of internal consistency (Cronbach's alpha = 0.79), as well as good test–retest reliability over a 3-month period. Factor analysis of the scale using principal–factor extraction with a varimax rotation produced a four-factor solution theoretically congruent with the alexithymia construct. The first three factors—difficulty identifying and distinguishing between feelings and bodily sensations (e.g., "I am often confused about what emotion I am feeling," "When I am upset, I don't know if I am sad, frightened, or angry"); difficulty communicating feelings (e.g., "I am able to describe my feelings easily" negatively keyed item, "It is difficult for me to find the right words for my feelings"); and reduced daydreaming (e.g., "Daydreaming is a waste of time," "I rarely daydream") corresponded to the main features of the alexithymia construct. The fourth factor, externally oriented thinking (e.g., "Knowing the answers to problems is more important than knowing the reasons for the answers"), correspond to the *pensée opératoire* initially described by Marty, de M'Uzan, and David (1963). Subsequent studies with clinical and nonclinical populations have shown that the factor structure of the TAS is stable and replicable. Construct validity of the TAS was further supported by results from several studies examining the relationship of the scale with other personality and psychopathological measures (Parker, Bagby, & Taylor, 1989).

The Spanish TAS 26-item scale showed a high level of internal consistency (Cronbach's alpha = 0.79), as well as good test–retest reliability over a two-month period (Test–retest = 0.63, N = 49). Confirmatory factor analysis of the Spanish scale produced a three factor solution theoretically congruent with the alexithymia construct. One factor was related to difficulty identifying and communicating feelings, a second factor with concern with external events, and a third factor with reduced imagery and fantasy (Paez & Velasco, 1993). Using the Taylor Manifest Anxiety Scale TMAS and the Marlowe-Crowne scale to define repressors (see Schwartz's chapter, this volume), we found that alexithymia, measured by the TAS scale, is positively associated with highly anxious subjects and is not related to repression (Paez, Vergara, & Velasco, 1991). In a sample of 180 students' relatives, the TAS (Spanish version) correlated moderately with the Beck Depression Inventory (BDI), with the Taylor Manifest Anxiety Scale (TMAS), and with a Psychosomatic Symptoms Checklist. In a sample of Spanish Multiple Sclerosis patients (N = 36), we found positive correlations with both the BDI and the Anxiety subscale of the SCL-90 (Paez, 1993). In a Spanish study on life events using normal adults, alexithymia covaried positively with an inhibition dimension and with negative affect. Adults ($N = 168$, 50.3% females, mean age $= 28.4$, range 17–54) were relatives of Basque Country psychology students and were asked to answer a short version of the Psychiatric Epidemiology Research Interview (PERI) and the Holmes and Rahe Life events scale. The questionnaire requires subjects to indicate which of these events they have experienced during the past year, choose the most important one, and answer how they coped with it (see the point on Types and Dimensions of Coping for dimensions and examples of the items: For instance the inhibition dimension was composed of "I hid from other people how I felt," "I avoided being with people," "I refused to believe that it had happened," and "I drank alcohol or took drugs in order to think less about it"). Original positive affect scores and alexithymia show, using causal modeling, a significant direct effect on positive affect. Causal modeling and multiple regression allow us to test the specific influence of one factor (alexithymia in this case) controlling statistically the influence of other relevant factors (social support, coping, initial affect) on a dependent variable (in this particular case affect two months later). These results mean that alexithymia is related to inhibitory coping reactions and predicts a lower positive affect two months later in a sample of adults, controlling the initial level of positive affect.

A very interesting question in this context, suggested by an anonymous reviewer, is what would happen if individuals high on alexithymia were asked to engage in disclosure? In a partial replication of Pennebaker's research (1989) subjects ($N = 108$, psychology students, 65% females) were randomly assigned to a control group or to write for 20 minutes during three different days once per day on traumatic and social events (instructions were exactly the same as those found in Pennebaker's research: to write about their feelings and thoughts related to the traumatic and social event). The dependent variables, measured during a first session previous to being assigned to the control or writing condition 1 and 2 months later, were rumination, avoidance (the short Spanish version of Horowitz's Impact of Event scale), event appraisal (just or unjust; controllable or uncontrollable, etc.), positive and negative affect (Bradburn's PNA scale), self reported physical symptoms (Pennebaker's LSE scale) and the impact of having to re-evoke (induced arousal and mood—see Rimé, chapter 14, this book). Subjects also answered the TAS scale and those subjects who scored above the median were considered as high on alexithymia. Correlations between the first session measures confirm that subjects high on alexithymia have high scores on negative affect balance, physical symptoms, show more rumination and cognitive avoidance of the traumatic and social event, shared the traumatic and social event less, made a bigger effort in order to avoid disclosure, and felt that they had not disclosed enough. These results are important because they show that subjects high on alexithymia are simultaneously prone to both ruminate and avoid, and to have problems with self-disclosure—they actively try to conceal disclosure and feel that they do not share sufficiently. We conducted a repeated measures Multiple Analysis of Variance, which allows us to examine, controlling the initial scores, changes in the dependent variables. As regards to the main effects of writing, and not taking into account the level of alexithymia, writing provokes a positive change in the impact of having to re-evoke (diminishes the negative mood induced by re-evocation), less physical symptoms (1 month later) and higher affect balance (higher positive affect and lower negative affect 2 months later). These results partially confirm the positive effects of induced disclosure and self-reflection (see Pennebaker and Rimé, chapters 1 and 14, this book). However, rumination, avoidance, and general appraisal of the traumatic and social event was not changed by induced disclosure—most of the events were previously shared and probably general appraisal as well as ruminatory and inhibitory memory processes were stabilized. An interesting result of this experimental research was the significant interaction between high and low alexithymia, time, and induced confrontation or disclosure. Individuals high on alexithymia assigned to the writing condition showed an improvement on affect balance. Moreover, individuals high on alexithymia who were asked to confront diminished the avoidance of remembering the traumatic and social event 2 months later. The high and low alexithymia control group shows no change on affectivity or on avoidance. Individuals low on alexithymia who were asked to write suffer a slight decrease on the affect balance and an increase in avoidance. This suggests that inducing social sharing or symbolic disclosure and confrontation in subjects high on alexithymia has more important positive effects on emotions and assimilation of the traumatic and social event. Subjects low in alexithymia who normally disclose, suffer slightly of induced disclosure on the short term. Because of the absence of direct health measures we do not know the effects on the physical state in the long term. However we should remember that disclosure provokes a global positive effect on self-reported physical symptoms 1 month later (Paez, Velasco, & Basabe, 1995). Briefly, our results suggest positive effects for induced disclosure in the case of subjects above the median of alexithymia in a healthy and young sample.

Previous criticisms suggest that alexithymia is not a clear construct, does not have a reliable instrument, and may be mistaken with the repressive coping style (Bonanno & Singer, 1990). Our results show that the alexithymia scale is reliable, shows concurrent and predictive validity with emotional distress, and is independent of repression. Finally, it is important to note some problems we may find with respect to alexithymia. Is it a personal disposition or is it related to deficits in social support? Some of our data show that both alexithymia and subjective social support are related to inhibition as coping reactions, and that the relationship between subjective support and alexithymia is negative, but of a weak or medium nature ($-.08$, *ns*, and $-.29$, $p < .05$, for a normal sample and breast cancer patients, respectively), suggesting that they are a more or less independent phenomena. Is alexithymia a stable trait or an effect of a traumatic event? Some data confirm the latter idea. Victims of traumatic events show emotional numbing and difficulties in personal relationships. Patients with serious illnesses also show emotional inhibition and a focus on the somatic aspects of their problems (Pedinielli, 1992). We can conclude, tentatively, that in some cases deficits in social sharing of emotions are due to the impact of strong negative stressful or chronic events, while in other cases they are related to deficits in social support, and probably in other cases are related to more stable personal dispositions.

INHIBITORY OR AVOIDANT AND APPROACHING–CONFRONTATION COPING AND EMOTIONAL ADJUSTMENT

Inhibition, or avoidant emotional coping, is potentially unhealthy in two ways (Pennebaker, 1989a). First of all, the work of inhibition serves as a cumulative stressor. Second, the failure to talk about, and to account for, the stressful event impedes the cognitive–affective assimilation process. Stressful events that are not assimilated are more likely to remain in the consciousness as unwanted and ruminative thoughts, and the suppression of these thoughts is associated with increased physiological arousal (Wegner, Shortt, Blake, & Page, 1990). A number of researches have shown that individuals who use inhibitory (repressive) coping strategies in the face of stressful life events exhibit increased objective health problems (Weinberger, 1990). Research on a sample of women with breast cancer using the Marlowe-Crowne and the Taylor MAS scales in order to classify repressors, and the three other subtypes, found that repressors reported significantly less negative emotion, yet their rate of remission was 46% lower than nonrepressors (Schwartz, 1990). In addition to health problems, repressors or subjects who do not confront emotions have a deficit of affective memory (a less clear, less articulated memory of negative emotions) (Davis, 1990). Similar results were found for affective memory in Spain (Paez, 1993). In our research with breast cancer patients, defining repressors with the TMAS and Marlowe-Crowne scales, the repressors displayed better affect adjustment. As we have previously said, and in agreement with some studies, repressors control negative affect and may be better able to accept the illness. Given that (fortunately) there is no "variability" in relapses or death rate, we do not know if being a repressor is associated with a worse illness development or not.

Inhibitory or avoidant (cognitive and behavioral) coping styles are related to depression, neuroticism, and health problems. However, we cannot simply conclude that cognitive approaches to negative affective reactions are healthy or improve emotional regulation. Suls and Fletcher's meta-analysis review of the relative efficacy of avoidant and nonavoidant coping strategies shows that avoidance was associated with more positive adaptation in the short term (Suls & Fletcher, 1985). Sensitizers, individuals who appeared to contrast with repressors by showing a vigilant and ruminative style of information processing and an overly disclosive pattern of self-presentation, also show vulnerability in the face of stress. Some data show that this coping style is associated with cardiovascular disease and that the repressor style is associated with cancer (Bonnano & Singer, 1990; Taylor, 1990). Pennebaker (1989a) also found that both chronic low-level thinkers (similar to repressors) and chronic high-level dwellers on emotions (similar to sensitizers) run the risk of emotional distress and health problems. A behavioral and cognitive ruminatory style, as opposed to a positive distraction coping style, is related to depression (Nolen-Hoeksema, 1991). Rumination can be conceived of as involuntary and obsessional thoughts or dreams related to a stressful event (Norris, 1990). On the other hand, rumination can be conceived of as a voluntary effort to think the event over. For instance, Morrow and Nolen-Hoeksema (1990) defined ruminative responses as cognition and behavior that repetitively focuses the depressed individual's attention on his or her symptoms and the possible causes and consequences of those symptoms. Rumination intensifies negative affective reactions (Nolen-Hoeksema, 1991; Nolen-Hoeksema & Morrow, 1991). Rumination can appear to increase the likelihood of individuals recalling negative information and making negative inferences about events; rumination can enhance the effects of existing maladaptive cognitive styles by bringing maladaptive cognitions to the individual's mind relatively more often, thereby amplifying the depressed mood. Finally, rumination interferes with attention, concentration, and the initiation of instrumental behavior (Morrow & Nolen-Hoeksema, 1990).

Nevertheless, some researchers have argued that rumination may provide benefits because it may enable one to find meaning in, and gain mastery over, traumatic events by developing an understanding of these events and by developing coping strategies (e.g., Horowitz, 1986; Martin & Tesser, 1989). Nevertheless, empirical research on coping shows that active cognitive coping and positive reappraisal (two forms of cognitive coping similar to Martin and Tesser's conception of mental rumination) reinforce negative affect (Billings & Moos, 1982; Folkman & Lazarus, 1988; Mattlin et al., 1990). Billings and Moos (1982) and Mattlin et al. (1990), documented in a multivariate analysis that cognitive and behavioral elements of active coping have opposite effects on emotional adjustment. The Mattlin et al. results suggest that approaching cognitive coping or active cognitive coping is maladaptive only when it is used outside larger versatile coping, and that thinking about ways to improve a situation raises levels of anxiety and depression when it is not followed by subsequent action. Similar results were found for another cognitive approach to coping: positive reevaluation or coping with stress by reappraisal or positive reinterpretation of events. Folkman and Lazarus (1988) found that positive reappraisal had a positive effect in a younger group, where it was associated with improved emotional states in three analyses. However, in an older group it was associated with an increase in distress (worry or fear) rather than a decrease. Folkman and Lazarus (1988) speculate that the reduction of distress achieved cognitively through positive reappraisal may be difficult to sustain when faced with external and internal cues in the form of intrusive thoughts and images associated with the inhibition of negative thinking brought about by positive reappraisal. Our results, with a sample of young adolescents, show that internal rumination (as a dimension distinct from active cognitive coping) and inhibitory coping independent from active coping, have deleterious effects on affect-controlling for stress and objective and subjective social support effects.

But the problem we face is this: When is confronting (i.e., expressing, talking, and thinking about) a negative affect event harmful and when is it adaptive? One possible answer to this question is suggested by Wood, Saltzberg, Neale, Stone, and Rachmiel's (1990) research. The Wood et al. measures of active coping and rumination had opposite relationships with negative mood, but they shared a common feature: thinking about the problem. The direct action measure asked not only whether respondents "actually did something," but also whether they "thought about solutions to the problem," and the rumination measure asked whether they found themselves "dwelling on it, focusing on how bad it was and even intensifying its negative aspects." One answer to the question we posited would then be as follows: Thinking about a problem is adaptive (improves negative affective state) when it is action-oriented (active cognitive coping or cognitive planning action). Thinking about the event can be related to other active cognitive coping strategies not directly related to direct action, such as positive reappraisal: "I look for something good in what is happening" (Mattlin et al., 1990; Folkman & Lazarus, 1988; Carver et al., 1989). In other words, thinking about an autobiographical event is harmful for emotional recovery when it is state-oriented (i.e., dwelling on one's past, present, or future state). In contrast to an understanding (reappraisal) or action orientation, (focusing on alternative plans of actions to achieve a goal), state orientation corresponds to brooding about a problem's negative aspects (Wood et al., 1990).

We can conclude that state-oriented, rigidly and reactively ruminating, and cognitive approaches to negative affective reactions can be unhealthy in the short term, and sometimes in the long-term (sensitizers' coping style). On the other hand, expressing emotion and confronting others may also be maladaptive. With regard to discharging emotions and emotional regulation, confrontive coping was consistently associated in research with worse emotional states (Folkman & Lazarus, 1988; Tavris, 1984). Our results with a sample of young adolescents show that confrontational or direct coping and emotional discharge have ambivalent results: They are related to positive and negative affect (Basabe et al., 1993). Perhaps expressing negative affect (i.e., sadness, anger, and hostility) does not always provide the relief that is suggested in the aphorism "Getting it off your chest makes you feel better." In fact the findings suggest that expressing anger and hostility may make a person feel worse. Support for this idea comes from research (Folkman & Lazarus, 1986; Barnett & Gottlib, 1988) which found that people who were high in depressive symptoms used more emotion discharge, seeking social support, and confrontive coping than did people who were low in depressive symptoms. However, confronting and sharing emotions may be adaptive (see Rimé, chapter 14, this book).

An anonymous reviewer has reminded us that most items in the emotional discharge coping scales are confounded with negative affect. Confounding negative affect with perceived stress and inadaptative coping is a real problem. Fortunately, the emotional discharge items were very general and not directly related to anger, fear and anxiety. On the other hand, if we separate the sample on the basis of the positive and negative life events, we found that the results were stable. Venting emotions has a positive correlation with both positive and negative affect when subjects were coping with negative events, and to our surprise also when they cope with positive life events. This suggests that the association between discharge and negative affect is not capable of explaning these results by itself.

Finally, timing is an important element related to the functional or dysfunctional role of inhibition and confrontation. The impact of timing as a mediator of social support may help explain why some studies find that social support, at least when it involves emotional coping by confrontation (i.e., talking about feelings), is beneficial after (e.g., Pennebaker, 1989b) but not before (e.g., Hobfoll & London, 1985) confronting the stressful event. Hobfoll and London (1985) found that Israeli women whose husbands had been mobilized experienced greater psychological distress if they had confidants with whom to talk. Intimacy with friends (e.g., "I have friends with whom I can speak freely about what is important to me") was positively correlated with anxiety. Also the amount of social support received during the crisis period (e.g., sharing of feelings, tangible assistance or advice received during the crisis period) was positively correlated with depression. Costanza, Derlega and Winstead's (1988) experimental research indicates that talking about one's feelings with a friend in anticipation of a stressful event is less beneficial than talking with a friend about problem-solving or unrelated contents. Talking about one's feelings was associated with a relatively high level of negative affect (anxiety and depression scores). Suls and Fletcher's (1985) meta-analysis shows that emotional monitoring was associated with more negative outcomes in the short term. With regard to long-term outcomes, avoidance indicates better outcome initially, but with time, attention was associated with a more positive outcome. These results—based not only on laboratory data, but also on field data (i.e., childbirth, coronary illness)—confirm Pennebaker's results with traumatic and stressful life events: Confronting negative affective reactions produces short-term negative effects, and avoiding negative affective reactions causes short-term positive effects. Nevertheless, confronting negative affective reactions produces long-term positive effects on health and affect (Pennebaker, 1989a, 1989b).

CHRONIC STRESSORS AND COPING EFFECTS

For chronic negative stressors (cancer, bereavement, etc.) results are partially different. Work conducted with cancer patients indicates that, from the patient's perspective, the most appreciated kind of help in the earlier stages (initial crisis, diagnosis) is emotional support and assistance in emotional coping (providing the patient an opportunity to express feelings) (Ferrero, 1993; Taylor, 1990). Similar results were found for bereavement. Jacobson (1986) states that during the transition period, emotional support (a social-sharing focus on understanding and assimilating the emotional event) is the most important and effective response.

With respect to cancer and confrontation coping, three American studies and a Spanish study (Ferrero, 1993) confirm that the so-called "Fighting Spirit" style of coping with cancer, related to direct coping and to challenge appraisal, is associated with better adjustment to the disease. Optimism with regard to the prognosis is related to better adjustment in two studies (Friedman et al., 1988 and Mishel, Hostetter, King, & Graham, 1993). Confrontation coping reactions in specific situations (attempts to cope directly with the problem, seeking information about it) were not related to adjustment in one study (Friedman, Baer, Lewy, Lane, & Smith, 1993). Approaching coping, as an active implication in the concrete effects of disease and treatment, was related to better adjustment (Penman, 1993).

With regard to avoidant coping reactions, denying the reality of which the patient was previously informed of ("It is not true, I don't have breast cancer"), is a very common reaction and shows no effect on adjustment in two studies (Nelson, Friedman, Baer, Lane, & Smith, 1989; Friedman, Nelson, Baer, Lane & Smith, 1990) a negative effect in two studies (Carver, et al., 1993, Friedman et al., 1988, quoted in Ferrero, 1993) and predicts well-being better in Ferrero's Spanish research (Ferrero, 1993).

Minimization of threat ("I'm sick, but it's not so serious and I'm optimistic") as a coping reaction predicts adjustment better in another study

(Orr & Meyer, 1993). Wishful thinking, as a coping reaction in cancer patients, predicts negative affect in one study (Felton & Revenson, 1984). Cognitive–behavioral avoidance or disengagement is related to high affective distress in five studies with cancer patients (Friedman et al., 1988, 1990; Penman, 1993; Viney & Westbrook, 1993; Carver et al., 1993). However, some forms of avoidant coping show positive effects. Distancing, or cognitive suppression, shows a positive relationship with mental health in general (Vaillant, 1990). Suppression or capacity to stop thinking about, and to distract oneself from, negative events and emotions is related to low psychological distress, and ruminating is associated with negative affect (Meyerowitz, 1993; Filipp, Klauer, Freudenberg, & Ferring, 1993). Predictive regressions suggest that rumination can be more a result than an antecedent of negative affect (Meyerowitz, 1993; Filipp, Klauer, Freudenberg, & Ferring, 1993). Distraction by involvement in social activities shows a positive transversal relation with affective adjustment, but does not predict better (or worse) affect balance (Filipp et al., 1993).

With regard to cognitive–approaching coping, results confirm mostly adaptive effects—excluding rumination, which shows negative effects. Reappraisal and growth coping (e.g., I realized what was important in life) was associated with better adjustment in one research but it does not show any relation in another (Friedman et al., 1988 and Taylor, 1993, quoted in Ferrero, 1993). Positive social comparison (downward evaluation as opposed to upward comparison) is common in cancer patients (80–90% of breast cancer patients perform social comparison) and sometimes shows adaptive effects. However in a Spanish sample of cancer patients this cognitive coping reaction was not related to adjustment, and in another study upward comparisons more often led to positive than negative affect (Helgeson & Taylor, 1993). Searching for cognitive social support (seeking information) as a coping reaction when faced with cancer does not show a clear relation with affective adjustment to illness: one positive result, four neutral and one negative (Felton & Revenson, 1984, positive results; Friedman et al., 1990, negative results; Friedman et al., 1988; Nelson et al., 1989; Filipp et al., 1993, and Ferrero, 1993, for neutral results). Ferrero's results show no relation in a Spanish breast cancer sample between searching for information, as a coping reaction, and affective adjustment.

Acceptance ("I am in the hands of God"; "I have had a good life, what will be, will be"), different from fatalism, is related to better adjustment in two studies (Carver et al., 1993). In other cases, even if passive acceptance shows a relation with distress, the distress is lower than in subjects who show helplessness and resignation, or in people who show rumination or anxious worry (Watson et al., 1988; Ferrero, 1993).

Finally, confrontive coping (showing and expressing anger) as opposed to fatalism and low negative affect, predicts a better chance of survival in breast cancer patients. Rodin and Salovey (1989) found that repressor subjects had a poorer prognosis in the case of breast cancer. Likewise, in the oldest research reviewed by Temoshok and Heller (1986), it was also found that subjects suffering from cancer, but who had a better survival rate, presented higher affective expressiveness, including negative affect explosions of anger and rage. Temoshok and Heller concluded that cancer patients had difficulty in expressing their emotions, so suggesting the relevance of alexithymia as a predictive factor of cancer.

To conclude, direct instrumental and confrontive coping shows a positive relationship with adjustment to illness, probably by improving the sense of control in addition to better concrete-problem solving. Rumination and seeking information do not show a positive relationship, suggesting that rigid cognitive processing reinforces emotional problems when faced with chronic illness. Some types of inhibition (cognitive–behavioral avoidance and wishful thinking) reinforce emotional distress in cancer patients, which is congruent with general literature on inhibition. However, some types of self-control (distancing, distraction), cognitive distortion (denial, minimization), and acceptance are related to better adjustment, suggesting that some levels of illusory optimism and of acceptance and distraction are adaptive.

Support Groups, Coping, Alexithymia, Repression, and Affect: A Longitudinal Study With Breast Cancer Patients

If we extrapolate the previous results to a situation of coping with a threat posed by a chronic illness that has a probable fatal outcome—cancer—we should find that alexithymic subjects, and those who use inhibition, avoiding coping styles and emotional discharge, will later show a worse emotional state with regard to the balance of positive–negative affect. Subjects with better social support will have a stronger tendency toward more active coping styles and a happier state of mind. The subjects in a social support and emotion confrontation treatment group should display better affective balance as well as more flexible and adaptive coping with the illness. In fact, Spiegel et al.'s classic study found that advanced breast cancer patients assigned to a weekly social support group lived longer than did a control group that met with physicians but did not participate in the social support group. It is interesting to note that the group session facilitators encouraged these women to share their emotions and coping strategies (Traue & Pennebaker, 1993). We performed a partial replication of this research (Gabaldon et al., 1993; see Table 1) with mastectomized patients treated between the years 1990–92 in the Obstetrics and Gynecological Section of the San Sebastian Hospital. There were 43 people between the age of 29 and 71 years, 18 in the control group and 25 in the experimental group. Because of deontological problems all the sample underwent individual support therapy. The subjects were evaluated when they underwent surgery (Time 1), and again 14 months after surgery (Time 2). Patients were randomly assigned either to an emotion confrontation support group or to a control group.

With the aim of verifying treatment effects, controlling for initial levels of positive affect, coping reactions, objective degree of seriousness of the illness, medical treatment, alexithymia ratings, being a repressor, and objective and subjective support, we applied multiple regression to affect in Time 2 using the above variables.

The multivariate coefficients confirm that a higher level of positive affect is positively associated with participation in the support group (treatment group = 2; control group = 1), with reappraisal and with repression. Results suggest that confrontation and positive cognitive processing of the illness improved adjustment. Affective discharge and avoidance were predictors of higher negative affect six to eight weeks after surgery. Alexithymia was negatively associated with affect balance (a positive associa-

| | Table 1 | | | |

Positive and Negative Affect: Multiple Regression Analysis and Correlations

	Positive Affect		Negative Affect	
Predictor Variable	r	beta	r	beta
Repressor (Yes = 1; No = 0)	.25*	.24&	−.26*	−.24&
Alexithymia	−.33**	−.09	.15	.27&
Objective Support	.11	.11	−.09	−.05
Subjective Support	.04	.03	.22&	.29&
Chemotherapy (Yes = 1; No = 0)	.13	.10	.17	−.24
Radiotherapy (Yes = 1; No = 0)	−.26*	−.50**	.21&	.18
Hormone therapy (Yes = 1; No = 0)	.19	.12	−.44**	−.55**
Illness Stage	.26*	.22	.02	.32&
Positive Affect Time One	.20&	.03	−.24*	
Negative Affect Time One	−.31*		.22&	.06
Group Therapy (No = 1; Yes = 2)	.41***	.33*	−.21&	−.24&
Reappraisal	.36**	.34*	.09	.26&

(& = $p < .10$; * = $p < .05$; ** = $p < .01$)

Note. Dependent Variables = Positive and Negative Affect—14 months after initial treatment—was measured by a Spanish version of Bradburn's PNA affect scale (the higher the rating the higher positive/negative affect).

tion with negative affect and vice versa). The regression shows that alexithymia specifically predicts only negative affect, but does not predict positive affect, probably because alexithymia is negatively related to reappraisal ($r = −.35, p < .01$).

Finally, negative affect is negatively associated with a higher level of repression (opposite to what happens to positive affect and repression), and positively with alexithymia and with affective discharge. We have found that support groups (emotion confrontation and problem resolution) improve quality of life (a better affect balance). This effect is particularly noticeable in the improvement of positive affect. Negative affect would appear to follow the ups and downs of stress and the objective threat posed by the illness.

Nevertheless, the lack of differences in coping strategies suggests that our group must have more structured and systematic ways of handling stress. We also believe that it is best to work with the couple (the patient's partner should be included), with the aim of improving help and stress management. Improving coping strategies (by reducing avoidance and affect discharge, by increasing direct coping and reframing of the situation) may allow us to improve even further the patient's quality of life. The predictive nature of coping styles reaffirm the importance of improving them to produce an increase in the quality of life.

These conclusions are in accordance with the "Adjuvant Therapy" orientation. This orientation is aimed precisely at getting patients to cope actively, increase their problem-solving abilities, regulate their negative thoughts and feelings, and to express their feelings and not inhibit or avoid them. It also suggests the need to include the partner and to improve social communication skills (Ibáñez, 1991).

GENERAL CONCLUSIONS

We were able to confirm the reliability and validity of the alexithymia scale. As regards the construct validity, results confirm that alexithymia is related to avoidant–inhibitory coping reactions and impedes cognitive reevaluation. Alexithymia is associated with inhibition (normal adults) and negatively related to reevaluation (breast cancer patients). Apart from being related to negative coping reactions and impeding positive ones, a high alexithymia score predicts low positive affect.

With regard to negative effects of passive and avoidant forms of coping, inhibition–coping predicts a negative affect balance. On the other hand, with regard to cognitive–confrontation coping, correlational and longitudinal research shows that rumination, and sometimes reappraisal, does not help affective assimilation. These results reaffirm the idea that rigid and chronic high levels of thinking on emotion can intensify distress. Similarly, venting or discharging emotion as a coping reaction is related to negative affect. These longitudinal results are coherent with coping literature: extreme expression of emotion and extreme rumination of stressful events are related to emotional distress. However, congruent with literature on inhibition, inhibition–avoidance reinforces the affective impact of negative events. Confirming the adaptive effect of cognitive confrontation for chronic stressors, reappraisal reinforces positive affect for breast cancer patients. For these patients reasserting the positive effects of social support and confrontation coping, and participation in a treatment group is related to a higher level of positive affect. Having a limited number of subjects does not allow us to test whether patients high in alexithymia improve more by participating in the treatment group. However, at least the results confirm that the group has a positive effect, even if subjects have a high alexithymia score. Clearer results were found with healthy young students. Induced disclosure of traumatic and social events improves affect, diminishes self-reported physical symptoms and the impact of re-evoking these events. This effect on affectivity was more positive for individuals high in alexithymia, at the same time, inducing a decrease in the cognitive and behavioral avoidance of cues related to the traumatic and social events. These optimistic results must be viewed with some caution because subjects in the sample were above median, and not extremely high scorers on the TAS scale. Globally, we may conclude that inducing self-disclosure has more positive effects on affect and affective memory processes for those subjects who share less and inhibit more the disclosure confrontation. Lower dispositional self-disclosure does not impede the positive effects of social support and confrontation coping.

REFERENCES

Barnett, P. A., & Gottlib, I. H. (1988). Psychosocial functioning and depression: Distinguishing among antecedents, concomitants and consequences. *Psychological Bulletin, 104*, 97–126.

Basabe, N., Valdoseda, M., & Paez, D. (1993). Memoria afectiva, salud, formas de afrontamiento y soporte social [Affective memory, health, coping, and social support]. In D. Paez (Ed.), *Salud, expresión y represión social de las emociones* [Health, expression and social repression of emotions] (pp. 339–376). Valencia, Spain: Promolibro.

Billings, A. G., & Moos, R. H. (1982). Stressful life events and symptoms: A longitudinal model. *Health Psychology, 1,* 99–118.

Bonanno, G. A., & Singer, J. L. (1990). Repressive personality style. In J. L. Singer (Ed.), *Repression and dissociation.* Chicago: The Chicago University Press.

Calvete, E., & Sampedro, R. (1990). Dimensiones de los eventos estresantes y estilos de afrontamiento [Dimensions of stressful life events and coping styles]. In J. Rodriguez Marín (Ed.), *Aspectos psicosociales de la salud y de la comunidad* [Psychosocial aspects of health and community]. Actas del II Congreso Nacional de Psicología Social. Alicante, Abril 6–8, 1988: PPU, pp. 150–160.

Carver, C. S., Scheier, M. F., & Weintraub, J. K. (1989). Assessing coping strategies: A theoretically based approach. *Journal of Personality and Social Psychology, 56,* 267–283.

Carver, C. S., Pozo, C., Harris, S. D., Noriega, V., Scheier, M. F., Robinson, D. S., Ketcham, A. S., Moffat, F. L., & Clark, K. C. (1993). How coping mediates the effects of optimism on distress: A study of women with early stage breast cancer. *Journal of Personality and Social Psychology, 65,* 375–391.

Costanza, R. S., Derlega, V. J., & Winstead, B. A. (1988). Positive and negative forms of social support: Effects of conversational topics on coping with stress among same-sex friends. *Journal of Experimental Social Psychology, 24,* 182–193.

Davis, P. J. (1990). Repression and the inaccessibility of emotional memories. In J. L. Singer (Ed.), *Repression and dissociation.* Chicago: The Chicago University Press.

Derlega, V., Metts, S., Petronio, S., & Margulis, S. T. (1993). *Self-Disclosure.* Newbury Park: Sage.

Endler, N. S., & Parker, J. A. (1990). Multidimensional assessment of coping: A critical evaluation. *Journal of Personality and Social Psychology, 58,* 844–854.

Felton, B. I, & Revenson, T. A. (1984). Coping with chronic illness: A study of illness controllability and the influence of coping strategies on psychological adjustment. *Journal of Consulting and Clinical Psychology, 52,* 343–353.

Ferrero, J. (1993). *El afrontamiento de un diagnóstico de cáncer* [Coping with a cancer diagnostic]. Valencia, Spain: Promolibro.

Filipp, S. H., Klauer, T., Freudenberg, E., & Ferring, D. (1993). The regulation of subjective well-being in cancer patients: An analysis of coping effectiveness. Psychology and Health, 4, 305.317. In J. Ferrero (Ed.) *El afrontamiento de un diagnóstico de cáncer.* Valencia, Spain: Promolibro.

Folkman, S., & Lazarus, R. S. (1986). *Estrés y procesos cognitivos* [Stress and cognitive processes]. Barcelona, Spain: Martinez Roca.

Folkman, S., & Lazarus, R. S. (1988). Coping as a mediator of emotion. *Journal of Personality and Social Psychology, 54,* 466–475.

Friedman, L. C., Baer, P. E., Lewy, A., Lane, M., & Smith, F. E. (1988). Predictors of psychosocial adjustment to breast cancer. *Journal of Psychosocial Oncology, 6,* 75–94.

Friedman, L. C., Nelson, D. V., Baer, P. E., Lane, M., & Smith, F. E. (1990). Adjustment to breast cancer: A replication study. *Journal of Psychosocial Oncology, 8,* 27–40.

Gabaldón, O., Mayoral, J. L., & Paez, D. (1993). Afectividad, apoyo social, represión, alexitimia y grupos de apoyo [Affect, social support, repression, alexithymia, and supportive groups]. *Boletín de Psicología, 41,* 31–55.

Helgeson, V. S., & Taylor, S. E. (1993). Social comparisons and adjustment among cardiac patients. *Journal of Applied Social Psychology, 23,* 1171–1195.

Hobfoll, S. E. & London, P. (1985). The relationship of self-concept and social support to emotional distress among women during war. *Journal of Social and Clinical Psychology, 3,* 231–248.

Horowitz, M. (1986). *Stress response syndrome.* Northvale, NJ: Aronson.

Ibáñez, E. (1991). *Psicología de la salud y estilos de vida* [Health psychology and lifestyles]. Valencia, Spain: Promolibro.

Jacobson, D. E. (1986). Types and timing of social support. *Journal of Health and Social Behavior, 27,* 250–264.

Laux, L., & Weber, H. (1991). Presentation of self in coping with anger and anxiety: An international approach. *Anxiety Research, 3,* 233–255.

Martin, L. L. & Tesser, A. (1989). Toward a motivational and structural theory of ruminative thought. In J. S. Uleman and J. Bargh (Eds.), *Unintended thought.* New York: Guilford Press.

Marty, P., de M'Uzan, M., & David, Ch. (1963). L'investigation psychosomatique. In P. Chauchard (Ed.), *La médecine psychosomatique.* París: P. U. F.

Mattlin, J. A., Wethington, E., & Kessler, D. C. (1990). Situational determinants of coping and coping effectiveness. *Journal of Health and Social Behavior, 31,* 103–122.

Meyerowitz, B. E. (1993). Postmastectomy coping strategies and quality of life. Health Psychology, 2, 117–132. In J. Ferrero (Ed.), *El afrontamiento de un diagnóstico de cáncer.* Valencia, Spain: Promolibro.

Mishel, M. H., Hostetter, T., King, B., & Graham, V. (1993). Predictors of psychosocial adjustment in patients newly diagnosed with gynecological cancer. Cancer Nursing, August 1984, 291–300. In J. Ferrero (Ed.), *El afrontamiento de un diagnóstico de cáncer.* Valencia, Spain: Promolibro.

Moos, R. H. (1988). Life stressors and coping resources influence health and well-being. *Evaluación Psicológica/ Psychological Assessment, 4,* 133–158.

Morrow, J., & Nolen-Hoeksema, S. (1990). Effects of responses to depression on the remediation of depressive affect. *Journal of Personality and Social Psychology, 58,* 519–527.

Nelson, D. V., Friedman, L. C., Baer, P. E., Lane, M., & Smith, F. E. (1989). Attitudes to cancer: Psychometric properties of fighting spirit and denial. *Journal of Behavioral Medicine, 12,* 341–355.

Nolen-Hoeksema, S. (1991). Responses to depression and their effects on the duration of depressive episodes. *Journal of Abnormal Psychology, 100,* 569–582.

Nolen-Hoeksema, S., & Morrow, J. (1991). A prospective study of depression and distress following a natural disaster: The 1989 Loma Prieta earthquake. *Journal of Personality and Social Psychology, 61,* 115–121.

Norris, F. H. (1990). Screening for traumatic stress: A scale for use in the general population. *Journal of Applied Social Psychology, 20,* 1704–1718.

Orr, E., & Meyer, J. (1993). Disease appraisals as a coping strategy with cancer threat. I. J. Psychiatry Relat. Sci. 27, 145–159. In J. Ferrero (Ed.), *El afrontamiento de un diagnóstico de cáncer.* Valencia, Spain: Promolibro.

Paez, D. (1993). *Salud, expresión y represión social de las emociones* [Health, expression, and social repression of emotions]. Valencia, Spain: Promolibro.

Paez, D., Velasco, C., & Basabe, N. (1995). Confrontation of traumatic and social events, Alexithymia and Affective Memory: An experimental research. Unpublished manuscript.

Paez, D. & Velasco, C. (1993). Alexitimia: una revisión de los conceptos, de los instrumentos y una comparación con la represión [Alexithymia: A review of concepts, instruments, and a confrontation with the concept repression]. In D. Paez (Ed.), *Salud, expresión y represión social de las emociones* (pp. 195–236). Valencia, Spain: Promolibro.

Paez, D., Vergara, A., & Velasco, C. (1991). Represión, alexitimia y memoria afectiva [Repression, alexithymia, and affective memory]. *Boletín de Psicología, 31,* 7–40.

Parker, J., Bagby, R. M., & Taylor, G. J. (1989). Toronto alexithymia scale, EPQ and self-report measures of somatic complaints. *Personality and Individual Differences, 10,* 599–604.

Pedinielli, J. L. (1992). *Psychosomatique et alexithymie.* Paris: Presses Universitaires de France.

Penman, D. T. (1993). Coping strategies in adaptation to mastectomy. Psychosomatic Medicine, 44 (1), 117. Abstract. In J. Ferrero (ed.), *El afrontamiento de un diagnóstico de cáncer.* Valencia, Spain: Promolibro.

Pennebaker, J. W. (1989a). Stream of consciousness and stress: Levels of thinking. In J. S. Uleman and J. Bargh (Eds.), *Unintended thought.* New York: Guilford Press.

Pennebaker, J. W. (1989b). Confession, inhibition and disease. In L. Berkowitz (Ed.), *Advances in Experimental Social Psychology,* (Vol. 22, pp. 211–244). New York: Academic Press.

Rodin, J., & Salovey, P. (1989). Health psychology. *Annual Review of Psychology, 40,* 553–579.

Schwartz. G. E. (1990). Psychobiology of repression and health: A systems approach. In J. L. Singer (Ed.), *Repression and dissociation.* Chicago: The Chicago University Press.

Singer, J. L. (1990). *Repression and dissociation.* Chicago: The Chicago University Press.

Suls, J., & Fletcher, B. (1985). The relative efficacy of avoidant and nonavoidant coping strategies: A meta-analysis. *Health Psychology, 4,* 249–288.

Tavris, C. (1984). On the wisdom of counting to ten. Personal and social dangers of anger expression. In P. Shaver (Ed.), *Emotions, relationships and health.* Beverly Hills, CA: Sage.

Taylor, G. J. (1984). Alexithymia: Concept, measurement and implications for treatment. *American Journal of Psychiatry, 141,* 725–732.

Taylor, G. J., Bagby, R. M., Ryan, D., Parker, J., Doody, K., & Keefe, P. (1988). Criterion validity of the Toronto Alexithymia Scale. *Psychosomatic Medicine, 50,* 500–509.

Taylor, S. E. (1990). Health psychology: The science and the field. *American Psychologist, 45,* 40–50.

Taylor, S. E. (1993). Adjustment to threatening events: A theory of cognitive adaptation. American Psychologist, November, 1161–1173. In J. Ferrero (Ed.), *El afrontamiento de un diagnóstico de cáncer.* Valencia, Spain: Promolibro.

Temoshok, L., & Heller, B. (1986). Sobre la comparación de manzanas y naranjas y ensaladas de fruta: una vista de conjunto, metodológica, de los estudios de resultados médicos, en oncología psicosocial [About the comparison between apples and oranges and fruit salad: A united methodological view of medical results in psychosocial oncology]. In C. Cooper (Ed.), *Estrés y cáncer.* Madrid: Díaz de Santos.

Thoits, P. (1986). Social support as coping assistance. *Journal of Consulting and Clinical Psychology, 54,* 416–423.

Traue, H. C. & Pennebaker, J. W. (1993). *Emotion, Inhibition and Health.* Seattle: Hogrefe & Huber.

Vaillant, G. E. (1990). Repression in college men followed for half a century. In J. L. Singer (Ed.), *Repression and dissociation. Implications for personality, theory, psychopathology, and health.* The University of Chicago Press, Chicago.

Viney, L. L., & Westbrook, M. T. (1993). Coping with chronic illness: Strategy preferences, changes in preferences and associated emotional reactions. Journal of Chronic Disease, 37, 489–502. In J. Ferrero (Ed.), *El afrontamiento de un diagnóstico de cáncer.* Valencia: Promolibro.

Watson, M., Greer, S., Young, J., Inayat, Q., Burgess, C., & Robertson, B. (1988). Development of a questionnaire measure of adjustment to cancer: The MAC scale. *Psychological Medicine, 18,* 203–209.

Wegner, D. M., Shortt, J. W., Blake, A. W., & Page, M. S. (1990). The supression of exciting thoughts. *Journal of Personality and Social Psychology, 58,* 409–418.

Weinberger, D. (1990). The construct validity of the repressive coping style. In J. L. Singer (Ed.), *Repression and dissociation.* Chicago: The Chicago University Press.

Wood, J. V., Saltzberg, J. A., Neale, J. M., Stone, A. A., & Rachmiel, T. B. (1990). Self-focused attention, coping responses and distressed mood in everyday life. *Journal of Personality and Social Psychology, 58,* 1027–1036.

11

Repression, Disclosure, and Immune Function: Recent Findings and Methodological Issues

Keith J. Petrie, Roger J. Booth, & Kathryn P. Davison

The health benefits of disclosing emotions have received increasing attention in the psychological literature. Research into the impact of repressing or disclosing emotions on immune function and health has a short history and draws on a wide range of methodologies. The past decade has seen a dramatic increase in the number of general psychoneuroimmunological investigations. A large number of these studies have been based on a simplistic model and many have focused solely on the effect of various forms of psychological stress on immunological variables (e.g., proportions of blood lymphocyte subpopulations, mitogenic responses, natural killer cell activity). As more attention has been given to the function of emotion in health, more sophisticated research designs have developed in order to address these more complex questions. In this chapter, we review recent research on the inhibition and repression of emotions and immune function as well as work on emotional disclosure and the

Preparation of this chapter was supported by the Auckland Medical Research Foundation and the Health Research Council of New Zealand.

immune system. In the final section, we examine some of the methodological difficulties facing researchers in this area.

INHIBITION AND THE IMMUNE SYSTEM

There is strong evidence that factors that reduce the ability of the individual to confide or discuss stressful events may aggravate immunological dysfunction and increase the likelihood of illness. Previous studies have
found that both acute and chronic stressors can compromise immune
function and increase the susceptibility to infectious illness (Arnetz et al.,
1987; Cohen & Williamson, 1991; Glaser et al., 1987; Kiecolt-Glaser, Dura,
Speicher, Trask, & Glaser, 1991). It also seems that individuals in situations that prevent disclosure of stressful situations are at increased risk of
negative health consequences. For example, a number of investigators have
found lower levels of social or spouse support to be associated with poorer
immunological function following stressful events (Glaser et al., 1993;
Kiecolt-Glaser et al., 1993; Kennedy, Kiecolt-Glaser, & Glaser, 1988). There
is also evidence that victims of stressful life events that are socially embarrassing or difficult to confide to others, such as sexual abuse and rape,
may have greater vulnerability to poor health (Golding, Stein, Siegel, Burnam, & Sorenson, 1988; Kimerling & Calhoun, 1994). Correlational studies have found significant associations between a history of sexual abuse
or other trauma and a higher incidence of illness (Pennebaker & Susman,
1988). Evidence from these studies also suggests that nondisclosure of upsetting events can aggravate the adverse health toll taken by such traumas
(e.g., Pennebaker & O'Heeron, 1984).

Repressors are typically classified as having a heightened recognition
threshold for anxiety-provoking stimuli, consistently avoiding such disturbing cognitions across a variety of perceptual, projective, and learning
tasks (Weinberger, Schwartz, & Davidson, 1979). Often this is characterized by a discrepancy between self-reports of distress and physiological
measures of stress such as muscle activity and skin conductance levels
(Watson, Pettingale, & Greer, 1984; Weinberger et al., 1979). Question-

naire measures of this style of defensiveness include the Byrne Repression–
Sensitization (R–S) Scale (Byrne, 1961); the Self-Concealment Scale (Lar-
son & Chastain, 1990); and the combination of a low score on the Taylor
Manifest Anxiety Scale with a high score on the Marlowe-Crowne Social
Desirability Scale (Weinberger, 1990).

There are considerable data now to suggest that when individuals actively inhibit emotional expression, they show measurable immunological changes consistent with poorer health outcomes. Repression of negative affect, as measured by a laboratory task involving disclosure of
emotional material, was found to be correlated with higher serum antibody titers in subjects with latent Epstein-Barr virus (EBV) infection (Esterling, Antoni, Kumar, & Schneiderman, 1990). Most adults carry a latent, persistent infection with this virus that can be reactivated by stressful
events. The appearance of anti-EBV antibodies in the blood is related to
EBV reactivation and an inability of the immune system to keep the virus
in check. In a normal, healthy college population made up of people previously exposed to EBV, subjects reporting high and middle levels of anxiety also had higher antibody titers to EBV (indicating poorer immunological control) as compared with the low anxiety group. Furthermore,
subjects who were highly defensive had higher antibody titers than their
low-defensive counterparts (Esterling, Antoni, Kumar, & Schneiderman,
1993). Using an outpatient clinic sample, Jamner, Schwartz, and Leigh
(1988) found that repressive and defensive high-anxious patients demonstrated significantly decreased monocyte counts. They also found repressive coping was associated with elevated eosinophil counts, serum glucose
levels, and self-reported reactions to medications. Shea, Burton, and Girgis (1993) also reported that subjects classified as repressors showed lower
cell-mediated immune responses than other groups of subjects.

The use of a repressive coping style has most frequently been associated with the onset or progression of cancer (Gross, 1989). A number of
investigations have found a repressive personality style was significantly
associated with poorer natural killer (NK) cell activity, the most readily
measurable element of immune function with relevance to the control of

tumors (Levy, Herberman, Maluish, Schlien, & Lippman, 1985). It was also associated with the diagnosis of malignancy (Greer & Morris, 1975; Kissen, Brown, & Kissen, 1969) and with subsequent death from cancer (Pettingale, Morris, Greer, & Haybittle, 1985; Shaffer, Graves, Swank, & Pearson, 1987; Graves & Thomas, 1981).

Lydia Temoshok (1987) has proposed a model of the cancer prone individual based on a constellation of traits that seemed to be consistent with a diagnosis of cancer and a poor disease prognosis. She identified this "Type C" personality as having three major characteristics: (a) the personality traits of stoicism, niceness, industriousness, perfectionism, sociability, and conventionality; (b) difficulty in expressing emotions; and (c) an attitude of resignation or of helplessness–hopelessness.

Schwartz (1983, 1990) has also proposed a theory of disregulation and disease based on general systems theory and cybernetics that integrates findings from biofeedback, neuroendocrinology, and the psychometrics of repression. In brief, the theory asserts that there exists a cerebral disconnectivity such that physiological signals of distress arising in the body are cortically overridden because of high levels of centrally circulating endogenous opioids. It is known that endogenous opioids, particularly beta endorphins, play an immunomodulatory role because receptors for those molecules have been identified on the surface of immune cells. The theory suggests that repressors are less likely to attend to threatening internal symptoms and are more likely to delay seeking medical assistance for such problems.

The weight of evidence relating to inhibition and health suggests that restrictions on the individual's ability to express emotions, because of either negative social consequences or personality style, seems to result in compromised immunological function and increased risk of health problems. How emotional expression works to modify the negative effects of psychological trauma is unclear. It may be that the effort required in suppressing painful or threatening emotions over time compromises immunological function, perhaps via increased autonomic activity (Pennebaker, 1989). Another possibility is that the expression of emotions also offers a way to make sense of traumatic experiences and integrate them into a new coherent view of the self. Thus, the reduced effort involved in the suppression of such emotional experiences is less likely to interfere with daily thoughts and activities (Wegner, 1989).

DISCLOSURE AND THE IMMUNE SYSTEM

If emotional inhibition or repression can have an impact on immune responsiveness, then expressing or disclosing emotions may also be influential. Spontaneous verbal or nonverbal expression of emotion is related to immediate reductions in autonomic nervous system activity and these physiological changes are most likely to occur among individuals who are either verbally or nonverbally highly expressive (Berry & Pennebaker, 1993). Expression of emotions (particularly negative emotions) in an experimental context has been associated with transient changes in blood lymphocyte reactivity to mitogens (Knapp et al., 1992; Zakowski, McAllister, Deal, & Baum 1992) and with small elevations in natural killer cell activity (Futterman, Kemeny, Shapiro, Polonsky, & Fahey, 1992). Labott, Ahleman, Wolever, and Martin (1990) examined the effects of either inhibition or expression of overt laughter and weeping in subjects watching sad and humorous videotapes. The humorous stimulus resulted in increased salivary immunoglobulin A (IgA) antibody levels, regardless of whether overt laughter was expressed. In contrast, overt crying decreased salivary IgA, whereas the inhibition of weeping in the context of the same sad stimulus did not. Although these effects may be partially the result of altered lymphocyte trafficking associated with arousal or excitement triggered by the experimental experience (Knapp et al., 1992) or by changes in salivary flow rates under different conditions (Labott et al., 1990), they seem to indicate a relationship between the expression of emotions and immune behavior.

Many of the studies examining expression of emotions and immune functions have used a writing experimental paradigm developed by James Pennebaker and his associates, where subjects are randomly assigned to write about emotional or control topics typically over a four-day period for 20 minutes each day. In the briefings for such studies, subjects in the emotional writing group are encouraged to write about traumatic and upsetting experiences and to focus on emotional issues that still concern them, but which they may not have discussed in detail with others. Measurement of immune parameters and health changes are then made in both the emotional writing and control groups following the writing period.

Research using this experimental paradigm has assessed immunological changes following writing about emotional or traumatic issues. Pennebaker, Kiecolt-Glaser, and Glaser (1988) demonstrated significant differences between emotional expression and control writing groups in the blastogenic response to concanavalin A (Con A) 6 weeks after the writing intervention. Although Con A blastogenic responses measure the proliferative capacity of T lymphocytes from blood, the test is highly variable from day to day (van Rood et al., 1991) and thus it is not clear whether the small changes observed are indicative of any immunologically significant effect.

Other workers have focused on the effects of emotional disclosure on the immune response to EBV. Esterling, Antoni, Fletcher, Margulies, and Scheiderman (1994) found that subjects assigned to express their emotions about stressful events verbally or through writing had lower titers of antibodies against EBV (suggesting better cell mediated control of the virus) compared with subjects in a control condition. Although this work and the Con A blastogenic study discussed above both suggest that the expression of emotions related to stressful events can influence the immune parameters in reliable ways, they do not demonstrate that such immune changes have real health consequences.

Another way of approaching this question is to assess the effects of emotional disclosure on responses to clinically relevant viral vaccines. Immunity induced by recombinant hepatitis B viral vaccines has been shown to be modulated by emotion-related variables. For example, Petry, Weems, and Livingstone (1991) found that higher levels of negatively perceived stress, irascibility, depression, and anxiety during the induction phase of immunization with hepatitis B vaccine were significantly associated with higher peak antibody titers. Glaser et al. (1992) studied the effect of examination stress on the ability to generate an anti-hepatitis response in students who received each of a series of three hepatitis B inoculations on the third day of a three-day examination series. They found that the 25%

of the students who seroconverted after the first injection were significantly less stressed and anxious than those who did not seroconvert at that time. In addition, students who reported greater social support exhibited a stronger immune response to the vaccine at the time of the third inoculation, as measured by antibody titers to hepatitis B antigen and by blastogenic response of blood lymphocytes to hepatitis B antigen in culture. Similar results were reported by Jabaaij et al. (1993), who found that antibody levels against hepatitis B vaccine measured at 7 months after the initial vaccine were negatively correlated with the stress index score assessed at 2 months. Thus, there is evidence that response to hepatitis B vaccination can be modulated by psychosocial factors measurable both at the time of immunization and during the course of the response. However, in contrast with the studies of EBV antibodies (Esterling et al., 1993; Glaser et al., 1992), coping styles and loneliness are not necessarily associated with antihepatitis antibody formation (Jabaaij et al., 1993). Because the immune mechanisms associated with reactivation of latent herpes viruses are different from those involved in responses to acute infection or to immunization with hepatitis B vaccine, it is conceivable that such mechanisms may be differentially affected by psychological variables.

We have sought to test the hypotheses that expression of negative affect by writing about traumatic events for four days immediately before beginning a three-dose vaccination schedule against hepatitis B virus would be associated with large decreases in autonomic activity as measured by changes in skin conductance during the course of writing and subsequently with high antibody titers against the vaccine (Petrie, Booth, Pennebaker, Davison, & Thomas, in press). Compared with a group assigned to write about trivial topics, the traumatic writing group showed a significant drop in mean skin conductance over the course of the four writing days. An analysis of immune responses subsequent to the writing process revealed that, compared with the control group, subjects in the emotional expression group showed significantly higher antibody levels against hepatitis B over the subsequent six month period. They also exhibited transiently reduced numbers of helper (CD4) T lymphocytes and basophils in their blood immediately after the four days of writing.

Thus, our work is consistent with the more general reports of the health benefits of disclosure but provides an important additional perspective that specific immune activity of fundamental importance in viral infections can be affected by emotional expression. Although we have observed only small effects of emotional disclosure on responses to vaccination, our experiments were conducted with young healthy subjects using a vaccination protocol designed to produce maximal immunity to hepatitis B in greater than 90% of normal individuals. It is conceivable therefore, that where conditions are more marginal or critical—such as in individuals with compromised immune systems, with vaccines that stimulate the immune system less effectively, or with individuals suffering from chronic immunologically related conditions—emotional disclosure may have much more profound effects on the development of immunity. Clearly, further investigation of this area is warranted and may lead to the development of new therapeutic approaches to chronic conditions that often prove intractable to current treatments.

DIFFICULTIES INVESTIGATING DISCLOSURE AND IMMUNE FUNCTION

While the immunological results reported in the previous section are of interest, only a relatively small number of experimental studies have investigated the effect of the disclosure of emotional experiences on the immune system. Significant methodological problems exist in this area that limit our ability to tie specific immunological changes to the process of disclosure in the writing experimental paradigm as it is currently used. A number of these difficulties come with the repression territory and others underline how little we currently know about the process of effective disclosure.

One significant problem is that of defining traumatic experiences. In most studies using the writing paradigm, the writing topic is set by the subject after being given a briefing that encourages the disclosure of traumatic or personally upsetting experiences (e.g., Esterling et al., 1994; Pennebaker et al., 1988). The main difficulty with this approach is that the choice of topic itself may represent a repressive process, with some subjects choosing to write about areas that have minimal real personal meaning or impact for them and therefore presumably little influence on immunological processes and health outcomes. Possibilities for encouraging subjects to write about personally meaningful topics may be to use more directed coaching before each writing session or perhaps to enlist subjects who have recently been involved in a clearly traumatic experience such as a bank robbery, rape or assault, and direct them to explore aspects of that experience.

An important related aspect is that of identifying what represents effective disclosure in writing and how these elements can be related to physiological changes. At present there is some suggestive evidence that subjects who gain most from writing use more negative emotion words overall and increase their use of insight type words over the course of the writing sessions (Pennebaker, 1993). The development of the CARMEN program for linking text with autonomic change offers new possibilities to explore this area, especially when these data are linked to a linguistic analysis of the subject's writing (Pennebaker & Uhlmann, 1994). Defining effective disclosure in writing will be a large methodological step forward in being able to link the expression of emotions with immunological changes. Without progress in this area it will be difficult to develop more detailed theoretical models of how disclosure affects immunological processes.

Another issue is the paucity of data on the immunological effects associated with the experience of common emotions. This would be useful in identifying links with existing data on the distinctive patterns of autonomic activity associated with different emotions (Ekman, Levenson, & Friesen, 1983). Some short-term immunological effects have been observed as a result of the induction of various emotions. Knapp et al. (1992) found the induction of negative emotion produced a decrease in mitogenic activity but increased NK cell activity in blood lymphocytes. Induction of positive emotions was also associated with a decrease in mitogenic activity but not to the same degree as negative emotions. Another study has found few significant changes from baseline to postinduction period in blood associated immune parameters, with the exception of elevations in NK cell numbers associated with a state of anxiety (Futterman et al., 1992). Both these studies indicated that immunological variability increased across all emotional states regardless of specific emotion, suggesting that it may be the experience of emotion, regardless of valence, that is critical in producing immune changes. Clearly, more work is required in this area to help clarify the nature of the relationship between emotions and changes in immunological activity.

A related problem concerns the nature of the human immune variables currently available for use in such studies. Measures derived from blood lymphocytes must be treated with caution because blood lymphocyte populations represent only a few percent of the total lymphocyte pool and their release into the circulation and their sequestration from the circulation by other lymphoid compartments can be quite rapid and affected by a variety of physiological circumstances (Booth, 1993; van Rood et al., 1991). Immune variables not subject to such transient fluctuations may have greater potential to provide a more relevant measure of immune behavior associated with emotional disclosure by providing information about more systemic properties of the immune system. Measuring immune variables such as antibodies associated with responses to infectious agents or vaccines is therefore one way of accessing a more distributed aspect of immune behavior with potentially more direct relevance to disease processes.

A further consideration in future psychoneuroimmunological work is distinguishing between different motivating factors in the development of repressive behavior. A distinction can be drawn between a *life events motive*, that is, the avoidance of acutely painful memories such as a history of abuse, rape, infidelity, or the death of a loved one, and a *personality motive* characterized by high sensitivity to socialization. This sensitivity may take the form of shyness, blunted affect or a submissive–helpless style. Although these motives may overlap in some individuals, they are conceptually different and, perhaps more importantly, may have their own distinctive effects on health and immunological parameters.

Researchers investigating the role of inhibition, disclosure, and immune function face considerable methodological challenges designing studies to examine this area. The writing experimental paradigm has been a major advance by allowing manipulation of aspects of emotional diclosure without the interactions from therapist variables. However, more basic data identifying effective disclosure at both a physiological and linguistic level would be valuable for developing more detailed theoretical models of the immunological effects of disclosure. The relevance of the immunological variables used in many studies to date has not been well justified and more work needs to be done on the immunological correlates of common emotions. The complexity of this area will undoubtedly mean that the writing paradigm as it exists will be modified in the future and replaced by more innovative experimental methodologies in order to address some of these issues.

In conclusion, we underline that the psychoneuroimmunological network represents a largely obscure and unclassified territory for examining the effect of repression or expression of emotions on health. Although work in this area is new, some provocative findings have already been reported. Researchers face major methodological difficulties in splicing ongoing emotional processes to reliable immunological changes. Researchers are also challenged to use relevant immunological measures that have real health consequences. Whereas considerable difficulties exist in this work, the area also offers the promise of developing stronger theoretical models concerning the role of psychological factors in health and illness.

REFERENCES

Arnetz, B. B., Wasserman, J., Petrini, B., Brenner, S. O., Levi, L., Eneroth, P., Salovaara, H., Hjelm, R., Salovaara, L., Theorell, T., & Petterson, I. L. (1987). Immune function in unemployed women. *Psychosomotic Medicine, 49,* 3–12.

Berry, D. S., & Pennebaker, J. W. (1993). Nonverbal and verbal emotional expression and health. *Psychotherapy and Psychosomatics, 59,* 11–19.

Booth, R. J. (1993). Exercise, overtraining and the immune system: A biological perspective. *New Zealand Journal of Sports Medicine, 21,* 41–45.

Byrne, D. (1961). The repression-sensitization scale. Rationale, reliability, and validity. *Journal of Personality, 29,* 334–349.

Cohen, S., & Williamson, G. M. (1991). Stress and infectious disease in humans. *Psychological Bulletin, 109,* 5–24.

Ekman, P., Levenson, R. W., & Friesen, W. V. (1983). Autonomic nervous system activity distinguishes among emotions. *Science, 221,* 1208–1210.

Esterling, B. A., Antoni, M. H., Fletcher, M. A., Margulies, S., & Scheiderman, N. (1994). Emotional disclosure through writing or speaking modulates latent Epstein-Barr virus antibody titers. *Journal of Consulting and Clinical Psychology, 62,* 130–140.

Esterling, B. A., Antoni, M. H., Kumar, M., & Schneiderman, N. (1990). Emotional depression, stress disclosure responses, and Epstein-Barr viral capsid antigen titers. *Psychosomatic Medicine, 52,* 397–410.

Esterling, B. A., Antoni, M. H., Kumar, M., & Schneiderman, N. (1993). Defensiveness, trait anxiety, and Epstein-Barr viral capsid antigen antibody titers in healthy college students. *Health Psychology, 12,* 132–139.

Futterman, A. D., Kemeny, M. E., Shapiro, D., Polonsky, W., & Fahey, J. L. (1992). Immunological variability associated with experimentally-induced positive and negative affective states. *Psychological Medicine, 22,* 231–238.

Glaser, R., Kiecolt-Glaser, Bonneau, R. H., Malarkey, W., Kennedy, S., & Hughes, J. (1992). Stress-induced modulation of the immune response to recombinant hepatitis B vaccine. *Psychosomatic Medicine, 54,* 22–29.

Glaser, R., Pearson, G. R., Bonneau, R. H., Esterling, B. A., Atkinson, C., & Kiecolt-Glaser, J. K. (1993). Stress and the memory T-cell response to the Epstein-Barr virus in healthy medical students. *Health Psychology, 12,* 435–442.

Glaser, R., Rice, J., Sheridan, J., Fertel, R., Stout, J., Speicher, C., Pinsky, D., Kotur, M., Post, A., Beck, M., & Kiecolt-Glaser, J. (1987). Stress related immune suppression: Health implications. *Brain Behavior and Immunity, 1,* 7–20.

Golding, J. M., Stein, J. A., Siegel, J. M., Burnam, M. A., & Sorenson, S. B. (1988). Sexual assault history and the use of health and mental health services. *American Journal of Community Psychology, 16,* 625–644.

Graves, P. L., & Thomas, C. B. (1981). Themes of interaction in medical students' Rorschach responses as predictors of midlife health problems or disease. *Psychosomatic Medicine, 43,* 215–225.

Greer, S., & Morris, T. (1975). Psychological attributes of women who develop breast cancer: A controlled study. *Journal of Psychosomatic Research, 19,* 147–153.

Gross, J. (1989). Emotional expression in cancer onset and progression. *Social Science and Medicine, 28,* 1239–1248.

Jabaaij, L., Grosheide, P. M., Heijtink, R. A., Duivenvoorden, H. J., Ballieux, R. E., & Vingerhoets, A. J. J. M. (1993). Influence of perceived psychological stress and distress on antibody response to low dose rDNA hepatitis B vaccine. *Journal of Psychosomatic Research, 37,* 361–369.

Jamner, L. D., Schwartz, G. E., & Leigh, H. (1988). The relationship between repressive and defensive coping styles and monocyte, eosinophile, and serum glucose levels: Support for the opioid peptide hypothesis of repression. *Psychosomatic Medicine, 50,* 567–575.

Kennedy, S., Kiecolt-Glaser, J. K., & Glaser, R. (1988). Immunological consequences of acute and chronic stressors: Mediating role of interpersonal relationships. *British Journal of Medical Psychology, 61,* 77–85.

Kiecolt-Glaser, J. K., Dura, J. R., Speicher, C. E., Trask, O. J., & Glaser, R. (1991). Spousal caregivers of dementia victims: Longitudinal changes in immunity and health. *Psychosomatic Medicine, 53,* 345–362.

Kiecolt-Glaser, J. K., Malarkey, W. B., Chee, M., Newton, T., Cacioppo, J. T., Mao, H. Y., & Glaser, R. (1993). Negative behavior during marital conflict is associated with immunological down regulation. *Psychosomatic Medicine, 55,* 395–409.

Kimerling, R., & Calhoun, K. S. (1994). Somatic symptoms, social support, and treatment seeking among sexual assault victims. *Journal of Consulting and Clinical Psychology, 62,* 333–340.

Kissen, D. M., Brown, R. I. F., & Kissen, M. (1969). A further report on personality and psychological factors in lung cancer. *Annals of the New York Academy of Science, 164,* 535–545.

Knapp, P. H., Levy, E. M., Giorgi, R. G., Black, P. H., Fox, B. H., & Heeren, T. C. (1992). Short-term immunological effects of induced emotion. *Psychosomatic Medicine, 54,* 133–148.

Labott, S. M., Ahleman, S., Wolever, M. E., & Martin, R. B. (1990). The physiological and psychological effects of the expression and inhibition of emotion. *Behavioral Medicine, 16,* 182–189.

Larson, D. G., & Chastain, R. L. (1990). Self-concealment: Conceptualization, measurement, and health implication. 439–455.

Levy, S. M., Herberman, R. B., Maluish, A. M., Schlien, B., & Lippman, M. (1985). Prognostic risk assessment in primary breast cancer by behavioral and immunological parameters. *Health Psychology, 4,* 99–113.

Pennebaker, J. W. (1989). Confession, inhibition and disease. In L. Berkowitz (Ed.), *Advances in Experimental Social Psychology* (Vol. 22, pp. 211–244). New York: Academic.

Pennebaker, J. W. (1993). Putting stress into words: Health, linguistic and therapeutic implications. *Behaviour Research and Therapy, 31,* 539–548.

Pennebaker, J. W., Kiecolt-Glaser, J. K., & Glaser, R. (1988). Disclosure of trauma and immune function: Health implications for psychotherapy. *Journal of Consulting and Clinical Psychology, 56,* 239–245.

Pennebaker, J. W., & O'Heeron, R. C. (1984). Confiding in others and illness rates among spouses of suicide and accidental death victims. *Journal of Abnormal Psychology, 93,* 473–476.

Pennebaker, J. W., & Susman, J. R. (1988). Disclosure of traumas and psychosomatic processes. *Social Science and Medicine, 26,* 327–332.

Pennebaker, J. W., & Uhlmann, C. (1994). Direct linking of autonomic activity with typed text: The CARMEN machine. *Behavior Research Methods, Instruments and Computers, 26,* 28–31.

Petrie, K. J., Booth, R. J., Pennebaker, J. W., Davison, K. P., & Thomas, M. G. (in press). Disclosure of trauma and immune response to a hepatitis B vaccination program. *Journal of Consulting and Clinical Psychology.*

Petry, L. J., Weems, L. B., & Livingstone, J. N., (1991). Relationship of stress, distress, and the immunologic response to a recombinant hepatitis B vaccine. *Journal of Family Practice, 32,* 481–486.

Pettingale, G. M., Morris, T., Greer, S., & Haybittle, J. L. (1985). Mental attitudes to cancer: An additional prognostic factor. *Lancet, 1,* 750.

Schwartz, G. E. (1983). Disregulation theory and disease: Applications to the repression/cerebral disconnection/cardiovascular disorder hypothesis. *International Review of Applied Psychology, 32,* 95–118.

Schwartz, G. E. (1990). Psychobiology of repression and health: A systems approach. In J. L. Singer (Ed.), *Repression and dissociation* (pp. 405–434). Chicago: University of Chicago Press.

Shaffer, J. W., Graves, P. L., Swank, R. T., & Pearson, T. A. (1987). Clustering of personality in youth and the subsequent development of cancer among physicians. *Journal of Behavioral Medicine, 10,* 441–447.

Shea, J. D., Burton, R., & Girgis, A. (1993). Negative affect, absorption, and immunity. *Physiological Behavior, 53,* 449–457.

Temoshok, L. (1987). Personality, coping style emotion and cancer: Toward an integrative model. *Cancer Surveys, 6,* 545–567.

van Rood, Y., Goulmy, E., Blokland, E., Pool, J., van Rood, J., & van Houwelingen, H. (1991). Month-related variability in immunological test results; implications for immunological follow-up studies. *Cellular and Experimental Immunolology, 86,* 349–353.

Watson, M., Pettingale, K. W., & Greer, S. (1984). Emotional control and autonomous arousal in breast cancer patients. *Journal of Psychosomatic Research, 28,* 467–474.

Wegner, D. M. (1989). *White bears and other unwanted thoughts.* New York: Viking Press.

Weinberger, D. A. (1990). The construct validity of the repressive coping style. In J. L. Singer (Ed.), *Repression and dissociation* (pp. 337–386). Chicago: University of Chicago Press.

Weinberger, D. A., Schwartz, G. E., & Davidson, R. J. (1979). Low-anxious, high-anxious, and repressive coping styles: Psychometric patterns and behavioral and physiological responses to stress. *Journal of Abnormal Psychology, 88,* 369–380.

Zakowski, S. G., McAllister, C. G., Deal, M., & Baum, A. (1992). Stress, reactivity, and immune function in healthy men. *Health Psychology, 11,* 223–232.

PART FOUR

Clinical and Social Dimensions of Disclosure

12

Emotionality and Health: Lessons From and for Psychotherapy

Michael J. Mahoney

E motional experiences have long been a central concern in psychotherapy. When Breuer and Freud established psychoanalysis in 1895 with their *Studies of Hysteria,* there was already an awareness that the theater of personal affective life was the metaphorical fountain of all other modes of psychological experience. For the past century, therapists and researchers have worked to understand the mysteries of the emotions and the dynamics of the life within. Increasingly, those who sought therapy did so out of affective concerns. Indeed, emotional distress is probably the single most common motivation for seeking and remaining in psychotherapy. This being the case, it should not be surprising that increasing numbers of practitioners and psychotherapy researchers have turned more and more of their attention to such matters as affect regulation, affective polarities, affect disorders, and emotional bonds (Bucci, chapter 5, this volume; Hobson, 1985).

In this chapter I shall venture some conjectures on the multiple roles of emotionality in psychological adjustment and development. My remarks are organized around three basic themes: (a) the role of affect regulation in personal development, (b) the most common problems with emotionality that are encountered in psychotherapy, and (c) possible processes operative in psychotherapy-related improvements in feeling and functioning. I will conclude with some reflections on the implications of the foregoing for the training as well as the well-being of psychotherapists.

AFFECT REGULATION IN PSYCHOLOGICAL DEVELOPMENT

The role of affect in life span psychological development has been studied substantially over the past half century. Setting aside such questions as whether there are a finite number of basic emotions, there is now general acceptance of the fact that affect regulation and biological patternings are closely related (Schore, 1994; Thayer, 1989). Indeed, these two domains constitute the first major developmental challenges for the human infant. In struggling to organize his or her multiple biological systems, the human infant experiences and expresses the developmental differentiation of affect. The physical and emotional presence of a sensitive and responsive caregiver first helps the infant to settle into and create basic patterns of activity and rest (Bowlby, 1988).

The same is true with regard to emotional patterning. The emergence of different emotional capacities in the child reflects important differentiations in adaptation and development. Children not only develop capacities and coping strategies across a range of affects, but they also learn to rely on their emotional experiences as navigational guides. Children literally feel their way toward a sense of an orderly world and a complex historical consistency, which later emerges as an individual self. Theories of affect regulation and research on emotionality have diversified considerably in the past two decades (Izard, Kagan, & Zajonc, 1984; Mahoney, 1991). The major conclusions emanating from that theory and research include the following:

1. Emotional processes are pervasively involved in the direction of an individual's attention and in all acts of perception, learning, and memory.

2. Emotional development is functionally inseparable from psychosocial experience patterns at all ages.

3. The closely related constructs of personality and personal identity ("self") are fundamentally emotional in nature.

Among other things, these conclusions have made it increasingly clear to psychotherapy researchers that optimal psychological services must reflect a deep appreciation for the lifelong primacy and power of emotional experiences in an individual's adjustment, development, and health (Borkovec et al., chapter 3, this volume; Greenberg & Safran, 1987; Guidano, 1987, 1991; Rimé, chapter 14, this volume; Schore, 1994).

COMMON EMOTIONAL PROBLEMS
IN PSYCHOTHERAPY

As practiced by the vast majority of professional service providers, psychotherapy is usually focused on disorder or dysfunction in the client; hence the strong conceptual and research ties among the specializations of personality, psychopathology, and psychological services. The affective disorders account for a substantial percentage of diagnoses, and other patterns of disorder are typically defined in a central way by their affective components (Watson & Clark, 1994). (I shall return to this matrix of meanings in the next section.)

Although an individual's motivations for entering psychotherapy are clearly related to his or her emotional experience in the course of such therapy, it may be heuristic to consider some of the problems most commonly encountered in psychotherapy: (a) the pain of acute or chronic negative affect, (b) fear of feeling, (c) emotional numbing, (d) perplexing emotional reactions, (e) emotional conflict or ambivalence, and (f) experiences (usually painful) associated with "unfinished" or inadequately expressed affect. These six categories reflect considerable overlap, of course, and their distinctions are often less clearcut in psychotherapy practice (Greenberg & Safran, 1987; Mahoney, in press). The pain of acute or chronic negative affect lies at the heart of those patterns of emotionality now termed the "affective and personality disorders." The traditionally negative emotions—anger, anxiety, depression, disgust, hate, embarrassment, guilt, and shame—are the most frequent concerns of psychotherapy clients. Besides being hedonically unpleasant, these emotions often interfere with various dimensions of functioning. Indeed, it is often their dysfunctional covariates that motivate interest in psychotherapy.

Not surprisingly, emotional numbing and fear of feeling are often related. I shall be terse in my elaboration here. Noteworthy is the generally accepted maxim among psychotherapy practitioners that the three most common and powerful messages exchanged among members of dysfunctional families are (a) don't feel, (b) don't trust, and (c) don't talk about it. Likewise, clinical levels of depression and anxiety are diagnostically defined in emotional terms (anhedonia, apathy, and blunting in the case of depression, and vigilance regarding emotional intensity in the case of anxiety). Common to depression and anxiety is the act of avoidance. Depressive individuals are characterized by passive avoidance, reflecting Beck's (1967) famous negative triad in depression: negative self, negative world, and negative future. Chronically depressed persons typically disengage from their social worlds, their work, and their self-care. Chronically anxious individuals, on the other hand, are relatively more active in their avoidance of interactions with others and themselves. They struggle with their ambivalence of hope and fear, and they are vigilant, rather than depressively hopeless, about issues of control. As appreciations for the complexities of emotionality have begun to permeate theory, research, and practice in psychotherapy, contemporary psychologists have increasingly acknowledged the common co-occurrence of anxiety and depression (not to mention other emotions) and the dynamic fluctuations of their dominance in personal phenomenologies (Greenberg & Safran, 1987; Guidano, 1987, 1991; Mahoney, 1991).

Perplexing emotional reactions are episodes of surprising emotionality. These episodes are usually presented by clients as a puzzling instance or pattern in which he or she responded with intense affect to a situation or context that was not expected to elicit emotional intensity (and for which the individuals usually have no explanation). Typical here are phenomenologically surprising experiences of anger or panic. Sensing that something is wrong or fearing that the perplexing reaction might happen again, with tragic consequences, the individual seeks professional help. A related pattern is that characterized by emotional conflict or ambivalence, in which individuals report being distressed by their inability to resolve a bivalent emotional attachment or, in less technical language, report feeling "stuck" or "torn apart" by what they experience as incompatible emotions or response options.

The sixth and final category in this impromptu classification of common problems in psychotherapy is that of unfinished emotional experiencing or expression. Rare is the practitioner who has not repeatedly encountered or recognized this pattern as a presenting or emergent concern of some clients. Research on bereavement, grief, and loss (of abilities, options, and significant others) has recently lent clarification to some of the factors that appear to contribute to the maintenance or developmental transformation of both acute and chronic emotional reactions. Consistent with the conjectures of both attachment and bereavement specialists, it appears that such reactions are ultimately more likely to be transformed or transcended in personal psychological development if their emotional pain is acknowledged, accepted, and ultimately "reframed" in survivors' personal meaning systems. Increasingly, psychotherapists seem to be acknowledging that intense and intimate emotional relationships (positive, negative, and—most often—mixed) are never really ended in the psychological sense. Even if the significant other has functionally or structurally died, clients exhibit clear signs of continuing to be influenced by their prior human relationships. As Mary Watkins (1986) so aptly put it, human beings "are all un/willing" and "un/witting" hosts of multiple "invisible guests" in our private psychological lives, and we are well advised to acknowledge and respect the phenomenological implications of this fact.

Of particular relevance to the present volume is the fact that the foregoing common emotional problems in psychotherapy have also been linked to both psychological and physical health (Pennebaker, 1990, 1993; chapter 1, this volume). Less clear at this point is how emotional experience, emotional expression, and health are related. Recent speculations on the nature of that relationship have raised some fascinating questions about psychological development and psychotherapy process. For example, what is the difference between experiencing and expressing an emotion? How do talking, writing, and otherwise symbolically expressing a trauma help to reduce associated emotional distress and health risks (Krantz & Pennebaker, 1994)? How important is the process of confiding in another (emotional disclosure) relative to that of expressive self-reflection in facilitating recovery from a trauma? These are questions at the forefront of contemporary research (e.g., Paez, chapter 9, this volume; Petrie, chapter 10, this volume; Traue, chapter 7, this volume).

EMOTIONAL EXPERIENCE AND PSYCHOTHERAPY PROCESS

Answers to questions such as these lie at the heart of some lines of inquiry in psychotherapy process research. One of its first clients (Anna O., who later became a therapist herself) gave psychotherapy the title of "the talking cure." In the century since that label was suggested, it has become patently clear that the curative effects of psychotherapy involve much more than talking. "Corrective emotional experiences" lie at the heart of effective psychotherapy, regardless of the theoretical orientation or strategic techniques of the practitioner (Hobson, 1985). For reasons that remain a matter of debate among specialists, the capacity to experience and express intense affect appears to be important to psychophysical well-being. Attempts to explain this relation could probably be classified in a number of different ways. One clarifying contrast here is that between toxic and constructivist conceptualizations of emotionality.

The toxic view of emotionality draws heavily on metaphors of containment, toxic build-up, and discharge. From this perspective, physical and psychological traumas generate negative affect, most notably anger, anxiety, guilt, sadness, and shame. This negative affect is considered toxic, and it must therefore be periodically discharged to minimize its hazards to the individual. Catharsis (from the Greek *katharsis*, a cleansing or purification process) has long been a favorite metaphor in attempts to define the essence of psychotherapy process. Research on emotional experience and expression during psychotherapy suggests, however, that the processes involved in psychological improvement are more complex than a simple catharsis model can accommodate. As Greenberg and Safran (1987) have documented, the expression of affect in the absence of personal meaning does not have the therapeutic effectiveness of emotional expressions that have personal and present relevance for the individual. Pragmatically, these studies suggest that it is less helpful to ask a person to act emotionally (such as by yelling or beating a pillow) than it is to ask him or her to recall significant life events and express the affect thereby evoked.

Constructivist views of emotionality and psychological development suggest that processes far more complex than discharge are involved in effective psychotherapy (Greenberg & Safran, 1987; Guidano, 1987, 1991; Mahoney, 1991, in press; Neimeyer & Mahoney, 1995). By and large, constructivists challenge the traditional separations drawn among the dimensions of affect, behavior, and cognition. They also challenge the assumption that negative affects are necessarily dangerous to the individual. Drawing on metaphors and models from developmental systems theories, constructivists maintain that affective distress and disorder are reflections of a complex living system's attempts to continually organize and reorganize itself in the face of past, present, and anticipated challenges. Of particular importance here is the constructivist attempt to reframe episodes and patterns of emotional intensity and disorganization in terms of ongoing experiments in self-organization (Guidano, 1987, 1991; Schore, 1994). From such a perspective, negative affect is neither an enemy nor the heart of an individual's psychological problems. Rather, such affect is viewed as a natural expression of the developmental dynamics of a self-organizing system.

The conceptual and practical significance of the contrast between toxic and constructivist views of emotionality is considerable. The therapist operating out of beliefs that intense negative affect is bad for the individual is likely to (consciously or otherwise) collude in the client's sense of crisis and urgency in eliminating or overcoming uncomfortable or disorganizing emotions. The therapeutic strategy is reduced to one of control, and affective patterns easily come to be seen as the problems to be solved, rather than as reflections of discrepancies in the ongoing development of the client's overall life. Likewise, when old emotional patterns return—as they often do in episodes of ambiguity, fatigue, and sudden life change—there is a tendency for both therapist and client to view such developments as regressive or recidivistic. The constructivist view encourages a more developmental conceptualization. Sensitivities and emotional vulnerabilities as well as episodes of affective intensity are respected as important and instructive reflections of the individual's complex and unique constellation of personal history, affective organization, and current contextual challenges and supports. Requests for interpersonal support—most of which occur outside the therapeutic relationship—and the reactions to those requests are important factors in the individual's efforts to function.

Related to this last point is the fact that affective requests and self-reports lie at the heart of both the therapeutic relationship and the process of psychotherapy itself. This has been recognized by psychodynamic practitioners for a century, and it has been a central theme in major religious traditions. Donoghue and Shapiro (1984) reported that the Sumerians (ca. 3000 B.C.) "were the first people to confess their sins to gods through intermediaries" (p. 14). Later, the Jewish holy day of Yom Kippur ("Day of Atonement") and the Christian tradition of confession (or reconciliation) were to become central aspects of religious practice in Western civilization. Between 500 and 1300 A.D., the Celts evolved their concept of the *anmcharas* ("soul friends") who offered personal and imaginal spiritual guidance, usually associated with an act of self-disclosure (confession) and some form of cleansing ritual (e.g., floor sweeping). With their inclination toward this sacrament of self-disclosure, the Irish eventually transformed the Roman Catholic stance toward confession and absolution (forgiveness). The act itself originated as a public ritual, but it eventually became private, resulting in the 874 Vatican decree that secrets shared by a parishioner with a priest were to be considered absolutely private. The need for this privacy and for some degree of anonymity was ritualized by Cardinal Charles Borromeo of Milan, Italy, in 1576. Borromeo worried about the dangerous temptations that might be energized by male priests hearing the intimate confessions of female parishioners. An astute inventor, Borromeo devised a box called the *capsa incertorum*—first intended for the private confessions of thieves and later generalized to all parishioners—that created a physical separation and some degree of anonymity between confessor and priest.

With large leaps in tradition and presentation, this protective distance was maintained in the inauguration of the profession now called psychotherapy. The prototype of the psychoanalyst is that of an appropriately distant and emotionally unreactive blank screen onto which the client can detail personal confessions and project his or her emotional conflicts. During the past two decades, researchers have become increasingly involved in the study of confession, dialogue, and personal narrative and their role in the organization and reorganization of human experience (Bruner, 1990; Carr, 1986; Danto, 1985; Dewart, 1989; Freeman, 1993; Friedman, 1992; Gonçalves, 1994; Joyce-Moniz, 1988; Mahoney, 1994; Manning & Cullum-Swan, 1994; Neimeyer & Mahoney, 1995). A recurring theme in these studies has dealt with the dialectical (contrast-generated) processes involved in shuttling back and forth across the boundaries between experiencing and explaining. Although the distinction between these two realms is not without its own semantic difficulties, specialists in narrative and constructivist psychotherapies have become increasingly interested in the processes that reflect exchanges and relations between the poles of relatively more mediated (reflective, symbolic) activities and relatively less mediated (immediate, bodily) experiences (Bozarth-Campbell, 1979; Dewart, 1989; Greenberg & Pascual-Leone, 1995; Guidano, 1987, 1991; Mahoney, in press). Besides encouraging a more diversified dialogue on the engines of psychological adaptation and development, these explorations have begun to shed new light on the legacy and limitations of mind–body dualism in health psychology.

CONCLUDING REMARKS

In a very condensed fashion, I have basically made three observations:

1. There is increasing consensus that emotional experience and affect regulation are central to all other psychological processes, especially those dealing with personality and identity development.

2. The most common emotional problems encountered in psychotherapy involve not only the pain of negative affectivity but also individuals' variable capacities to experience and express intense emotions.
3. Discharge models of therapeutic benefits are now being challenged
   by constructive (developmental systems) models of ongoing self-
   organization.

It is in this last domain that dialogical and narrative approaches have converged with constructivist perspectives on the potential role of bridging
processes that relate feeling and telling in psychological adjustment and
development.

I shall conclude with some brief reflections that have particular relevance to psychotherapists. It seems clear that clients' relations with their
own emotional experiences can be importantly influenced by their therapists' models of and reactions to emotion (their own as well as that of
their clients). Generally speaking, psychotherapists who are relatively more
aware, accepting, and respectful of their own emotional processes are more
likely to foster such awareness, acceptance, and respect on the part of their
clients. As psychotherapy researchers continue to document, the emotional
presence of the therapist and the emotional experiencing of the client are
significant predictors of psychotherapy outcome (Greenberg & Pinsof,
1986). The definition and measurement of emotional presence are not
simple, however, and much work remains to be done on these process variables in psychotherapy.

There is a fascinating theoretical and practical paradox here that also
merits further investigation. Being emotionally present to clients is neither easy nor free of hazards for psychotherapists (Bugental, 1978, 1981;
Guy, 1987; Mahoney, 1991). Therapist stress and burnout may be ampli-
fied by the challenges of being emotionally present to, and sometimes feeling responsible for, the affective lives of clients. Good psychotherapeutic
work is positively correlated with the caring and emotional presence of
the therapist. At the same time, however, caring and emotional presence
are the most demanding and stressful aspects of being a psychotherapist.

How are these two to be reconciled in a manner that respects both the rights and needs of the client and the responsibilities and personal limitations of the psychotherapist? In my opinion, this is a question that is likely to energize psychotherapy research well into the 21st century, if not beyond. As a psychotherapist, how does one witness and participate in the intensely emotional aspects of so many human lives without being adversely affected? Because most psychotherapy clients are not the proverbial "happy campers," how does the psychotherapy practitioner cope with such intense and selective involvement in human pain, be it anger, anxiety, depression, grief, guilt, shame, or whatever? Research on the personal lives of psychotherapists suggests that they may be particularly vulnerable to depression, relationship difficulties, and substance abuse (Guy, 1987; Mahoney, 1991), and that these vulnerabilities may be related to emotional distancing, exhaustion, and emotional numbing. Recent research also suggests that a career as a psychotherapist may substantially accelerate and expand psychological development (Mahoney, in press).

It is for these reasons that psychotherapists are well advised to monitor their own emotional lives and to prioritize psychological self-care as an important aspect of their own well-being. Whatever their theoretical orientation, the practicing psychotherapist is destined to encounter and vicariously witness a wide range of human experiences. Because of the contemporary nature and focus of the profession, a substantial majority of those experiences are likely to involve trauma—abuse, accidents, injustices, natural disasters, oppression, and so on. While counseling their clients on how best to cope with such trauma, psychotherapists cannot help but be personally affected. Conscious and tacit assumptions about life, human nature, pain, and psychological development are likely to be challenged by the breadth and depth of a psychotherapist's vicarious professional experiences. All of those experiences are emotional in nature, and a therapist's "feelings about feelings" are likely to be a significant moderator variable in his or her professional services as well as his or her personal life. What does this mean for the selection and training of psychotherapists? What does it mean for their developmental trajectories and the risks and benefits of counseling others about life experiences? These are, as yet, unaddressed—let alone answered—questions in psychotherapy. Needless to say, I emphasize their importance to our understanding and optimal enactment of the role of professional life counselors.

REFERENCES

Beck, A. T. (1967). *Depression: Clinical, experimental, and theoretical aspects.* New York: Hoeber.

Bowlby, J. (1988). *A secure base.* New York: Basic Books.

Bozarth-Campbell, A. (1979). *The word's body: An incarnational aesthetic of interpretation.* Tuscaloosa, AL: University of Alabama Press.

Breuer, J., & Freud, S. (1966). *Studies of hysteria.* New York: Avon. (Original work published in 1895)

Bruner, J. (1990). *Acts of meaning.* Cambridge, MA: Harvard University Press.

Bugental, J. F. T. (1978). *Psychotherapy and process.* Reading, MA: Addison-Wesley.

Bugental, J. F. T. (1981). *The search for authenticity.* New York: Irvington.

Carr, D. (1986). *Time, narrative, and history.* Bloomington, IN: Indiana University Press.

Danto, A. C. (1985). *Narration and knowledge.* New York: Columbia University Press.

Dewart, L. (1989). *Evolution and consciousness: The role of speech in the origin and development of human nature.* Toronto, Canada: University of Toronto Press.

Donoghue, Q., & Shapiro, L. (1984). *Bless me, father, for I have sinned.* New York: Donald I. Fine, Inc.

Freeman, M. (1993). *Rewriting the self: History, memory, narrative.* New York: Routledge.

Friedman, M. (1992). *Dialogue and the human image.* London: Sage.

Gonçalves, O. F. (1994). *Cognitive narrative psychotherapy.* Unpublished manuscript, University of Minho, Braga, Portugal.

Greenberg, L. S., & Pascual-Leone, J. (1995). A dialectical constructivist approach to experiential change. In R. A. Neimeyer & M. J. Mahoney (Eds.), *Constructivism in psychotherapy* (169–191). Washington, DC: American Psychological Association.

Greenberg, L. S., & Pinsof, W. (Eds.). (1986). *The psychotherapeutic process.* New York: Guilford.

Greenberg, L. S., & Safran, J. D. (1987). *Emotion in psychotherapy.* New York: Guilford.

Guidano, V. F. (1987). *Complexity of the self.* New York: Guilford.

Guidano, V. F. (1991). *The self in process.* New York: Guilford.

Guy, J. D. (1987). *The personal life of the psychotherapist.* New York: Wiley.

Hobson, R. F. (1985). *Forms of feeling: The heart of psychotherapy.* London: Tavistock.

Izard, C. E., Kagan, J., & Zajonc, R. B. (Eds.). (1984). *Emotions, cognition, and behavior.* Cambridge, England: Cambridge University Press.

Joyce-Moniz, L. (1988). Self-talk, dramatic expression, and constructivism. In C. Perris, I. M. Blackburn, & H. Perris (Eds.), *Cognitive psychotherapy: Theory and practice* (pp. 276–305). Heidelberg, Germany: Springer-Verlag.

Krantz, A. M., & Pennebaker, J. W. (1994). Expression of traumatic experience through dance and writing: Psychological and health effects. Manuscript submitted for publication, Southern Methodist University, Dallas.

Mahoney, M. J. (1991). *Human change processes.* New York: Basic Books.

Mahoney, M. J. (Ed.). (1994). *The cognitive and constructive psychotherapies: Recent developments.* New York: Springer.

Mahoney, M. J. (in press). *Constructive psychotherapy.* New York: Guilford.

Manning, P. K., & Cullum-Swan, B. (1994). Narrative, content, and semiotic analysis. In N. K. Denzin & Y. S. Lincoln (Eds.), *The handbook of qualitative research* (pp. 463–477). London: Sage.

Neimeyer, R. A., & Mahoney, M. J. (Eds.). (1995). *Constructivism in psychotherapy.* Washington, DC: American Psychological Association.

Pennebaker, J. W. (1990). *Opening up: The healing power of confiding in others.* New York: Morrow.

Pennebaker, J. W. (1993). Putting stress into words: Health, linguistic, and therapeutic implications. *Behaviour Research and Therapy, 31,* 539–548.

Schore, A. N. (1994). *Affect regulation and the origin of self.* Hillsdale, NJ: Erlbaum.

Thayer, R. E. (1989). *The biopsychology of mood and arousal.* Oxford, England: Oxford University Press.

Watkins, M. (1986). *Invisible guests: The development of imaginal dialogues.* Hillsdale, NJ: Analytic Press.

Watson, D., & Clark, L. A. (Eds.). (1994). Special Issue on Personality and Psychopathology. *Journal of Abnormal Psychology, 103,* 3–77.

13

The Roles of Disclosure and Emotional Reversal in Clinical Practice

Benjamín Domínguez, Pablo Valderrama,
María de los Angeles Meza, Sara Lidia Pérez,
Amparo Silva, Gloria Martínez, Victor Manuel Méndez,
and Yolanda Olvera

Love, pleasure, and pain play central roles in human experience. Despite the importance of emotions in everyday life, scientific efforts to try to understand them and their links to the mind and brain have proved troublesome. Particularly problematic from a clinical perspective are creating and instituting ways of controlling emotions (especially negative ones) in clients and even in psychologists. The present chapter examines two overlapping clinical issues in helping individuals to manage stress and emotions among adults in Mexico City. The first focuses on the role of written disclosure on the control of biological and subjective stress. A second strategy considers the role of disclosure as a technique to bring about emotional reversal. As we discuss, processes related to disclosure and emotional reversal may not conform to traditional notions of stress and linear causal relations.

If we are to understand the effects of emotional stress on human behavior, we need to be able to distinguish between an emotional and a nonemotional state. Unfortunately a pure physiological definition of emotion of stress is limited. Selye (1983) defines *stress* as the result of any demand on the body, using objective indicators such as bodily and chemical changes that appear after any demand. The perception and interaction of such arousal is an important psychological issue. It is the perceived experience of an emotional change that determines its effect on other mental processes, such as attention and short-term memory (Horgan, 1994). It is the perception of arousal as well as the preoccupation with probable stressors that interferes with continuous conscious processing (Mandler, 1993).

Current theories view emotions as consisting of an interaction of a cognitive evaluative schema with visceral arousal. In this context, evaluative cognitions provide the qualitative component of an emotional experience, and visceral activity provides its intensity and peculiar "emotional" characteristics. Some strokes, for example, may cause peculiar conditions known as prosopagnosia, in which the patient is unable to recognize faces, even those as familiar as a spouse's or child's. Even though the patient is unable to recognize them, looking at the face of someone emotionally close will increase the heartbeat rate. Thus the visual stimulus can evoke an emotional response even if the verbal association is lost (Klivington, 1989). Observations such as these have led to the idea that visceral arousal is necessary for emotional experience, but that the nature of emotional experience will depend on an individual's thoughts, memories, and current circumstances. According to this view, individuals will evaluate any experience as a positive or negative emotion depending on what they expect of it, their social context, and whether they feel in control of a situation.

Most relevant to the present discussion is the emotional state of stress. Historically, people have believed that stress-relevant psychological factors affect disease susceptibility and course (see Georges, chapter 2, this volume). A number of recent studies have shown that various stressors can adversely affect immune function and that some psychological interventions may reduce stress, thereby improving immune function (e.g., Kiecolt-Glaser & Glaser, 1992). An important current task is the development of effective psychological interventions for immune-related illness that is linked to "out of control" emotional states. The controlled intervention design, in which potentially valuable applications of psychoimmunologic research are tested, represents a scientifically superior method for revealing causal or perhaps nonlinear relationships between psychosocial and physiological processes.

MOVING BEYOND SIMPLE CAUSAL MODELS

Lazarus (1993) argued that stress is an inevitably "unclean" variable that depends on a dynamic and changing interaction between person and environment. He also noted that it is possible to break down a complex stressful situation into interdependent variables—in other words, within linear cause–effect approaches—especially when it comes to studying people in natural, clinical, and everyday situations. From our view, however, reducing complex relationships into simple causal components is probably not possible.

Clinical interventions often try to modify the presumed causes of a client's behavior or emotional problems. For example, responses to psychosocial stressors are often the focus of treatment programs for different chronic pain populations (Domínguez, Valderrama, Pérez, & Meza, 1994). Given the central role played in this clinical context of causal variables in the treatment programs, many authors (Haynes, Huland, & Oliveira, 1993) have emphasized that an empirically based causal analysis is important to the development of effective treatment programs for clients. Errors in causal analysis of any given problem are also likely to lead to poor treatments.

With most clients and patients, the identification and diagnosis of emotional problems is necessary, but not sufficient for the identification of causal variables. That is because there can be many possible causes for single psychological stress problems as well as differences across clients in the impact of various causes of the same emotional state problem. Consequently it is usually not possible to select among social skills, cognitive, biofeedback, or pharmacological interventions just on the basis of the client's diagnosis of, for example, posttraumatic stress disorder.

Most of the current methods for detecting causal relationships presume that the relationships are linear (i.e., the strength of the relationship between the variables is equal across their values). An accumulating body of research suggests, however, that the causal relationship often demonstrates functional plateaus, critical levels, varying causal latencies, duration of effects, and more complex nonlinear functional relationships (Haynes et al., 1993).

Causal relationships can change across time. They are unstable and dynamic. There is strong empirical support for the hypothesis that the causes of many distress-associated disorders, such as chronic pain, substance abuse, or depression, may change across time and developmental periods (Haynes et al., 1993). Consequently, the relative strength of causal variables can change across the course of effective treatments. According to Barton (1994), the general characteristics of self-organizations (a concept that denotes a process by which a structure or pattern emerges in an open system without specifications from the outside environment) are shared by chemical, biological, and psychological systems and include among others (a) readiness to exhibit multiple stable states that change suddenly from one to another if a parameter value crosses a critical threshold (e.g., chronic pain patients who go from a suffering to a relaxation state); (b) cyclical state changes (as the ones that happen within a Monday–Friday cycle linked to work stress); (c) the structural coupling of component processes; (d) temporal, spatial, and behavioral organization (e.g. patients' relaxation skills that progress from muscular-response to language mediated change); (e) localized instabilities that can lead to one part of the system to organize itself differently from another part of the system (e.g., the clinical finding of patients with "relaxed" peripheral temperature index and stressed verbal reports); (f) the ability of one unit to cause other units to oscillate at a harmonically related frequency (entrainment); and (g) behaviors that could be modeled by a system of nonlinear equations (e.g., inverted-U functions, as in the Yerkes-Dodson Law).

There are clinically relevant implications in considering transitions from one to another emotional state as a causal variable. First, the degree of change of a variable (or the degree of contrast between current and previous magnitudes of the causal variable) is an important target of assessment (psychophysiological stress profile). Second, the effects of intervention may dissipate with time, rendering this causal phenomenon difficult to detect. Third, patients and clients with equal values on psychophysiological measurements are not necessarily equal on that state (stress impact, or subjective pain).

IDENTIFYING AND TREATING STRESS WITHIN A CLINICAL CONTEXT: RELAXATION AND DISCLOSURE

In 1985, Mexico City experienced a devastating earthquake. After the earthquake, it soon became widely accepted that virtually anyone could become psychologically or physically affected by current or recalled stressors. This social reaction created the appropriate conditions for psychologists' professional intervention. Within this context, a primary preventive level approach to stress management was soon adopted by many top managers in goverment. In recent years, there has been a growing recognition of the important role that stress plays in the etiology and maintenance of both psychological and somatic disorders. Consequently, the demand for effective stress management programs has been increasing in clinical psychology as well as in medicine. Unlike many other treatment approaches, stress management is not targeted toward any particular symptom syndrome or diagnostic category. Stress or negative emotion expression or inhibition may play a role in any disorder or illness.

There may be instances in which a subject reports feeling stressed but shows no obvious physiological sign of sympathetic arousal (the de facto sign of stress). In such cases, psychophysiological analyses offer little constructive contribution to the understanding of the phenomenology of stress. Conversely, there may be instances where a person shows clear patterns of physiological reactivity to an eliciting stimulus but reports no emotional signs of distress. How should psychologists interpret such disjunction among behavior, subjective experience, and physiological response? Is it reasonable to assume that psychophysiological responses alone define a stress response? Or is the proper definition of stress, in the final analysis, a phenomenological one? Psychophysiological measurement, as a subdiscipline of the broader interdisciplinary field of behavioral neuroscience, is distinguished by its use of surface recordings of bioelectric activity rather than invasive procedures for the study of emotional activity linked to biological changes.

Among the many biological measures of stress, we have tended to rely on hand temperature. Circulation in the hands and fingers is controlled by the autonomic nervous system through sympathetic vasoconstricting nerves as well as by circulating vasoactive hormones. It is generally assumed that feedback-induced vasodilation results from lowered sympathetic activation (Surwit, Pilon, & Fenton, 1978). Temperature feedback studies employing brief training sessions (Keefe, 1978) generally have demonstrated significant vasodilation, whereas those employing longer sessions have failed to do so (Surwit, 1977).

Disclosure Within a Stress Management Setting

In 1992, we began a large scale stress management program using peripheral temperature as a biological indicator of the effectiveness of each of several interventions. The stress management program involved 174 male (46.8%) and 198 female (53.2%) adults ranging in age from 23 to 63. The sample was selected by management based on administrative criteria outlined by the the Director of Training within a large governmental office. Workshops of 15 hours consisting of small groups of approximately 14 people were run for three to five consecutive sessions. The project had two main goals. First, we attempted to provide relaxation response training in order to help participants decrease or restructure their dysfunctional coping style to job stressors. Second, we offered participants a ready to use technique based on self-disclosure through writing to moderate or decrease active inhibition effects on cognitive and somatic measures of stress (Pennebaker, 1993).

General results linked to the first goal were achieved with autogenic relaxation training techniques. Using skin temperature as the dependent measure, the autogenic training data were ultimately compared with a second training technique, which we call "Pennebaker's exercises" wherein participants wrote about their stressors. The physiological data were then compared in terms of temporal shifts in temperature and correlation between subjective emotional change and physiological changes.

In the writing phase of the project, participants wrote about their painful secrets for four separate days different perspectives each day. The different perspectives were based on correlational findings by Pennebaker (1993) that indicated that people who consistently use negative emotions in their "writing secrets" sessions subsequently evidence greater health improvements than those who overuse positive emotions. In addition, those who move from conveying very little to a high degree of insight and causal thinking over the 3–5 days of writing also demonstrate health improvements.

On the 1st day of writing, subjects received the standard trauma writing instructions (Trauma Writing-I condition): Do not pay attention to grammatical rules while writing, use first person, anonymity guaranteed, write nonstop about painful secrets. On the 2nd day, participants were told to write about traumas using specific language rules, including the use of a high number of negative emotion and low number of positive emotion words and encouragement to use causal words within their natural writing style (Language Guided condition). On the 3rd day, participants repeated the standard trauma writing that had been employed on the 1st day (Trauma Writing-II condition). Finally, on day 4, participants were encouraged to avoid using first person in their writing in order to promote psychological distancing from the original emotional state (Third Person condition).

As can be seen in Figure 1, hand temperature increased markedly in the two Trauma Writing conditions and decreased in the Third Person condition. Interestingly, only the Language Guided condition failed to evidence a significant increase in peripheral temperature from before to after writing. Particularly striking is the comparison of changes in hand temperature for the various writing conditions with the results from the autogenic relaxation training. Overall, the within-session increase of hand temperature from before to after relaxation was 0.7° C. Averaging across the two Trauma Writing conditions, hand temperature increased 1.5° C— over twice as much.

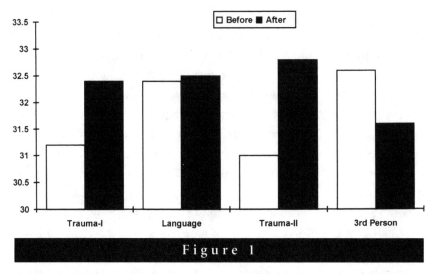

Figure 1

Changes in skin temperature (in centigrade) from before to after writing as a function of condition. Trauma-I and Trauma-II refer to individuals' writing about traumas; Language refers to the language-guided condition; 3rd Person refers to people writing about traumas from the third person perspective. From Domínguez et al. (1994) based on data from 372 workers between 1992 and 1993.

Analyzing the data on a case-by-case basis, it was possible to find a general pattern of temperature temporal patterning as early as during the first trauma writing that served as a predictor of which subjects would evidence emotional improvements and who would not. Beginning the first writing session, dominant hand temperature started to increase, then at the middle of session (when people report disclosure of negative emotions) temperature decreased significantly from the initial temperature. Although preliminary, these observations suggest that we can gain tremendous insight by looking at specific fluctuations in temperature on a minute-by-minute basis.

In summary, autogenic training and disclosure through writing are both effective in reducing stress, as measured by increased hand temperature. Whereas the writing produced more striking increases, the degree to which the relaxation training may have actually augmented the writing's effects is not known . To explore these issues in greater detail, we attempted to adapt these techniques to a chronic pain sample.

Potential Value of Disclosure Among
Chronic Pain Patients

According to an evolutionary approach, negative as well as positive emotions play functional roles in human behavior. Pain, too, has survival value in helping organisms avoid further injuries to tissues (Domínguez, 1994). Chronic pain has often been distinguished from acute pain, which is a response to a trauma and dissipates once healing has taken place. Acute pain serves the biological function of warning the body that tissue damage is present and that a change in behavior may be necessary for repair and healing to occur.

Chronic pain, on the other hand, is pain that persists for at least 3 to 6 months, often in the absence of specific evidence of tissue damage. The bulk of the research on chronic pain has focused on identifying characteristics of specific pain syndromes (e.g., headache and chronic back pain), developing psychometric instruments for assessing pain, and delineating various psychological parameters associated with pain, such as cognitive and affective responses. Research has also addressed the efficacy of both medical and psychological treatments on the relief of chronic pain and improvements in behavior despite the subjective reports of pain.

Although research in this field has yielded encouraging results, pain continues to be a complex phenomenon for clinicians to diagnose and track (Wall & Jones, 1991). One important area where confusion prevails concerns basic definition. For example, researchers disagree on how to define pain in general and how to describe specific syndromes (Flor & Turk, 1989).

The position that the clinician adopts in defining pain has both assessment and treatment implications. The decision to employ a specific clinical procedure with a particular pain syndrome often appears to depend more on history and intuition than on empirical findings. Although a number of empirically sound procedures are available for the noninvasive management of chronic pain, it remains unclear how the clinician should determine which of these procedures is likely to be the most effective for a particular patient with a specific pain problem (Domínguez, Alvarez, Cortes, & Olvera, 1993).

The fastest growing area of research on the assessment of chronic pain deals with cognitive variables. One topic of current interest is patient beliefs about pain. One reason for assessing pain beliefs is that they may predict response to treatment. Williams and Thorn (1989) found that patients who believed that their pain was likely to be a chronic condition failed to comply with physical therapy or behavioral therapy assignments.

Another cognitive process that is relevant to the understanding of pain responses—self-efficacy—is based on people's judgments of their abilities to execute given levels of performance and to exercise control over events (Bandura, O'Leary, Taylor, Gauthier, & Gossard, 1987). Chronic pain patients differ in the degree to which they view themselves as having control over pain (internal or proprioceptive control) versus other external factors having control over pain (e.g., inhibition or social sharing of painful emotional experience).

Coping style reflects another aspect of cognitive processing. In a recent review of coping among chronic pain patients, Turner (1991) emphasized the roles of attentional control and other psychological factors related to the ability of people to cope with pain. First, chronic pain patients who remain passive or who use catastrophizing, ignoring and reinterpreting, attention diversion, and praying and hoping as coping strategies typically have high levels of physical and psychological disability. Second, patients who rate their perceived control as high or who rely on active or attentional coping function much more effectively. Researchers need to identify which of these constructs is more useful in understanding pain disability and if there are other basic processes, such as active inhibition, that support observed variability and outcomes.

It has been clear from the beginning that the kind of questions and answers raised about pain reflect different sets of needs that are not always convergent. Whereas the scientist seeks to explain data and predict future emotional and disability states, the healthcare expert searches for tools to promote effective treatment options. The patient, of course, seeks pain relief and improved quality of life. These divergent needs help explain the persistence of unresolved issues in the field, both in the research enterprise and in the clinical setting. For example, the recognition that emotion and biology do not function as isolated entities has been one of the important advances in thought about pain. Still, beliefs from earlier decades tend to perpetuate the view that pain is either in the body or in the mind (Merskey, 1985). In clinical practice (and to a lesser degree in published research), pain continues to be attributed to psychological causes when physical findings are lacking and pain persists despite medical intervention.

Supported by several clinical case studies, we have begun exploring the disclosure paradigm as a research strategy to help clarify the psychological variables that increase a patient's risk for developing a chronic pain problem. Early prospective studies designed to assess verbal negative emotional and psychological status soon after an injury or early in the presentation of a pain complaint permit comparisons between those whose pain resolves and those whose pain fails to do so.

Although it may be possible to identify a group at increased risk for chronic pain on the basis of psychological features, it does not follow that the majority of patients whose pain becomes chronic are members of this group. For this to be achieved it is still necessary to compare them with healthy groups within the same paradigm.

Since 1988, we have been involved in a wide assessment and noninvasive treatment program for chronic pain patients at the General Hospital of Mexico City Pain Clinic. Data collected by Jose Montes, chief of immunology services, indicated that 12 to 22% of the 41,000 monthly outpatient visits were for headache. Our initial research was based on a sample of 800 chronic pain patients who attended the General Hospital. By way of comparison, we were able to identify a group of adult workers who were defined as "clinically healthy" who participated in a program of Labor Stress Management (1992–1994) that was conducted at the request of the Secretary of Labor of Mexico, as part of its National Program of Training for Total Quality.

Initially, we identified subjects in both groups who presented notable limitations in their capacity to express and communicate emotional states. These individuals considered themselves as "isolated and with not many friends," and suggested that "I don't like it that no one knows what is going on with me." Interestingly, chronic pain subjects with these characteristics evidenced the highest distress and suffering levels and showed highly variable physical symptomotology.

We started an exploratory clinical study with pain patients that consisted of biofeedback, hypnosis and autogenic relaxation, and the stress disclosure paradigm exercises with the therapeutic target of reducing the active inhibition mechanism and its psychophysiological consequences (high systolic pressure and low peripheral temperatures).

Patients were informed that during four sessions they should write about their painful secrets with the intention of reducing their distress. The instructions for each of the exercises were verbally provided by the therapist in charge who stayed with the patient during 20 minutes of writing. Before and after the exercise, arterial pressure and pulse were measured. In addition, peripheral temperature of the dominant hand was measured continuously across the sessions. At the end of the writing exercise, patients were asked to give a verbal report about their emotions. From the first session, patients reported different relief levels at the end of writing, which was compared with a relaxation state. Overall, changes in peripheral temperature from before to after the writing sessions were 2.5° C higher than for temperature changes from before to after relaxation.

With some patients it was necessary to repeat the writing exercise during the days between sessions. Preliminary data from 14 chronic pain patients suggested the temporal patterns of emotional change and peripheral temperature that appeared during the first exercise predicted the ultimate outcomes of the patients. Typically, patients began writing with a low temperature (28–30° C). Within 2 or 3 minutes the temperature increased (30–33° C) and then decreased (a mean of 1.5° C). Finally during the last 2 or 3 minutes they increased above the baseline (3 or more degrees).

When we compare group temperature patterns over time for healthy subjects with chronic pain patients, several differences emerge. First, psychophysiological variability is much greater for healthy subjects than for chronic pain patients. Second, a smaller proportion of chronic pain patients could initiate control of skin temperature during biofeedback than could healthy controls. Finally, the ways that skin temperatures fluctuated over time during the disclosure-writing sessions tended to predict who would demonstrate faster clinical improvements.

USING DISCLOSURE TO ACHIEVE EMOTIONAL REVERSAL

Unlike adults, young children can move quickly from one emotional state to another. Through maturation, however, people tend to lose this ability. For adults in distress, it is virtually impossible for them to alter their emotional states. Indeed, the act of trying to change their emotions can produce even more stress. When this occurs, some people look for medical or psychological help. At this point, the specialist in human behavior must intervene with at least two goals in mind: (a) to choose the most effective techniques to help clients acquire greater flexibility in making a transition from one emotional state to another and (b) to make sense of the relations between a particular emotional state, its psychophysiological correlates, its linguistic correlates, and social consequences.

Our experience in designing psychological treatment programs for stress-affected persons in Mexico City has led us to consider that stress shares many characteristics with negative emotions. In this context, the most important therapeutic target is to choose and apply techniques that can create favorable conditions to allow individuals to pass from a negative emotional state to a positive one within a relatively brief time. An excellent example of this kind of psychological intervention can be seen with the application of relaxation techniques, wherein a stressed individual is able to move into a state of serenity within a few minutes after only 2–4 weeks of training. Acquiring a voluntary relaxation response does not require a great deal of effort on the part of the patient. However, the ability to exercise emotional control in other situations is often more necessary and difficult to do.

In our opinion, one factor that hinders peoples' abilities to master the relaxation response is the difficulty of maintaining a state of active inhibition. Interestingly, the writing-disclosure technique may be ideally suited to reducing active inhibition in chronic pain patients. Writing exercises, then, may directly and indirectly decrease the psychophysiological effects of inhibition and, at the same time, increase the ability of individuals to pass from one emotional state to another (Apter, Fontana, & Murgatroyd, 1985).

According to our clinical research findings, the main value of the disclosure-writing paradigm lies in the kind of emotional reversal process that can be attained within a short time. This emotion reversal ability results when healthy and chronic pain patients attain insight from expressing and becoming aware of their deepest emotional secrets or pains and their related thoughts and psychophysiological patterns of response.

Of further interest are the open-ended verbal reports that our subjects have given after writing sessions, which illustrate positive long-term effects of the disclosure paradigm. Specifically, clients report that a writing intervention produces the fastest transition from one emotional state (e.g., distress and suffering) to another (e.g., relaxation) than any other psychological techniques we have employed, including autogenic training and biofeedback. Even within-session analyses of the skin temperature change patterns ("micro patterns") appear to have diagnostic and predictive functions, both for healthy and chronic pain samples.

The empirical finding that some chronic pain (low back) patients show an initial increase in muscle activity (EMG) and a delayed return to baseline only in the paraspinal muscles and only when verbally discussing personally relevant stress (Flor & Turk, 1989) represents additional support for what happens physiologically when people put their feelings about secret traumatic events into words. Finally, it is worth noting that successful control of physiological activity associated with nonverbalized negative emotional activity made evident by biofeedback may serve to enhance patients' perceived control regarding their ability to move from one to another emotional state.

REFERENCES

Apter, M. J., Fontana, D., & Murgatroyd, S. (1985). *Reversal theory: Applications and developments.* Cardiff, Wales: University College Cardiff Press.

Bandura, A., O'Leary, A., Taylor, C., Gauthier, J., & Gossard, D. (1987). Perceived self-efficacy and pain control: Opioid and non-opioid mechanisms. *Journal of Personality and Social Psychology, 35,* 563–571.

Barton, S. (1994). Chaos, self-organization, and psychology. *American Psychologist, 49,* 5–14.

Domínguez, B. (1994). La importancia de sentirse mal [The Importance of Feeling Badly]. *El Nacional Dominical, 231,* 24–27.

Domínguez, B., Alvarez, L. M., Cortes, J., & Olvera, Y. (1993). Multiple-psychophysiological, self-report, and other measurement in order to obtain clinical significance: A case study of chronic pain and synthetic opioid addiction. *Biofeedback and Self-Regulation, 18,* 159–160.

Domínguez, B., Valderrama, P., Perez, S. L., & Meza, M. A. (1994). *Relaxation, health and chaos theory.* Paper presented at Annual Meeting of the Society for Chaos Theory in Psychology and the Life Sciences. The John Hopkins University, Baltimore, MD.

Flor, H., & Turk, D. (1989). Psychophysiology of chronic pain: Do chronic pain patients exhibit symptom-specific psychophysiological responses? *Psychological Bulletin, 105,* 215–259.

Haynes, S. N., Huland, E. S., & Oliveira, J. (1993). Identifying causal relationships in clinical assessment. *Psychological Assessment, 5,* 281–291.

Horgan, J. (1994). Can science explain consciousness? *Scientific American, 270,* 72–78.

Keefe, F. (1978). Biofeedback vs. instructional control of skin temperature. *Journal of Behavioral Medicine, 1,* 323–335.

Kiecolt-Glaser, J. K., & Glaser, R. (1992). Psycho-neuroimmunology: Can psychological interventions modulate immunity? *Journal of Consulting and Clinical Psychology, 60,* 569–575.

Klivington, K. (1989). *The science of mind.* Boston: MIT Press.

Lazarus, R. S. (1993). From psychological stress to the emotions: A history of changing outlooks. *Annual Review of Psychology, 44,* 1–21.

Mandler, G. (1993). Thought, memory, and learning: Effects of emotional stress. In Goldberger & Bernitz (Eds.), *Handbook of stress. Theoretical and clinical aspects* (2nd Ed.). New York: Free Press.

Merskey, H. (1985). A mentalistic view of pain and behaviour. *Behavior and Brain Sciences, 8,* 65.

Pennebaker, J. (1993). Putting stress into words: Health, linguistic, and therapeutic implications. *Behaviour Research and Therapy, 31,* 539–548.

Selye, H. (1983). The stress concept: Past, present, and future. In C. L. Cooper (Ed.), *Stress research: Issues for the eighties.* New York: Wiley.

Surwit, R. (1977). Simple versus complex feedback displays in the training of digital temperature. *Journal of Consulting and Clinical Psychology, 45,* 146–147.

Surwit, R., Pilon, R., & Fenton, C. (1978). Behavioral treatment of Raynaud's disease. *Journal of Behavioral Medicine, 1,* 323–335.

Turner, J. (1991). Coping and chronic pain. In M. Bond, J. Charlton, & C. Woolf (Eds.), *Pain research and clinical management* (Vol. 4. Proceedings of the 6th World Congress on Pain). New York: Elsevier

Wall, P., & Jones, M. (1991). *Defeating pain: The war against a silent epidemic..* New York: Plenum.

Williams, D., & Thorn, B. (1989). An empirical assessment of pain beliefs. *Pain, 36,* 351–358.

14

Mental Rumination, Social Sharing, and the Recovery From Emotional Exposure

Bernard Rimé

M ajor negative life events and traumatic emotional conditions are known to have a long-lasting impact. People commonly reexperience traumatic events in intrusive recollections, distressing dreams, memory flashbacks, or overreactions when exposed to cues reminding them of the traumatic situation (American Psychiatric Association, 1994). Such thoughts and memories are involuntary and recurrent, and they can often persist for long periods of time. Tait and Silver (1989) observed that an average of 22.8 years following the most negative event in their life, 71% of investigated elderly subjects reported that they continued to experience thoughts, memories, and mental images of the event. Such tacit repetitive memories often parallel another type of manifestation: Victims of a major negative life event also commonly evidence an insatiable need to talk about their negative emotional experience. This phenomenon is poorly documented on empirical grounds (for an exception, see Pennebaker, 1993), yet it has been abundantly mentioned by investigators of reactions to undesirable life events (e.g., Bulman & Wortman, 1977; Silver & Wortman, 1980). Available data suggest this phenomenon to be pervasive. Surveys consistently evidence that more than 85% of people recently exposed to a major life event feel the need to share their experience verbally with others (Ersland, Weisaeth, & Sund, 1989; Mitchell & Glickman, 1977; Schoenberg, Carr, Peretz, Kutscher, & Cherico, 1975). As for memory reminiscences, the need for social communication observed after major negative life events seems to be long lasting. Lehman, Wortman, and Williams (1987) observed that 4 to 7 years after the accidental death of their spouse or child, 60% of spouses and 67% of parents still reported having spoken about the event in the recent past.

In contrast with a major negative emotional condition, the ordinary emotion typically appears at first sight as a very short-lived phenomenon. Obviously, defining the duration of an emotion is problematic because emotions are multicomponent phenomena (e.g., Scherer, 1984). They involve facial–expressive displays, physiological responses, experiential and cognitive changes, and action tendencies. Each of these components is likely to have different time courses (Frijda, Mesquita, Sonnemans, & Van Goozen, 1991). The duration of emotions also varies as a function of the relative permanence of emotion-eliciting circumstances. In fear, the emotion-eliciting object may show up and disappear within seconds, whereas in sadness, the elicitor may be the permanent loss of a loved one (Frijda et al., 1991). For these reasons, it is generally conceived that emotion ends with both the extinction of the elicitor and the return to baseline of the various response components. Whether emotion actually ends at that point, however, is questionable.

MENTAL RUMINATION AND SOCIAL SHARING AFTER EMOTION

Recent evidence shows that emotions are generally followed by processes that clearly parallel those observed after exposure to a major negative event (Mesquita, 1993; Rimé, Mesquita, Philippot, & Boca, 1991a; Rimé, Noël, & Philippot, 1991b; Vergara, 1993). Indeed, data show that in the hours, days, and even weeks following an emotional episode, memories of the episode tend to intrude into people's thoughts. The process occurs most often in a repetitive manner and manifests itself in two different forms.

One is mental rumination, a form of conscious thinking directed toward a given object for an extended period of time, involving both automatic and controlled processes (Martin & Tesser, 1989). The other is the social sharing of the emotional experience, a telling about this experience to some addressee in a socially shared language (Rimé, 1989). In its strongest form, the social sharing of emotion occurs in the course of conversations in which individuals openly communicate about the emotional circumstances and about their own feelings and reactions. In attenuated forms, the addressee is present only at the symbolic level, as is the case when people write letters or diaries.

Recalled Emotional Episodes, Mental Rumination, and Social Sharing

Evidence in support of the view that emotional experiences are usually prolonged in mental rumination and in social sharing was first found from studies using a retrospective procedure. Volunteer subjects were instructed first to recollect and briefly describe an emotional episode corresponding to a specified basic emotion (e.g., joy, anger, fear) that they recently experienced. They then answered a number of questions about their rumination and social sharing behaviors in relation to this episode during the hours and days that followed it. In several of these studies (Rimé, Mesquita, et al., 1991; Rimé, Nöel, et al., 1991), subjects' mental rumination was assessed by the following question: Did the event spontaneously come back to your mind afterwards? The proportion of subjects who answered negatively to this question was systematically very low in each of the studies (from 2.0 to 4.2%). A majority of subjects (from 50.0 and 59.2%) reported that spontaneous thoughts about the event occurred to them once or twice, or from time to time. Still, a considerable proportion of people (from 38.7 to 45.8%) mentioned that they have had such thoughts often or very often. These figures were observed for all types of emotion, of both positive and negative valence—joy, fear, anger, or sadness. Thus, these self-descriptive data were strongly in line with the prediction that ordinary emotion would be followed by repetitive thoughts about the emotional experience. Moreover, more intense emotional experiences elicited more frequent intrusive thoughts afterwards ($r = .44, p < .002$; Rimé, Mesquita, et al., 1991, study 6).

Further questions dealt with subjects' social communication behaviors related to the described emotional episode: Did they talk about the episode with other people? With whom? After what delay since the emotion? How often? Eight independent studies based on this procedure were reviewed by Rimé, Philippot, Boca, & Mesquita (1992). In total, 913 subjects, ranging in age from 12 to 60 years, reported on 1,384 emotional episodes. The observed proportion of cases in which the subject reported having talked with people about the emotional episode varied from 90.0 to 96.3% of the sample. These figures are very similar to those quoted above from the literature on the consequences of major negative life events. They did not vary with age or with sex. Neither the type of basic emotion, whether fear, anger, joy, sadness, or shame, nor the valence of the emotional experience, whether positive or negative, predicted the proportion of socially shared episodes. Furthermore, within the limits of investigated cultures (i.e., various Western European countries), no effect of culture was evidenced with respect to the global rate of socially shared episodes (Rimé et al., 1992; Vergara, 1993). However, investigating the social sharing of emotion in a cross-cultural study on Dutch, Surinamese, and Turkish subjects, Mesquita (1993) also observed comparable rates of social sharing, but found important differences in social sharing content. Data from these studies revealed that social sharing begins almost immediately after an emotional event and is predominantly a repetitive process. Indeed, the modal answer given by respondents was that they talked about the episode first "on the same day," and that they spoke "several times with several persons" about it (Rimé, Mesquita, et al., 1991; Rimé, Noël, et al., 1991). As was the case for mental rumination, quantity of social sharing was found to be positively correlated with the intensity of the emotional disruptiveness ($r = .49, p < .001$, Rimé, Mesquita, et al., 1991). It was also observed that when involved in some form of social sharing of an emotional episode, subjects predominantly reported experiencing (a) vivid mental images of the episode, (b) marked bodily sensations, and (c) intense subjective feelings (Rimé, Noel, et al., 1991).

Daily Emotional Events, Mental Rumination, and Social Sharing

Overall, thus, in these studies employing the retrospective procedure, mental rumination and social sharing were reported by subjects in more than 90% of the described emotional episodes. Yet these self-descriptive data may be somewhat limited in testing the hypothesis that any emotion, even if of mild intensity, is followed by private and public rehearsal. Indeed, subjects were left free to choose the emotional episode to be reported about. One could suspect them to have selected from their long-term memory relatively more intense and relatively more distinct emotional memories. Moreover, they might have selectively remembered episodes that they did think about and that they did socially share. Thus, the possibility cannot be ruled out that the self-descriptive data collected to assess the extent and frequency of these two processes were unduly inflated. In order to overcome limitations inherent in the retrospective method, investigations based on alternative procedures further tested the hypothesis that emotions are followed by mental rumination and by social sharing. Among the alternative procedures used were (a) the diary method, (b) follow-up investigations, and (c) experimental induction of emotion.

The diary method allowed subjects to report their mental rumination and social sharing during the hours and days immediately following the related emotional event. Such a method largely prevents potential reconstructive memory bias. In this procedure, subjects filled out a questionnaire every night before going to bed for a period of 2 to 3 weeks, depending on the study. Subjects first briefly described the event that had affected them the most during that day, or the day before, depending on the study. They then answered various questions, including questions on their social sharing or their mental rumination about the described event. Three such studies were conducted (Rimé, Philippot, Finkenauer, Legast, Moorkens, & Tornqvist, 1994). In one of them, 53 subjects reported every night on the event that affected them the most during that day. They did so, on average, for 22.5 consecutive days, creating a sample of 1,046 emotional events. For each event, subjects reported whether they talked about the event. In this sample, 66.8% of emotional events were socially shared.

In a second study, 34 subjects reported, for each of 14 consecutive nights, the most emotional event of the day. Among these 461 emotional events, 57.9% were reported as having been socially shared. It is remarkable that the figures observed in these two studies were both comparable with or even slightly superior to those recorded in retrospective studies for the social sharing that took place during the day of the emotional event, that is, 59.2% (Rauw & Rimé, 1990), 50% (Rimé, Mesquita, et al., 1991), 57.5% (Rimé, Noël, et al., 1991, study 1), 57.33% (Rimé, Noël, et al., 1991, study 2), and 52.8% (Rimé, Noël, et al., 1991, study 3).

Finally, both social sharing and mental rumination were assessed in a third diary study in which 17 subjects reported during 20 or 21 consecutive days about the most emotional event of the previous day. As compared with the other two studies, the monitored period was thus increased in length. In such conditions, the proportion of events that were reported as having been socially shared amounted to 74.1%. The social sharing was repetitive in most cases (49.0%), with 24.4% of all events shared twice, and 24.6% of them shared three times or more. In the majority of the cases (51.4%), the event was shared with more than one person. As regards mental rumination, 83.0% of subjects reported having thought of the event at least once during the day. As was the case for social sharing, in spite of the shortness of the monitored period, mental rumination appeared clearly repetitive in 34.8% of the events, with 19.5% of reported events thought of "several times," and 15.3% of them thought of "constantly." Thus, overall results from these diary studies were clearly consistent with studies conducted with the retrospective method.

Mental Rumination and Social Sharing After Negative and Positive Emotional Events

In a second research strategy, potential selection bias was prevented by having the experimenters preselect this target event, in so-called "follow-up studies." In this procedure, subjects are first contacted at the time of their exposure to some important emotional situation, and are then followed up by researchers during the course of the following weeks. One such study was conducted in an emergency care clinic, with 39 subjects just exposed to traffic, domestic, or work accidents (Boca, Rimé, & Arcuri, 1992). Subjects were contacted 6 weeks later in order to investigate their event-related social sharing behaviors. In close confirmation of the above observations, 93% of these subjects were found to have talked about their accident, and 60% of them did so in the course of the first day following the accident. These data also confirmed the repetitive character of social sharing, because it occurred more than twice in 83% of the cases, and was mentioned as having occurred about everyday by no less than 35% of the subjects. All of these figures are consistent with those observed in the diary studies.

In a further follow-up study, the target emotional event was child delivery, as experienced by 31 young mothers (Rimé et al.,1994). When leaving the maternity ward (on average 5 days after the delivery), these women were given five copies of questionnaires to be completed on a fixed day during each of the 5 subsequent weeks. These questionnaires were composed of items on the mental rumination and social sharing of their delivery experience. The gynecological check-up, scheduled 6 weeks after the delivery, was used to collect the questionnaires. During the 1st and 2nd weeks at home, the percentage of women who reported spontaneous social sharing was extremely high, 96.8% and 90.3% respectively. These figures progressively decreased during the subsequent weeks, with successive figures of 54.8%, 51.6%, and 32.3%. A very similar pattern was observed for assessments of mental rumination. Again, the data from this alternative research procedure replicated the very high rates of social sharing and mental rumination observed in retrospective studies.

Mental Rumination and Social Sharing in the Laboratory

The third alternative procedure used to test the hypothesis that mild or moderate emotional episodes elicit mental rumination as well as social sharing is the experimental induction of emotion. The notion that mental rumination naturally develops after mild or moderate emotional episodes was already supported by experimental investigations conducted by Horowitz and colleagues many years ago. Subjects were exposed to an emotion-inducing movie depicting sexual body injuries in adolescent circumcision rituals (e.g., Lazarus & Opton, 1966). In a postfilm observational session, these subjects were indeed found to have more frequent movie-related intrusive imagery and repetitive thoughts than subjects who were previously exposed to a neutral movie (Horowitz, 1969; Horowitz & Becker, 1971). In a subsequent study, Horowitz and Becker (1973) compared the memory impact of an emotionally arousing unpleasant movie (the circumcision film) with an emotionally-arousing pleasant one (a sex education movie depicting a young couple enjoying sexual intercourse). Both emotion-inducing movies were shown to have a comparable impact on subsequent movie-related intrusive imagery and repetitive thoughts. Thus, the hypothesis linking moderately intense emotional experience and subsequent mental rumination was again supported by experimental data.

Experiments resting upon a similar procedure were recently conducted in order to examine whether a laboratory-induced emotional condition would also elicit postemotion social sharing behaviors (Bouts, Luminet, Manstead, & Rimé, 1994). Three movie excerpts of 3 minutes each were used to induce emotions. The first movie depicted wildlife in the Himalayas, the second one showed a cock fight, and the third one displayed the consumption of the brain of a monkey by tourists in an Asiatic restaurant. Subjects came to the session with a same-sex friend. They were randomly assigned to one of the movies while their friend was assigned to an irrelevant task in another room. During movie exposure, subjects' faces were unobtrusively video recorded. These recordings were later assessed by judges for intensity of facially displayed emotions, and for duration of gaze aversion. These analyses showed that the monkey movie induced the most intense emotional responses. The emotional effects of the Himalaya and the cock fighting movies did not differ significantly from each other. After the movie, subjects were left for a 5-minute period in a waiting room together with their friend. Their conversation was unobtrusively tape-recorded and later assessed for time spent talking about the movie and for number of words from conversation transcripts that referred to the movie. Results revealed that, as compared with subjects in the two other conditions, subjects exposed to the highly emotional movie talked much more about their emotional exposure. Further analyses took into account individual differences in intensity of emotional reactions to the movies, and found marked correlations between intensity of emotional reaction and social sharing. The more subjects were emotionally aroused by the movies, the more they talked about it with their friend in the waiting room situation that followed. Thus, these laboratory investigations showed that a 3-minute exposure to a emotion-inducing movie is enough to generate the process of social sharing.

EFFECTS OF EMOTIONAL REHEARSAL ON RECOVERY FROM EMOTION

Considering the data summarized so far, there seems to be little doubt that mental rumination and social sharing are an integral part of emotion. If this is so, then the question must be raised about the function that these rehearsal processes serve. It is tempting to conclude that mental rumination and social sharing represent spontaneously initiated ways of emotional information processing that help people to integrate the emotional experience, to recover from it, and to achieve emotional relief.

Does Rehearsing an Emotion Contribute to Emotional Relief?

This view was taken by, among others, Martin and Tesser (1989). According to these authors, rumination fulfills important coping functions by helping one to develop better understanding of the event, and to elaborate strategies to accommodate, overcome, or bypass the blocking of goal-orientation resulting from the event. Yet other authors disagreed with such a view. Pennebaker (1989) argued that mental rumination does not contribute to the understanding and assimilation of events. A similar view was proposed by the response styles theory of depression (Nolen-Hoeksema, 1987). This theory holds that individuals who engage in ruminative responses to depressed mood will experience amplification and prolongation of the mood, whereas individuals who engage in distracting responses to their depressed mood will experience relief from it. Morrow and Nolen-Hoeksema (1990) provided experimental data in support of this proposition.

As far as social sharing is concerned, however, empirical evidence does support the view that it can have positive consequences. Pennebaker and colleagues examined the health consequences of having or not having confided traumatic experiences (Pennebaker & Hoover, 1986; Pennebaker & O'Heeron, 1984). Subjects who had suffered a traumatic experience were more prone to later health problems if they had not shared their experience with others than if they had. Subsequent studies showed that encouraging people to disclose traumatic experiences had positive long-term consequences on several health indicators (Pennebaker, Barger, & Tiebout, 1989; Pennebaker & Beall, 1986; Pennebaker, Hughes, & O'Heeron, 1987). Taken together, the results of these studies suggest that socially sharing a past emotional experience is potentially important in recovering from the experience. Yet, here too, disagreements exist. Other psychologists suggested that communicating a major negative personal experience could reactivate the emotional disruption rather than resolve it (e.g., Tait & Silver, 1989). Indeed, the need to confide in others about a major life event is frequently unmet (e.g., Dunkel-Schetter & Wortman, 1982), and social responses to the expression of difficulties or distress are often negative (Lazarus, 1985; Strack & Coyne, 1983).

Field Studies of Emotional Rehearsal and Emotional Recovery

It can thus be seen that although a very tempting idea, the hypothesis that emotional rehearsals have some instrumental functions in the recovery from negative emotional experiences is still controversial. One of our retrospective studies (Rimé et al., 1991a, study 6) attempted to shed some light in this matter by simultaneously measuring emotional disruption, mental rumination, social sharing, and emotion recovery. Adult subjects were invited to remember specific emotional events. They then reported (a) their emotions and reactions at the time of the event, (b) the rumination and social sharing that happened after the event, and (c) how their emotional reactions felt when remembering the event. Emotional disruption, rumination, and social sharing were each assessed by multiple questions. Emotional recovery was assessed by subtracting the intensity of the disruptiveness the event still had from the disruptiveness it had when it occurred. In order to address the role of social sharing and rumination in the process of recovery, partial correlations were computed between recovery and these variables. This analysis controlled for the intensity of the disruption as well as for possible correlations between social sharing and rumination. Results showed that neither rumination nor the amount or the delay of social sharing was correlated in any significant manner to recovery.

This finding is hardly compatible with the view that social sharing and rumination serve beneficial functions. Yet, in this retrospective study, the intensity of the disruption originally caused by the emotional event was assessed post hoc, in temporal simultaneity with the assessment of the disruption still experienced at the time of the investigation. This could have had the effect of reducing the difference between the two ratings, biasing the data. It thus seemed desirable to reexamine the correlations in a methodological context that would allow the assessment of emotional disruption at clearly distinct times. The diary method was well suited for this purpose.

Long-Lasting Rehearsal Correlates With Poor Recovery

The hypothesis that emotional rehearsals have some instrumental functions in the recovery from negative emotional experiences is tempting, but controversial. In one of the diary studies already mentioned above (Rimé et al., 1994), subjects filled out a short questionnaire every evening for 3 consecutive weeks. In these questionnaires, they described briefly the most emotional event of the previous day, and answered a set of questions on their reactions to this event, including emotional impact, social sharing, and mental rumination. Then, 2 to 3 weeks later, subjects came back to the laboratory for a follow-up session. At this session, subjects answered additional questions about six events taken from their diary reports. Three of these events were randomly selected from those that had a strong emotional impact, and three others from events that had a weak impact. On average, 32 days separated the target event from the follow-up session, with a minimum of 19 days and a maximum of 45 days. When reexposed to this material, subjects first read their own account of the event as extracted from their diary. Then, on the same scales as those used in the daily questionnaire, they rated the extent to which they had shared and ruminated the event during the 3 preceding days. Finally, subjects rated the emotional impact the event still had on them.

For each of the events considered at the follow-up session, a recovery index was calculated by subtracting follow-up impact from initial impact. Correlations between this index and the subjects' ratings of social sharing and mental rumination were then calculated both for initially weak and initially strong emotional events. For events with a weak initial impact, no significant relationship was observed between the recovery index and initial social sharing or mental rumination, suggesting that neither type of rehearsal affected the recovery process. However, a significant correlation was found with rehearsal that subjects still evidenced at the time of the follow-up. Specifically, a negative correlation was recorded between the recovery index and follow-up social sharing ($r = -.36$, $p < .01$), indicating that subjects were more likely to still share events from which they had less well recovered. For events with a strong initial impact, the recovery index was not found to be related to initial social sharing, but to be related well to initial mental rumination ($r = -.30$, $p < .05$), indicating that originally more ruminated events were those less recovered from at the time of the follow-up. Finally, marked relationships occurred between recovery and both the follow-up ratings of frequency of rumination ($r = -.56$, $p < .0001$) and of frequency of social sharing ($r = -.42$, $p < .005$), respectively. The latter results suggested that events still ruminated and events still shared at the follow-up were those from which subjects were less recovered.

These data consistently and markedly point to a fact that was not at all expected. When rehearsals about an emotional experience extend over a long period, a poorer recovery can be expected. This was most clearly shown, for both mental rumination and social sharing, in the case of strong emotional events. But even in the case of weaker emotional events, such a negative relationship was observed for social sharing. This suggests two possibilities. Either emotional rehearsals are symptomatic of a relative inability of the person to recover and to assimilate the episode, or they act to feed the emotional disruption elicited by this episode. With regard to emotional rehearsals occurring in the hours following the episode—recall that the daily reporting in this study questioned subjects about events of the preceding day—the view that mentally ruminating would be associated with a poorer recovery was supported. However, contrary to what was expected, the initial extent of social sharing was unrelated to the recovery index.

A further diary study including the experimental manipulation of social sharing was thus conducted (Rimé et al., 1994). All subjects were instructed to report during 14 consecutive days the most emotional episode of the day. Daily self-reports also requested subjects to report on their immediate spontaneous social sharing of their emotions related to the event. At a follow-up session 4 weeks after the end of the diary period, subjects were presented in a random order with their own summaries of six episodes, three of which were selected from among episodes that were initially socially shared and three from among episodes that were not. Subjects rated each episode on three items: (a) how often they talked about this episode during the two previous weeks, (b) with how many people they spoke about this episode during the weeks that followed, and (c) whether they presently felt emotional when thinking of this episode.

These data collected at the follow-up allowed us to examine emotional recovery as a function of spontaneous social sharing. In spite of the elapsed time, emotional events continued to have important arousing power at follow-up. Subjects still reported an average residual impact of 4.03 (as compared with 5.30 initially) on a 10-point scale. However, recovery was in no manner affected by the extent of spontaneous sharing on the day of the event. As was done in former studies described above, the difference between the initial and the follow-up ratings of the emotional impact of each event created an index of recovery. No significant effect was found for this variable.

Quantitative Versus Qualitative Social Sharing

The various sets of data discussed so far are quite consistent as regards the question of the instrumental role of social sharing. In each of the three studies in which this question was considered, no instrumental role was found. But does this necessarily mean that the social sharing of emotion has no instrumental effect on emotional recovery? This would be inconsistent with data from the various studies conducted by Pennebaker and his colleagues (for a review, see Pennebaker, 1989). This work reveals positive effects of sharing previously unrevealed trauma upon health indicators assessed in later follow-up. Yet, these studies suggest that the critical factor for recovery lies less in quantitative aspects of social sharing, as I have been considering up to now, and more in qualitative. This is suggested by Pennebaker and Beall (1986), who asked subjects to write essays about previously unrevealed trauma. In three conditions, subjects were told to describe the fact of the episode, the feelings of the episode, or both facts and feelings. As compared to a fourth, control condition in which subjects wrote about trivial topics, follow-up health assessments evidenced positive effects for subjects who described their feelings or their feelings and the facts, but not for those who gave facts-only descriptions. In a related manner, Mendolia and Kleck (1993) exposed subjects to an emotion-inducing movie, and then instructed them to talk either about the felt emotions (emotion condition) or about the sequence of movie events (fact condition). At a reexposure to the movie 48 hours later, subjects who had talked about their feelings evidenced lower levels of arousal and reported more positive affect than subjects who talked only about the movie facts. Thus, previous studies failed to find that talking about factual aspects of an emotional episode affected recovery. Yet, their data definitely suggest that instructions emphasizing the feeling dimension may be the most relevant for examinations of the potential consequences of social sharing.

The question of the potential impact of the feeling dimension of the social sharing process upon the emotional recovery was examined through experimental conditions that were included in the follow-up study of 31 young mothers discussed earlier in this chapter (Rimé et al., 1994). Sixteen of these subjects were randomly assigned to an experimental condition and 15 to a control condition. On the 3rd or 4th day after their delivery, subjects in the two conditions participated in a 45-minute interview conducted in their room at the maternity ward by a female experimenter, who presented to them a list of 12 standard emotions adapted from the Differential Emotions Scale (Izard, Dougherty, Bloxom, & Kotsch, 1974): interest, surprise, fear, disgust, joy, anger, distress, guilt, shame, sadness, contempt, and relaxation or well-being. Women in the experimental condition were instructed to concentrate on each successive emotion word, and to verbalize the extent to which they experienced the corresponding emotion at some moment of the delivery situation. For each emotion, the experimenter encouraged subjects to express in depth all the related feelings, thoughts, and physical sensations she had experienced during the delivery situation. Women in the control condition used the list in a comparable manner, but considered emotions experienced due to the impact of their pregnancy on their everyday life. When leaving the maternity ward (on average 5 days after the delivery), subjects in both conditions rated a number of items, including the felt emotionality of the delivery. They were then given five copies of a questionnaire to be completed on a fixed day during each of the 5 subsequent weeks. On each of these weekly questionnaires, subjects rated (a) the frequency of their ruminations about the delivery during the preceding week, (b) the frequency with which they had been talking about the delivery, and (c) the number of persons with whom they had shared the event. Additionally, the questionnaire to be filled on the last week invited women to rate the emotionality that the memory of the delivery still elicited in them. The gynecological check-up scheduled 6 weeks after the delivery was used to collect the questionnaires and to answer any questions about the study.

Assessments of their delivery completed immediately after release from the 5-day stay at the maternity ward showed that the emotional impact of the delivery at the time it happened was rated in a comparable manner by women of both groups. Both evidenced very high ratings of emotionality with no significant difference between them. The weekly ratings of extent of mental rumination and social sharing collected in the two groups were then compared. As regards mental rumination, a significant condition effect indicated less frequent mental rumination among experimental than among control subjects. Social sharing was also observed to be generally lower among experimental than control subjects, and significantly so for the 4th week after the delivery. Finally, ratings of the number of persons with whom the delivery was shared also showed a trend suggesting that women in the experimental condition shared the delivery with fewer people than women in the control condition. Overall, compared with women in the control condition, women in the experimental condition reported less mental rumination, and also tended to socially share the delivery less often and with fewer people. Assessments of the emotional impact the delivery at the end of the 6th week after returning home allowed us to create a recovery index by subtracting these ratings from the emotional impact the delivery had had initially. This index showed that subjects in the experimental group recovered better than those in the control group. Thus, although the two groups did not differ in their ratings of the emotionality of the delivery at the time they returned home, they differed in emotional recovery at a later assessment. It is possible that this effect was only indirectly a consequence of the social sharing interviews, through the impact these interviews had on later rehearsals.

CONCLUSION

In this chapter, I have shown that as is the case after major negative life events and traumatic emotional episodes, ordinary emotions, too, are commonly accompanied by intrusive memories and the need to talk about the episode. In various studies, I then considered the hypothesis that such mental rumination and social sharing would represent spontaneously initiated ways of processing emotional information. The most consistent finding from these studies was not predicted. It was observed that when rehearsals about an emotional experience extend over a long period, a poorer recovery from the emotional episode is to be expected. These investigations also offered some support to the negative view on the effects of mental rumination. Episodes that were more mentally ruminated immediately after they occurred were found associated with a poorer recovery. As far as social sharing was concerned, however, no significant relationship was observed with emotional recovery across three different studies. This was confirmed in a further diary study in which an experimental induction of social sharing was used.

In a final investigation, qualitative rather than quantitative aspects of social sharing were considered. Women who had recently given birth provided an experimenter with in-depth verbalization of feelings and emotions experienced in the course of the delivery. As compared with the control group, these women evidenced superior indices of emotional recovery at the follow-up. Consistent with previous studies (e.g., Mendolia & Kleck, 1993; Pennebaker & Beall, 1986), these results confirm that talking about feelings experienced in an emotional episode has an effect on emotional relief. Such data also suggest some explanation for the absence of relationship between social sharing and emotional recovery in our previous field studies. The feelings-focused interview conducted with the young mothers lasted an average of 45 minutes. Similarly, Pennebaker and Beall's (1986) confession sessions lasted 20 minutes each, and were repeated 4 days in succession for the same emotional episode. Thus, social sharing situations evidenced as affecting emotional recovery not only were specific from a qualitative point of view; they also involved an investment in time. Natural social situations are not likely to offer people opportunities to verbalize in depth and at length feelings experienced during an emotional episode. It may thus be that what people evidence as social sharing behaviors in everyday life would rather be uncompleted attempts at processing episode-related emotional information. One can probably conclude that in the field of emotion, there is ample place for professional intervention.

Finally, the data described in this chapter are raising a new research question. If the social sharing of emotion spontaneously developed after emotional exposure does not affect the recovery process, why does it accompany emotional experiences almost systematically? Future studies should address this question by focussing on the processing of emotional information as well as on the social consequences of experiencing an emotion.

REFERENCES

American Psychiatric Association. (1994). *Diagnostic and statistical manual of mental disorders.* (4th. ed., revised). Washington, DC: Author.

Boca, S., Rimé, B., & Arcuri, L. (1992, January). Uno studio longitudinale di eventi emotivamente traumatici [A Longitudinal Study of Emotionally Traumatic Events]. Paper presented at the Incontro Annuale delle Emozioni, Padova, Italy.

Bouts, P., Luminet, O., Rimé, B., & Manstead, A. S. R. (1994). Social sharing of emotion: Experimental evidence. Manuscript submitted for publication.

Bulman, R., & Wortman, C. B. (1977). Attributions of blame and coping in the "real world": Severe accident victims react to their lot. *Journal of Personality and Social Psychology, 35,* 351–363.

Dunkel-Shetter, C., & Wortman, C. B. (1982). The interpersonal dynamics of cancer: Problems in social relationships and their impact on the patient. In H. S. Friedman & M. R. DiMatteo (Eds.), *Interpersonal issues in health care* (pp. 69–100). San Diego, CA: Academic Press.

Ersland, S., Weisaeth, L., & Sund, A. (1989). The stress upon rescuers involved in an oil rig disaster: "Alexander Kielland"—1980. *Acta Psychiatrica Scandinavica, 80,* 38–49.

Frijda, N. H., Mesquita, B., Sonnemans, J., & Van Goozen, S. (1991). The duration of affective phenomena or emotions, sentiments, and passions. In K. T. Strongman (Ed.), *International Review of Studies on Emotion, Vol. 1.* (pp. 187–225). New York: Wiley

Horowitz, M. J. (1969). Psychic trauma: Return of images after a stress film. *Archives of General Psychiatry, 32,* 1457–1463.

Horowitz, M. J., & Becker, S. S. (1971). Cognitive response to stress and experimental demand. *Journal of Abnormal Psychology, 78,* 86–92.

Horowitz, M. J., & Becker, S. S. (1973). Cognitive response to erotic and stressful films. *Archives of General Psychiatry, 29,* 81–84.

Izard, C. E., Dougherty, F. E., Bloxom, B. M., & Kotsch, N. E. (1974). *The Differential Emotions Scale: A method of measuring the meaning of subjective experience of discrete emotions.* Nashville: Vanderbilt University.

Lazarus, R. S. (1985). The trivialization of distress. In J. C. Rose & L. J. Solomon (Eds.), *Primary prevention of psychopathology: Vol. 8. Prevention in Health Psychology* (pp. 279–298). Hanover, NH: University Press of New England.

Lazarus, R. S., & Opton, E. M., Jr. (1966). A study of psychological stress. In C. D.

Spielberger (Ed.), *Anxiety and behavior* (pp. 225–262). San Diego, CA: Academic Press.

Lehman, D. R., Wortman, C. B., & Williams, A. F. (1987). Long-term effects of losing a spouse or child in a motor vehicle crash. *Journal of Personality and Social Psychology, 52,* 218–231.

Martin, L. L., & Tesser, A. (1989). Toward a motivational and structural theory of ruminative thought. In J. S. Uleman & J. A. Bargh (Eds.), *Unintended thought* (pp. 306–326). New York: Guilford Press.

Mendolia, M., & Kleck, R. E. (1993). Effects of talking about a stressful event on arousal: Does what we talk about make a difference? *Journal of Personality and Social Psychology, 64,* 283–292.

Mesquita, B. (1993). Cultural variations in emotion: A comparative study of Dutch, Surinamese and Turkish people in the Netherlands. Unpublished doctoral dissertation, University of Amsterdam, Amsterdam, The Netherlands.

Mitchell, G. W., & Glickman, A. S. (1977). Cancer patients: Knowledge and attitude. *Cancer, 40,* 61–66.

Morrow, J., & Nolen-Hoeksema, S. (1990). Effects of responses to depression on the remediation of depressive affect. *Journal of Personality and Social Psychology, 58,* 519–527.

Nolen-Hoeksema, S. (1987). Sex differences in unipolar depression: Evidence and theory. *Psychological Bulletin, 101,* 259–282.

Pennebaker, J. W. (1989). Confession, inhibition and disease. In L. Berkowitz (Ed.), *Advances in Experimental Social Psychology,* (Vol. 22, pp. 211–244). San Diego, CA: Academic Press.

Pennebaker, J. W. (1993). Social mechanisms of constraint. In D. W. Wegner & J. W. Pennebaker (Eds.), *Handbook of mental control* (pp. 200–219). Englewood Cliffs, NJ: Prentice Hall.

Pennebaker, J. W., Barger, S. D., & Tiebout, J. (1989). Disclosure of traumas and health among holocaust survivors. *Psychosomatic Medicine, 51,* 577–589.

Pennebaker, J. W., & Beall, S. K. (1986). Confronting a traumatic event: Toward an understanding of inhibition and disease. *Journal of Abnormal Psychology, 95,* 274–281.

Pennebaker, J. W., & Hoover, C. W. (1986). Inhibition and cognition: Toward an understanding of trauma and disease. In R. J. Davidson, G. E. Schwartz, & D. Shapiro (Eds.), *Consciousness and self regulation* (Vol. 4, pp. 107–136). New York: Plenum.

Pennebaker, J. W., Hughes, C., & O'Heeron, N. C. (1987). The psychophysiology of confession: Linking inhibitory and psychosomatic processes. *Journal of Personality and Social Psychology, 52,* 781–793.

Pennebaker, J. W., & O'Heeron, R. C. (1984). Confiding in others and illness rate among spouses of suicide and accidental-death victims. *Journal of Abnormal Psychology, 93,* 473–476.

Rauw, M.C., & Rimé, B. (1990). Le partage social des emotions chez les adolescents [Social Sharing of Emotions in Adolescents]. Unpublished raw data.

Rimé, B. (1989). Le partage social des emotions [Social sharing of emotions]. In B. Rimé et K. R. Scherer (Eds.), *Les emotions* (pp. 271–303). Neuchatel: Delachaux et Nestle.

Rimé, B., Mesquita, B., Philippot, P., & Boca, S. (1991). Beyond the emotional event: Six studies on the social sharing of emotion. *Cognition and Emotion, 5,* 435–465.

Rimé, B., Noël, P., & Philippot, P. (1991). Episode emotional, reminiscences mentales et reminiscences sociales [Emotional episode, mental reminiscences, and social reminiscence]. *Les Cahiers Internationaux de Psychologie Sociale, 11,* 93–104.

Rimé, B., Philippot, P., Boca, S., & Mesquita, B. (1992). Long-lasting consequences of emotion: Social sharing and rumination. In W. Stroebe, & M. Hewstone (Eds.), *European Review of Social Psychology* (Vol. 1, pp. 225–258). Chichester, England: Wiley.

Rimé, B., Philippot, P., Finkenauer, C., Legast, S., Moorkens, P., & Tornqvist, J. (1994). Mental rumination and social sharing in current life emotion. Manuscript submitted for publication.

Scherer, K. R. (1984). On the nature and function of emotion: A component process approach. In K. Scherer & P. Ekman (Eds.), *Approaches to emotion* (pp. 293–318). Hillsdale, NJ: Erlbaum.

Schoenberg, B. B., Carr, A. C., Peretz, D., Kutscher, A. H., & Cherico, D. J. (1975). Advice of the bereaved for the bereaved. In B. Schoenberg, I. Gerber, A. Wiener, A. H. Kutscher, D. Peretz, & A. C. Carr (Eds.), *Bereavement: Its psychological aspects* (pp. 362–367). New York: Columbia University Press.

Silver, R. L., & Wortman, C. B. (1980). Coping with undesirable life events. In J. Garber & M. E. P. Seligman (Eds.), *Human helplessness* (pp. 279–340). San Diego, CA: Academic Press.

Strack, S., & Coyne, J. C. (1983). Shared and private reaction to depression. *Journal of Personality and Social Psychology, 44,* 798–806.

Tait, R., & Silver, R. C. (1989). Coming to term with major negative life events. In J. S. Uleman and J. A. Bargh (Eds.), *Unintended thoughts* (pp. 351–382). New York: Guilford Press.

Vergara, A. (1993). Sexo e identidad de genero: Diferencias en el conomiento social de las emociones en el modo de compatirlas [Sex and gender identity: Differences in the social knowledge of emotions and in the way to share them]. Unpublished doctoral dissertation, Universidad del Pais Vasco, San Sebastian, Spain.

15

Cultural Similarities and Differences Regarding Emotional Disclosure: Some Examples From Indonesia and the Pacific

Jane Wellenkamp

A s the chapters in this book demonstrate, there is a growing body of research conducted by Western psychologists that suggests that the ways
in which individuals respond to and manage their reactions to intense emotional experiences can have positive or negative consequences for their mental and physical health. Some studies, for example, indicate that individuals
have a tendency or need to disclose intensely felt emotional experiences—
by talking to others, writing in a journal, and so forth—and that such disclosures can have a positive effect on one's psychological and physical health;
other studies suggest that active nondisclosure, rumination, and worry are
detrimental to one's health and well-being (e.g., Pennebaker, 1989; Tait &
Silver, 1989; Traue & Pennebaker, 1993; Rimé, 1995; Borkovec, chapter 4,
this volume; Wegner, chapter 3, this volume).

As a psychocultural anthropologist, my initial reaction to these research findings is to ask several questions: Is there evidence in the ethnographic record that would lend support to findings linking emotions to
health? Do the forms and patterns of emotional disclosure in modern,
Western cultures vary significantly from those in other cultural settings?
What social or cultural variables might affect the need for individuals to

disclose their emotional experiences, and the relationship between disclosure and health?

In what follows, I begin to explore these questions. I start by pointing out that in some non-Western cultures, one finds traditional beliefs that parallel Western research findings suggesting a connection between emotions and health. My examples are drawn from my own research among the Toraja of Indonesia, and from anthropological research conducted among other cultural groups in Indonesia and the Pacific. I then discuss the possibility that the need for disclosing emotions may vary cross-culturally as a consequence of local practices and beliefs, and that certain forms of disclosure may be effective in some cultural settings but not others. Finally, I suggest that cultural attitudes toward disclosure may affect the relationship between disclosure and health.[1]

ETHNOGRAPHIC AND METHODOLOGICAL BACKGROUND

Before discussing Toraja beliefs about emotions and health, I will provide a brief introduction to the Toraja, and describe my general methodological approach.

The Toraja are one of a handful of related groups inhabiting the mountainous interior of the southwestern peninsula of the island of Sulawesi (Celebes) in Indonesia. Numbering around 350,000 and speaking an Austronesian (Malayo-Polynesian) language, the Toraja make their living through wet-rice agriculture. Up until around the beginning of the twentieth century, the Toraja were nonliterate, relatively isolated from other groups, and politically decentralized. Prior to the arrival of the Dutch in 1906, intervillage warfare occurred intermittently and headhunting was

[1]My research was conducted in 1981–1983 with the permission of the Lembaga Ilmu Pengetahuan Indonesia (Indonesian Institute of Sciences) and the sponsorship of the Universitas Hasanuddin in Ujung Pandang. Funding for the research was provided by the Wenner-Gren Foundation for Anthropological Research and by a National Institute of Mental Health Traineeship. I am grateful to Jamie Pennebaker for kindly inviting me to attend the conference, and I warmly thank Bernard Rimé whose thought-provoking questions helped to shape this chapter.

practiced. Yet the Toraja generally avoid conflict and are nonviolent (see Hollan, 1988; Wellenkamp, 1988a).

The majority of Indonesians are Islamic and yet the Toraja—in part due to their long isolation—were largely unaffected by Islamic influences and continued to practice their traditional religion, Aluk To Dolo or Alukta, until the arrival of the Dutch, who introduced Christianity to the area. Today over one half of the Toraja are Christian, primarily Protestant, and the remaining Toraja are largely Alukta. Alukta is based on the worship of ancestors and gods and spirits (*nene' sola deata*). To obtain the blessings and protection of these spiritual beings, villagers are obligated to perform various rituals and to observe numerous prohibitions, many of which serve to separate two distinct ritual spheres: the "smoke-ascending" sphere, oriented toward the attainment of health, fertility, and prosperity, and the "smoke-descending" sphere, which includes death rituals (for further elaboration, see Wellenkamp, 1988a; Nooy-Palm, 1986).

Traditionally there were three major social strata—nobles, commoners, and dependents or slaves—and status distinctions continue to be important today. While status distinctions are salient, gender differences are not highlighted in Toraja (Waterson, 1981; Hollan & Wellenkamp, 1994). The rural areas of Tana Toraja (the administrative region in which the Toraja reside) remain relatively isolated today. Although there are churches, schools, and health clinics in the remote rural areas, there are also villages—such as Paku Asu, the village in which I lived—that do not have electricity, running water, or all-weather roads.

When I left to conduct research among the Toraja, my intent was to learn about psychological responses to death in a culture with elaborate and unusual death practices (involving, for example, the storing of the deceased's body in the house for weeks or months prior to the funeral, and the periodic reopening of burial tombs [see Wellenkamp, 1988b, 1991, 1992]). Before looking specifically at issues concerning grief and mourning, however, I first investigated Toraja beliefs and practices regarding emotions in general and other psychologically or oriented topics. I began by using standard anthropological methods such as participant observation and informal and formal interviewing with a variety of informants (villagers, government officials, clinic workers, etc.). After living several months in Paku Asu (a pseudonym), Douglas Hollan (1989, 1990, 1994) and I then conducted a series of open-ended, "person-centered" interviews with a small number of village residents (11 in all). The interviews, which were tape-recorded, covered a range of topics including respondents' recollections of childhood and adolescence and their experiences with marriage, divorce, dreams, possession trance, animal sacrifice, and so forth (for further details, see Hollan & Wellenkamp, 1994; Hollan & Wellenkamp, in press). Following these interviews, I conducted open-ended interviews with other villagers specifically about their bereavement experiences. The quotations that appear below are taken from these two sets of tape-recorded interviews (the transcriptions total around 1,200 pages). Some of the quotations include questions or comments of the interviewer; these are placed in parentheses to distinguish them from the comments of the respondent. Words placed in brackets are not a part of the original transcript; they provide clarification or an expansion of the respondent's or interviewer's remarks. Two of our respondents were married to one another; in keeping with Toraja naming conventions, the same teknonym is used to refer to both individuals: Nene'na ("Grandparent of") Tandi. To clarify matters, however, (m) for "male" is placed after the husband's name, while (f) for "female" is placed after the wife's name.

BELIEFS REGARDING EMOTIONS AND HEALTH AMONG THE TORAJA

Early on in my research, I found that the Toraja have very clear ideas about the relationship between emotions and one's physical and mental health. Like many other cultural groups in Indonesia (particularly western and central Indonesia), the Toraja value emotional restraint and equanimity in daily life; among the Toraja, the experience and expression of "negative" feelings such as anger and sadness are normally avoided. One reason for this is that the Toraja believe that emotional distress can have an adverse affect on one's health. Negative or stressful experiences are believed possibly to cause weight loss and minor health problems, and prolonged emotional and mental distress—caused, for instance, by the absence or death of loved ones, financial difficulties, a spouse's infidelity, a legal dispute, or inauspicious dreams—is thought to be capable of causing more serious health problems including stomach and heart ailments, tuberculosis, and even premature death. Prolonged distress is also seen as a major cause of mental disturbances.

The topic of emotions and health came up often in daily conversation as well as during the interviews. People talked about the dangers of distress in general and about particular individuals whose death or illness was attributed to distress and rumination. People also talked about their own difficulties. Several examples from the interviews are provided below.

Indo'na ("Mother of") Tiku:

> People who cannot limit their distress, eventually it will ruin their body. It will ruin their thinking. So if our thinking is ruined, it means we're no longer normal. . . . [If a person cannot be consoled], often she/he will die.

Nene'na Tandi (m):

> If people realize that someone's thinking is damaged, they know that person will soon die. Everyone like that dies because they think [too much]. . . . (Are a lot of people like that, whose thinking is troubled and they can't be treated. . . ?) Ah, the dead person up [the trail] from here, [she died] from thinking, too! . . . because her primary wish was to become Christian, [she] wanted to be baptized. Her children [who live elsewhere] promised to come [for her baptism], but they didn't and so her thinking . . . wandered and wandered . . . night and day. . . . Until she died.

Nene'na Tandi (m):

> Think about this: . . . my first wife, after I divorced [her], died. The second one, I divorced, died. What was the cause? The cause was that I have a good heart. It wasn't possessions that they desired but sweet words, a good heart. . . . [They thought], "Where can I find a man like that?" . . . Why did they die right away? . . . just because of thinking [too much]. (Just thinking?) Yes, just thinking.

Indo'na Sapan:

> There was someone next to us [a neighbor] . . . one of the children went to Manado, a girl. . . . when it was morning like this, her mother would already start crying [because the daughter was absent]. . . . I always told her . . . "Don't always remember/think of her." She would say, "Wah, I can't tolerate it. . . . Of several children, she's the only girl." . . . And then that person died [from thinking about her absent daughter]! What a pity.

Ambe'na ("Father of") Toding (whose financial ventures have met with limited success):

> I . . . want to find happiness, but I don't find it. What about good fortune. . . ? I don't have any. . . . So there are many things [I think about]. That's why I'm thin. [I think so much that] it is often midnight before I can fall asleep. . . . Thoughts like that make people sick. If someone is happy, he/she must be fat, [because] there's nothing that he/she thinks about. Indeed [he/she] thinks about things, but only about matters having to do with the next day. Not other [distressing] things.

Indo'na Rante (who has a "weak heart" and as a consequence cannot have sugar in her coffee and must be careful not to become anxious or distressed):

> [I've had a weak heart] for five years. When my heart starts to pound/palpitate, I go again to the clinic [where] I'm injected [with medicine]. . . . (Do you know why you have that condition?) Because that's what happens . . . if we always are experiencing hardship. If we just think [ruminate] about things. For example, if we just sit like this and our thinking wanders/drifts. Later, we get heart illness. (What do you think about?) About difficulties! . . . for example, about death. Because my [deceased] mother isn't here. My [deceased] siblings aren't here. My [deceased] children aren't here. That's what I think about.

As these comments indicate, prolonged distress, rumination, and worry are seen as clearly posing a danger to one's health. These comments also indicate that Toraja villagers are not always successful in avoiding what they view as the negative consequences of emotional distress. But because of the perceived dangers of distress, there are several techniques that are commonly used in an effort to reduce distress, rumination, and worry. These include avoiding potentially upsetting situations, trying to remain "calm" (*rapa' penaa*) and "conscious" (*mengkilala*) when emotionally upsetting situations are unavoidable, trying not to think about or imagine distressing events, and reminding oneself of the potentially dangerous consequences of distress and rumination (for a discussion of other techniques and strategies, see Hollan & Wellenkamp, 1994, pp. 199–203). There is also an expectation that when people are upset, other villagers should attempt to distract them and encourage them to refrain from rumination and to place their experiences into perspective (e.g., by reminding a person whose relative has died that death strikes every household and he or she is not alone).

Nene'na Tandi (m) relates how he reminds his wife that they should not worry about things: "I always tell Nene'na Tandi [his wife], 'Let's not think long, we must instead think of the time just ahead—tomorrow and the next day. . . . If we think at length, we'll be ruined. We, ourselves, will be ruined . . . everything will be ruined.' . . . Thus, we must be quiet." Elsewhere, Nene'na Tandi (m) says that he tries not to visualize the faces of his deceased relatives, whom he misses, for if he did, "I might get tuberculosis. Or go crazy. That is how illnesses of the mind arise. Don't think [of them]. Don't visualize [them]."

Indo'na Tiku, who is an elementary school teacher, describes how she deals with her feelings of irritation and anger that arise during the course of her work by reminding herself of how her health could be adversely affected if she allows herself to get upset. According to Indo'na Tiku, because teachers are often getting angry at children

> they often get . . . TBC [tuberculosis]. . . . So indeed . . . we must be careful about [our] anger. . . . if we can, we must limit it. [We] shouldn't always be angry. . . . (Does that mean [anger] is stored in one's heart, or is that not the case?) Actually lots of people store their

anger in their hearts. . . . But I think it is better to let it out [storing negative emotions is seen by some as especially dangerous] . . . (Then how is it limited?) For example . . . even if the children do something [upsetting] we just reprimand [them] but [we] don't let our hearts get hot. We must make ourselves aware/conscious . . . for example, we want to get angry. But then we must remember, "Wah, if I get angry now, what's the use? My body will be disturbed/affected." The best thing—no matter what the children [do]—it's sufficient if [they] are [just] well reprimanded. In order to prevent illness [in ourselves].

One exception to the general attempt to remain calm in the face of upsetting events concerns grieving over a death: Although excessive crying following a death is thought to be harmful, occasional periods of crying and wailing (a combination of crying and calling out to the dead) are encouraged as a way of preventing later illness. According to Indo'na Sumpu, those who are too shy to wail

will quickly become ill. Because within his/her heart there are feelings that are fluttering that he/she wants to release. (Thus, it is better to release them?) Yes, it is better to release them because those who cry, all of the contents of their heart is said. Thus, when they have stopped, although usually they are still sad, they are quiet. But if one does not cry, usually . . . one is attacked by thoughts (see Wellenkamp, 1988b, and Hollan & Wellenkamp, 1994, for a discussion of other exceptional occasions when people are encouraged to express negative feelings or behave aggressively).

For Indo'na Sapan, talking to others is the only real option for dealing with a distressing experience: "(If [you] feel troubled, is there something that—) Can make it go away? [She pauses and then continues] Maybe there isn't. There is, but it only [helps] a little, you know? . . . if we talk to others." As noted above, when people are upset, it is expected that other villagers will talk to them and attempt to distract and console them. Indo'na Rante explains, for example, what someone should do if another person has experienced a death in the family:

. . . it's important for Toraja [that] we gather there [at the deceased's house] . . . We converse so that the person who has experienced the death is consoled. So that he/she doesn't continuously think troubling thoughts. . . . [People] talk about inconsequential things so that his/her thinking is divided [between] listening to the people who are relating [something], and thinking of the person who died.

Another person, Nene'na Tandi (m), says: ". . . as I've told you before, we give them [people who are troubled] advice as a treatment. . . . We coax/flatter them . . . so that their heart is quiet, their thinking is healthy, ah, that is effective." In another interview, Nene'na Tandi (m) says that while Toraja customarily bring pigs and water buffalo to the funerals of their deceased relatives, what is most important to provide the deceased's survivors are words of advice: "That is the most powerful medicine [there is]! . . . if we give deep understanding [or] good advice [to the bereaved], that's what they can consume, more so than buffalo, more so than gold."

The importance that individuals attach to receiving such attention and support when they are distressed is indicated by comments made by Nene'na Tandi (f):

(If someone experiences a death, are they happier if lots of people come to the house, or would they prefer to be alone?) Eee, it's not good to be alone. If lots of people come, it consoles [one's] heart, what a pity. Yes, [one] doesn't feel good if no one comes. That's why people here . . . [think], "We must befriend everyone." Because of that—if something upsetting happens [a death] and no one comes [to the house], [it is because] we like to get angry at others! . . . [But if we befriend others], people will remember us, they will say, "What a pity, that person has a good heart, let's go sit with him/her." . . . So it's better if we are nice toward everyone. . . . [Otherwise], when something upsetting happens, no one will look at us, not even with one eye.

It is noteworthy that Toraja villagers' ideas and practices regarding their emotional lives are strongly preventative in orientation. That is, by attending to their emotional and mental states and those of others on an ongoing basis, Toraja attempt to prevent illness and maintain health. While in many traditional cultures, there are healing practices or treatment procedures for individuals who have already become ill that may include the confession or expression of previously unexpressed feelings and desires, a preventative health orientation, especially one that focuses on the daily management of emotions, appears to be less common, although as discussed in the next section, other Austronesian language speaking groups share a similar orientation.

BELIEFS ABOUT EMOTIONS AND HEALTH AMONG OTHER INDONESIAN AND PACIFIC GROUPS

The Toraja are not an isolated case in terms of the connection they make between emotions and health, and in their preventative approach to the management of emotions. Several other Austronesian language speaking groups in Indonesia and the Pacific hold similar beliefs. Hildred Geertz (1961), for example, who conducted research among the Islamic Javanese in east central Java (Indonesia), reports that it is "a typical Javanese attitude" that it is best "to avoid emotional upset because sickness and possibly death" can result from mental suffering (p. 134). One Javanese woman, Juminah, told Geertz):

> If my husband does anything wrong again, I will ask for a divorce. This is better than loving him and his not responding, for then I might get sick and die. . . . Even though I have children, I still feel this way. I can always get married again, and if no one will take me, I can go to work. . . . If you don't do something like that and just let your husband get away with it, things will just get worse later, and then you will come down with tuberculosis, and your mother will miss you when you are dead. (p. 134)

Another Javanese, an urban laborer and laundryman, told Geertz (1961) that there were several individuals in the neighborhood who "were 135 and 150 years old" (p. 135). When Geertz asked him how it was that people could live so long he said that it was because their hearts were peaceful; they never got angry, never got upset about anything, and so they could live very long. When asked how one could become so peaceful, he said that he did not know—that if one is lucky, nothing very serious will happen to upset one. He said, "One thing that sometimes helps is that if you have a lot of wives you just keep changing them, and as soon as you start having trouble with one you leave and go marry another" (p. 135).

Clifford Geertz (1976), also writing about the Javanese, says that "the psychological causation of physical illness is a commonplace" p. 97. The example he gives from his fieldwork suggests that storing or holding onto unexpressed negative emotions is seen as especially dangerous for one's health:

> When Pak Ardjo went to Djakarta to visit his son whose wife had just died, he went by train with the mother of the wife. On the trip he began to feel ill, and by the time he got there he was very sick and spent the entire visit in bed. He said the reason he got sick . . . was that he was angry . . . toward the woman whose daughter it was who had died because she seemed not to be grieving at all over her daughter's decease. . . . he was angry at her but didn't show it, and this being held inside him was what made him sick. (p. 97)

Even more so than the Javanese, the Balinese of Indonesia (who are predominantly Hindu) appear to have well-developed and widely shared ideas regarding emotions and health. In several recent writings (e.g., Wikan, 1989, 1990), Wikan describes in detail North Balinese notions about emotions, the importance that Balinese place on health concerns in daily life, and the clear connection that is made between emotions and health. One Balinese woman, for instance, told Wikan "Anger eats away at the heart, destroys the intestines, makes you grow old, ruins your life . . ." (Wikan, 1990, p. 28). The woman went on, according to Wikan, "to expound on the evils of the bad—*jele*—emotions, reciting insights that are basic premises of Balinese culture" (p. 28). Among these premises is the notion that one should carefully manage one's emotional reactions both out of concern for one's health and the health of those with whom one interacts (because one's emotional state can affect the emotional states of others), and because of moral concerns (for an explanation of the latter, see Wikan, 1990). One important preventative technique used by the Balinese involves the cultivation of a feeling of calm. According to Wikan (1990), this entails

> a state of adjustment to the circumstances in which one finds oneself: an attitude of "not caring," forgetting the bad, letting bygones be bygones, and giving without expectation of return. Relaxed at the center, one avoids disappointment, does not get worked up, combats anger, does not bear grudges, and dispels fear. One feels generally "light and fresh" (*somboh*) and strong (*kuat*) (p. 182).

Beliefs that link emotions to health are found among several Pacific groups as well. Among the Ifaluk of Micronesia, getting rid of unpleasant or troubling thoughts and feelings is encouraged in part to avoid illness (Lutz, 1988). In contrast to the Indonesian groups discussed above, Ifaluk beliefs and norms emphasize the direct verbal expression of emotions as a way of accomplishing this. According to Lutz, Ifaluk advise one another to

> separate the good from the bad, or "divide the head," and then to "throw away" disruptive thoughts/emotions. This is universally the advice to the troubled, while at the same time, advice is given to express verbally one's thoughts/emotions as a preliminary step in ridding oneself of them. . . . When some problem or conflict results in such a situation of unresolved, unpleasant thought/emotion [that is, the thoughts/emotions won't leave the person's insides], the person involved will go to another with the express purpose of "saying my thoughts/emotions so that they will leave me." (p. 97–98)

Explicit cultural beliefs "about the illness- or misfortune-inducing effects of hidden bad feelings" are also found among Kwara'ae and A'ara speakers in the Solomon Islands in Melanesia, and among Hawaiians and Nukulaelae Islanders in Polynesia (White & Watson-Gegeo, 1990, p. 14).

In addition, with the exception of Nukulaelae Islanders, among these cultural groups there are explicit procedures for airing "bad feelings" and dealing with interpersonal conflicts, some of which are viewed as preventative in nature. Among the A'ara, for example, "disentangling" meetings—during which people "talk out. . .bad thoughts and feelings" that, if hidden, would "pose a danger to personal and community well-being"—are held either as a therapeutic measure to address "the psychosocial causes of illness or misfortune" or as "a preventative measure . . . to dispel bad feelings that could interfere with collective projects such as turtle hunting" (White, 1990, p. 56).

In sum, then, there are several traditional groups in Indonesia and the Pacific that emphasize the importance of not "storing" or keeping hidden negative emotional reactions and experiences, and of avoiding rumination and worry, in order to prevent illness. As for the specific mechanisms by which storing or hiding feelings, ruminating, and worrying are believed to lead to illness, ideas about these vary among the cultural groups discussed above (see, e.g., Geertz, 1976; Wellenkamp, 1988b), and in some cases are not well-articulated. Also, I should note that it is not clear to what extent the specific techniques used by these cultural groups are effective in reducing rumination and worry and in promoting health. Wegner's (1992) research, for example, suggests that one technique used by the Toraja—the conscious suppression of certain thoughts and images—often is not successful and may in fact present "more of a problem than a solution" in that in order to suppress unwanted thoughts and images, the mind must be especially alert to them and this, in turn, may increase their intrusiveness.

Although I believe that it is noteworthy that there are cultural groups that hold beliefs that parallel recent research findings linking emotions to health, I should make clear that there are other traditional, non-Western cultural groups that do not hold such beliefs. Rosaldo's (1980, 1984) accounts of the highland Ilongot of the Phillipines, for example, indicate that Ilongot ideas about emotions and how emotions "work" and are experienced are very different. According to Rosaldo, Ilongot say that they can be compensated with gifts for angry feelings that then dissolve (without discussion) and they can forget angry feelings whose expression would prove undesirable. And while Ilongot recognize that feelings can be hidden, they do not "think of hidden or forgotten affects as disturbing energies repressed" (Rosaldo, 1984, p. 144).

Such differences in the ways in which members of different cultural groups describe their emotional lives require further study (for instance, it may be that while Ilongot do not typically "disclose" their feelings about certain things, they also may not actively suppress or hide their feelings). It is my guess, however, that emotions are managed very differently in different cultural settings, beginning from when individuals are very young, and that in some groups, means of actively encouraging the disclosure of emotions are important for individuals' health, whereas in other groups, they are much less important.

VARIABLES THAT MAY AFFECT THE NEED FOR DISCLOSURE, AND THE FORMS AND EFFECTIVENESS OF DISCLOSURE, IN DIFFERENT CULTURAL SETTINGS

Having presented some ethnographic material that seems to support recent research regarding the disclosure of emotions and its relationship to health, I would like to now briefly consider the possibility that there may be cultural variation in the need for disclosure, and in the forms and effectiveness of disclosure.

Cultural Practices That May Reduce the Need for Later Disclosure

One factor that may reduce the need for later disclosure is the presence of cultural practices and rituals that may help individuals address and deal with intense emotional experiences as they occur. Among the Toraja, for example, there are many cultural practices surrounding death that potentially assist bereaved individuals in their adjustment to loss. One such practice (among Alukta adherents) is the custom of constructing a substitute body when the deceased's body cannot be recovered (e.g., in the case of drownings). The substitute body is treated as if it were the deceased's body—it is wrapped, held and cried over, and entombed. Another traditional practice involves the performance of a simple marriage ritual (*pakendek*) that unites the spouse of the deceased with another widowed individual. Following the *pakendek* ceremony, the couple stay together for a few nights, during which time they are permitted, but not required, to have sexual relations. After this, if the couple so desires, they may continue to live together as husband and wife. Otherwise, a simple divorce ceremony is performed and then each is free to marry whomever he or she pleases.

The one case of prolonged mourning that I encountered during my research involved a man, Ambe'na Doko, who had not participated in the *pakendek* ceremony because he was a Christian. His wife and child had died suddenly over two years before, and yet Ambe'na Doko was still very much upset and preoccupied with his loss. Sighing repeatedly, he said that since the death of his wife "[when] people come bringing women here, I don't accept them. I refuse them! Because . . . I think within my heart, I imagine in my eyes or in my heart, that my wife is probably within the house."

Another factor that would seem to reduce the need for later disclosure in many traditional cultures, as compared with the West, is the absence of Western notions of privacy, together with housing conditions and physical arrangements that do not afford much privacy. That is, in some places it would seem to be much easier to keep a traumatic or stressful experience private and hidden from others, whereas in other places, it would be very difficult. In Toraja, for instance, people say that villagers do not steal and engage in other forms of wrongdoing because it is very difficult to keep things secret and it is inevitable that others will eventually find out. One man, To Minaa Sattu (a *to minaa* is a type of ritual specialist), tries to imagine a situation in which it would be possible to commit adultery without being detected, but concludes: "Even if no one saw; if we did it [committed adultery] . . . by the second night [afterwards], surely by the third night, everyone would know!" Indo'na Tiku imagines a situation in which two children secretly steal some food but eventually their misdeed is discovered after someone says they saw the children at a distance, or when the owner hears that some children took his vegetables and the children are questioned at school: "So truly, our criminal deeds are always found out. Yes, it's just like the proverb: 'No matter how well something is wrapped, if it is rotten it is going to smell.' So what that means is even if it has been several years since we did something that others don't know about, in the end it will be found out."

Forms of Disclosure

While research studies conducted among Western populations indicate that there can be positive effects associated with disclosing emotions through a variety of forms (e.g., talking to someone, as well as writing in a private journal), it is likely that certain forms of disclosure are much more effective than others in different cultural settings. For example, judging from statements made by Toraja respondents about private versus public forms of absolution, it is likely that private forms of disclosure would not be effective for at least some Toraja individuals. For instance, Nene'na Tandi (m), who is himself a Christian, prefers Alukta responses to illness—which involve closely questioning the ill person to determine what "mistakes" or misdeeds he or she may have performed that resulted in the illness—as opposed to Christian responses, which do not entail public examination and confession:

> Village [Alukta] people must look for [a mistake] until they find it, beginning from the roots all the way to the leaves. But Christians don't, [they] only ask, "What kind of sickness do you have?" He/She may say, "I have a fever, I have a headache, I have a cough." After that, we just pray. . . . But it could be said that this is not right. Why do I say not right? Because this questioning only looks on the outside, not the inside. The village people, it is true, start on the outside, too, but they also look on the inside. They open everything for inspection. We Christians just look with [our] eyes. . . . But village people [not only] look with their eyes, but search within the heart. . . . But we Christians don't! That's why I say that Christians store their sins in their pockets.

Attitudes Toward Disclosure

Finally, I would like to raise the possibility that cultural attitudes toward disclosure may have a bearing on whether or to what degree, disclosures have positive psychological and physical health consequences. If, for example, there are strong cultural norms that work against disclosing emotions, or if there are cultural beliefs about the dangers of talking about certain experiences, these may influence the experience and consequences of disclosure, just as the presence or absence of a receptive audience may affect whether disclosure is a positive or negative experience.[2]

REFERENCES

Geertz, C. (1976). *The religion of Java*. Chicago: University of Chicago Press.

Geertz, H. (1961). *The Javanese family: A study of kinship and socialization*. Prospect Heights, IL: Waveland Press.

Hollan, D. (1988). Staying cool in Toraja: Informal strategies for the management of anger and hostility in a nonviolent society. *Ethos, 16,* 52–72.

Hollan, D. (1989). The personal use of dream beliefs in the Toraja highlands. *Ethos, 17,* 166–186.

Hollan, D. (1990). Indignant suicide in the Pacific: An example from the Toraja highlands of Indonesia. *Culture, Medicine, and Psychiatry, 14,* 368–379.

Hollan, D. (1994). Suffering and the work of culture: A case of magical poisoning in Toraja. *American Ethnologist, 21,* 74–87.

Hollan, D. W., & Wellenkamp, J. C. (1994). *Contentment and suffering: Culture and experience in Toraja*. New York: Columbia University Press.

Hollan, D. W., & Wellenkamp, J. C. (in press). The thread of life: Toraja reflections on the life-cycle. Honolulu: University of Hawaii Press.

Lutz, C. A. (1988). *Unnatural emotions: Everyday sentiments on a Micronesian atoll and their challenge to Western theory*. Chicago: University of Chicago Press.

Nooy-Palm, H. (1986). *The Sa'dan Toraja: A study of their social life and religion, Vol. 2. Rituals of the east and west*. Dordrecht, Netherlands: Foris.

---

[2]Similarly, psychologists should recognize that the experimental situation is not necessarily neutral or value-free: When individuals are asked as part of an experiment to disclose their thoughts and feelings, the situation is predefined to some degree as a positive one, in that by conforming to the experimenter's request, the subject presumably will be helping the experimenter or contributing to research.

Pennebaker, J. W. (1989). Confession, inhibition, and disease. In L. Berkowitz (Ed.), *Advances in experimental social psychology* (vol. 22, pp. 211–244). New York, NY: Academic Press.

Rimé, B. (1995). The social sharing of emotional experiences as a source for the social knowledge on emotion. In J. M. Fernández-Dols, A. S. R. Manstead, J. A. Russell, J. C. Wellenkamp (Eds.), *Everyday conceptions of emotion* (pp. 475–489). Norwell, MA: Kluwer Academic Publishers.

Rosaldo, M. Z. (1980). *Knowledge and passion: Ilongot notions of self and social life.* New York: Cambridge University Press.

Rosaldo, M. Z. (1984). Toward an anthropology of self and feeling. In R. A. Shweder & R. A. LeVine (Eds.), *Culture theory: Essays on mind, self, and emotion* (pp. 137–157). New York: Cambridge University Press.

Tait, R., & Silver, R. C. (1989). Coming to terms with major negative life events. In J. S. Uleman & J. A. Bargh (Eds.), *Unintended thoughts* (pp. 351–382). New York: Guilford Press.

Traue, H. C., & Pennebaker, J. W. (Eds.). (1993). *Emotion, inhibition, and health.* Göttingen, Germany: Hogrefe & Huber Publishers.

Waterson, R. (1981). *The economic and social position of women in Tana Toraja.* Unpublished doctoral dissertation, University of Cambridge, England.

Wegner, D. M. (1992). You can't always think what you want: Problems in the suppression of unwanted thoughts. *Advances in experimental social psychology* (Vol. 25, pp. 193–225). San Diego, CA: Academic Press.

Wellenkamp, J. C. (1988a). Order and disorder in Toraja thought and ritual. *Ethnology, 27,* 311–326.

Wellenkamp, J. C. (1988b). Notions of grief and catharsis among the Toraja. *American Ethnologist, 15,* 486–500.

Wellenkamp, J. C. (1991). Fallen leaves: Death and grieving in Toraja. In D. R. Counts & D. A. Counts (Eds.), *Coping with the final tragedy: Cultural variation in dying and grieving* (pp. 113–134). Amityville, NY: Baywood.

Wellenkamp, J. C. (1992). Variation in the social and cultural organization of emotions: The meanings of crying and the importance of compassion in Toraja, Indonesia. In D. D. Franks & V. Gecas (Eds.), *Social perspectives on emotion* (Vol. 1, pp. 189– 216). Greenwich, CT: JAI Press.

White, G. M. (1990). Emotion talk and social inference: Disentangling in Santa Isabel, Solomon Islands. In K. A. Watson-Gegeo & G. M. White (Eds.), *Disen-*

tangling: Conflict discourse in Pacific societies (pp. 53–121). Stanford, CA: Stanford University Press.

White, G. M., & Watson-Gegeo, K. A. (1990). Disentangling discourse. In K. A. Watson-Gegeo & G. M. White (Eds.), *Disentangling: Conflict discourse in Pacific societies* (pp. 3–49). Stanford, CA: Stanford University Press.

Wikan, U. (1989). Managing the heart to brighten face and soul: Emotions in Balinese morality and health care. *American Ethnologist, 17,* 294–310.

Wikan, U. (1990). *Managing turbulent hearts: A Balinese formula for living.* Chicago: University of Chicago Press.

Author Index

Numbers in italics refer to listings in the reference sections.

Schalling, D., 189, *193*
Scheiderman, N., 228, *234*
Scheier, M. F., 134, 146, *148, 151,* 197, *218*
Scherer, K. R., 101, *122,* 272, *290*
Schlenker, B. R., 71, *88*
Schlien, B., 226, *235*
Schlote, B., 156, *174*
Schmidt, H. J., 185, *192, 193*
Schneider, D. J., 32, *46,* 53, *70*
Schneider, W., 60, 61, *69*
Schneiderman, N., 4, *9,* 177, 188, *192,* 225, *234*
Schoen, M., 125, *150*
Schoenberg, B. B., 272, *290*
Scholz, O. B., 162, *173*
Schore, A. N., 242, 243, 247, *253*
Schwartz, G. E., 137, *149,* 177, 178, 180, 181, 182, 185, 187, 188, 189, 190, 191, *192, 193, 194,* 206, *221,* 224, 225, 226, *235, 236, 237*
Schwartz, J. I., 190, *193*
Schwartz, L., 162, *174*
Schwartz, N., 126, *151*
Searle, J. R., 73, *88*
Sechrest, L., 84, *91*
Seligman, M. E. P., 144, *150*
Selye, H., 255, *270*
Semmel, A., 144, *150*
Severino, S. K., 108, *120*
Shadick, R. N., 51, 60, *67, 69*
Shaffer, D. R., 73, *88*
Shaffer, J. W., 226, *236*
Shaffer, L. F., 125, *150*
Shapiro, D., 227, *234*
Shapiro, D. A., 76, 78, 79, 84, *87, 88, 90*
Shea, J. D., 225, *236*
Shea, T., *86*
Shedler, J., 6, *9*
Sheridan, J., *234*

Shiffrin, R. M., 60, 61, *69*
Shortt, J. W., 54, *70,* 206, *222*
Shrout, P. E., 42, *44*
Shuster, P. L., 81, 82, *90*
Siegel, J. M., 224, *234*
Sifneos, P. E., 138, *148, 151*
Silver, R. C., 271, 280, *291, 293, 310*
Silver, R. L., 138, *151,* 271, *290*
Simmel, G., 26, *45*
Simon, H. A., *22,* 97
Singer, J. L., 138, *148,* 181, 191, *193,* 205, 207, *218*
Slater, M. A., *174*
Sloan, W. W., Jr., 71, 78, 85, 86, *89, 90*
Smith, F. E., 211, *219, 220*
Sonnemans, J., 272, *288*
Sorenson, S. B., 224, *234*
Sotsky, S. M., *86*
Speicher, C. E., 224, *234, 235*
Spera, S. P., 4, *10*
Stein, J. A., 224, *234*
Stekel, W., 40, *45*
Stengers, I., 84, *88*
Stern, D. N., 101, *122*
Stern, R., 58, *70*
Stevens, A. A., 127, *150*
Stiles, W. B., 26, *45,* 71, 72, 73, 74, 76, 77, 78, 80, 81, 82, 83, 84, 85, *86, 86, 87, 88, 89, 90, 91*
Stone, A. A., 208, *222*
Stones, M. H., 138, *151*
Stout, J., *234*
Strack, S., 280, *290*
Struening, E. L., 42, *44*
Strupp, H. H., 80, *91*
Suls, J., 207, 210, *221*
Sultan, F. E., 76, *91*
Summit, R. C., 39, 40, 41, *45*
Sund, A., 272, *288*
Surwit, R., 260, *270*
Susman, J. R., 47, *69,* 224, *236*
Swank, R. T., 226, *236*

Subject Index

About the Editor

James W. Pennebaker is a professor and the chair of the Department of Psychology at Southern Methodist University in Dallas, Texas. Since receiving his PhD in 1977 from the University of Texas at Austin, he has studied the links between the mind and body, including how people perceive physical symptoms, how and when traumatic experiences affect biological activity, and why writing or talking about emotional upheavals can improve physical and mental health. His research, which has been funded by the National Science Foundation and the National Institutes of Health, has resulted in 5 books and over 100 scientific articles.